THE DEVELOPING CHILD

Recent decades have witnessed unprecedented advances in research on human development. In those same decades there have been profound changes in public policy toward children. Each book in the Developing Child series reflects the importance of such research in its own right and as it bears on the formulation of policy. It is the purpose of the series to make the findings of this research available to those who are responsible for raising a new generation and for shaping policy in its behalf. We hope that these books will provide rich and useful information for parents, educators, child-care professionals, students of developmental psychology, and all others concerned with the challenge of human growth.

Jerome Bruner
New York University

Michael Cole
University of California, San Diego

Annette Karmiloff-Smith
Medical Research Council, London

SERIES EDITORS

The Developing Child Series

Children with Autism

A Developmental Perspective

Marian Sigman & Lisa Capps

Harvard University Press
Cambridge, Massachusetts
London, England

Library of Congress Cataloging-in-Publication Data

Sigman, Marian.
    Children with autism : a developmental perspective / Marian Sigman
and Lisa Capps.
        p.   cm.—(The developing child)
    Includes bibliographical references and index.
    ISBN 0-674-05314-1 (cloth : alk. paper).—ISBN 0-674-05313-3
(pbk. : alk. paper)
    1. Autism in children. 2. Child development. I. Capps, Lisa.
II. Title. III. Series.
RJ506.A9S533   1997
618.92′8982—dc21
96-54384
CIP

This book is dedicated to children with autism
and their families

Acknowledgments

This book draws from the accomplishments of many individuals, laboratories, and clinics around the world. Our own research has profited from the extraordinarily creative and dedicated efforts of Shoshanna Arbelle, Rosalie Corona, Cheryl Dissanayake, Michael Espinosa, Connie Kasari, Jung-Hye Kwon, Mary McDonald, Peter Mundy, Norman Kim, Ellen Ruskin, Tracy Sherman, Judy Ungerer, and Nurit Yirmiya. Over the last 18 years our research was made possible by financial assistance from the National Institutes of Child Health and Human Development (NICHD), Mental Health (NIMH), and Neurological Disorders and Stroke (NINDS). This continuity has been essential in carrying out our longitudinal studies, and we thank the staff members at these institutes who have been extremely helpful, most recently Drs. Marie Bristol and Giovanna Spinella. Dr. Betty Jo Freeman has facilitated participation, shared clinical insights, and remains an invaluable resource for us at UCLA. We are grateful for the contributions of the many talented and devoted research assistants who have worked with us over the years; Jennifer Kehres and Alma Lopez have also been instrumental in bringing this book to completion. Margie Greenwald's boundless energy and extensive knowledge of university rules and institutional foibles have buoyed our spirits and maintained our research group on a more or less even keel. Finally, we want to thank David Sigman and Nathan Brostrom for their generous and steadfast support.

Contents

Children with Autism

1 / What Is Autism?

Jeremy, three and a half years old, has big brown eyes and a sturdy body. His mother carries him down the corridor toward the examiner, who greets them. Jeremy glances at the examiner's face but does not smile or say hello. They walk together into a play room. Jeremy's mother puts him down and he sits on the carpet in front of some toys. He picks up two blocks, bangs them together, and begins to stack the blocks, one on top of the other, not stopping until he has used the entire set. Jeremy does not look at the examiner or his mother while he works, nor when he finishes. And he does not make a sound. The examiner asks him to give her a red block. He does not respond. On their way out, Jeremy and his mother stop to look at a poster of a waterfall surrounded by redwood trees. "Yosemite Valley," Jeremy reads out—the name beneath the picture. His voice sounds automated, almost robotic. Turning toward the examiner, he then reads the identification badge she is wearing: "Neuropsychiatric Institute." These are the only words Jeremy utters during his visit to our laboratory, and will be the only words we hear him say over his two-month stay in our hospital unit.

Jeremy was the first autistic child Marian Sigman had ever met. As a child clinician and researcher at a large university hospital, she had spent eight years observing infants and children. Like Jeremy, many of these children were developmentally delayed. But this boy was different. While mentally retarded children typically seem younger than their years, their abilities are evenly developed—or rather, equally delayed—across cognitive and social domains. Jeremy presented a distinctly uneven repertoire of behaviors and abilities. He appeared extremely advanced in some areas, displaying skills one would not expect of his normally developing peers. Yet he lacked basic skills in other, often closely related, areas. For example, although he was able to read "Yosemite" and "Neuropsychiatric Institute," he appeared unable to comprehend simple words and instructions.

This variation in abilities mystified Marian, and it continues to contribute to the mystery of autism. The disorder has other compelling features. For instance, like other children with autism, Jeremy gave the impression that he was capable of more than he showed. Was he unable or unwilling? And why was it impossible to tell? Jeremy was extremely difficult to fathom. He seemed removed and unreachable, as if there were something blocking the communicative channels through which humans establish contact. To borrow the words of the mother of an autistic child, he seemed to be enclosed "in a glass ball," visible but unreachable, giving the impression that if one could shatter this ball, a normal person would emerge. Frustrated attempts to engage with others heighten our awareness of the ease with which we routinely expect to establish social connections. Thwarted, we feel uncomfortable and unsure of ourselves. Because we experience ourselves in relation to other people, when another person does not provide the response we seek and expect, or any response at all, it not only affects our perception of that person but how we experience ourselves.

This inexplicable lack of connection, coupled with questions about its cause and how it might be overcome, was noted in the very first accounts of children with autism. Cases of socially isolated, noncommunicative children entered clinical and popular lore long before the syndrome was formally identified. The most famous of these was the French physician Itard's account of the *Wild Child of Aveyron,* a boy who was found in a forest at the apparent age of twelve, having had no prior contact with humans.[1] Although subsequent reports cast doubt on whether the child was truly autistic, he displayed many features of the disorder: he did not speak or respond to questions or react to loud noises, and he was asocial, paying closer attention to objects than to people.

Formal documentation of autism dates back to 1943, when a child psychiatrist living in the United States, Leo Kanner, published a paper describing a group of eleven children and the difficulties they shared.[2] He proposed that these children suffered from a psychological malady, which he named "infantile autism." Quite remarkably, one year after Kanner's report appeared, a pediatrician living in Germany, Hans Asperger, described a set of symptoms, later called Asperger Syndrome, which was similar to Kanner's account of autism.[3]

Kanner's original description of his autistic patients focused on their social isolation: "There is from the start an extreme autistic aloneness that, whenever possible, disregards, ignores, shuts out anything that comes to the child from the outside." He went on to record these children's tendency to engage in repetitive behavior and their compulsive efforts to preserve order, both in terms of the organization of objects and the mainte-nance of daily routines. Kanner attributed this intense concern for order to "the desire for sameness." In addition to such peculiarities, he documented uncanny displays of exceptional skills, for example in vocabulary or memorization. One otherwise mentally retarded autistic child was able to recite pages from an encyclopedia from memory. Because such skills stood out against more pervasive impairment, Kanner called them "islets of abilities." His conclusion was that autistic children "have come into the world with an innate inability to form the usual biologically provided affective contact with people, just as other children come into the world with innate physical or intellectual handicaps."

Like Kanner, Asperger ascribed the syndrome he observed in his young patients to a core social impairment. Asperger highlighted the children's poor eye contact, limited empathy, impaired nonverbal communication, pedantic and monotonic speech, intense absorption in circumscribed topics such as the weather, and marked resistance to change. However, unlike Kanner's autism, Asperger Syndrome did not involve significant delays in language or cognitive development but did include impairment in fine and gross motor skill. Perhaps because his paper was published in Germany during World War II, Asperger Syndrome was essentially unknown in the English literature until quite recently. Hence it was Kanner's account of infantile autism that served as the foundation for changing conceptualizations of the disorder.[4]

Given the early observers' emphasis on impaired social relationships, autism initially was seen as a subtype of childhood schizophrenia. This association was made explicit in the name of the publication devoted to research on autism, the *Journal of Autism and Childhood Schizophrenia*. Like autism, childhood schizophrenia is characterized by pervasive difficulties disrupting language, reasoning skills, and social interactions. Today, however, the vast majority of clinicians and researchers agree that autism and childhood schizophrenia are clearly separate. (The journal was renamed the *Journal of Autism and Developmental Disorders.*) Children with autism do not suffer from the kind of hallucinations and delusions that trouble children with schizophrenia. And children with schizophrenia do not display many of the behaviors shown by children with autism, such as ritualized treatment of objects (like placing all of one's possessions in a row), fascination with things that rotate, obsessive preoccupation with a particular topic, self-stimulating behaviors (like hand-flapping). While both autistic and schizophrenic groups display language disorders, each manifests a different pattern of idiosyncracies. Further, unlike children with schizophrenia, a great many children with autism do not develop speech and are mentally retarded.

The sets of symptoms used in formal diagnosis of autism have varied over time and across cultures. In general, however, all systems emphasize limited verbal and communicative behaviors and abnormal social relationships.[5] Most also designate additional symptoms, such as obsessions, self-stimulation, and ritualized behaviors. Autism can be diagnosed narrowly or broadly, depending on whether individuals with fewer and milder symptoms are included. Such diagnostic variability is evident in the debate about the relationship between autism and Asperger Syndrome.

Persons with autism vary with respect to their intellectual level. The majority (75%) are mentally retarded. Those who are not mentally retarded are often called "high-functioning." Although they suffer social and emotional impairment, they are not cognitively delayed and generally develop fluent speech. High-functioning autistic individuals resemble those portrayed by Asperger, except that they do suffer language delays and do not necessarily display motor clumsiness. Questions about the extent to which Asperger Syndrome and high-functioning autism are distinct conditions have not yet been resolved. In 1994, however, Asperger Syndrome was "officially" recognized by the American Psychiatric Association as a clinical diagnosis separate from that of autism under the overarching class of Pervasive Developmental Disorders.[6] Diagnostic criteria also vary from country to country. For example, a child who is diagnosed with autism in Japan, where the classification is more inclusive, may not be so described in the United States or Great Britain, where the criteria are more stringent.[7] Further, while variation in diagnostic criteria may be attributable to theoretical differences concerning the nature of autism, it is also related to the structuring of eligibility for health care services.

The reported incidence of autism varies depending upon how the disorder is defined and diagnosed. Surveys conducted in Europe, Japan, the United States, and Canada report that the incidence ranges between four and ten autistic children in every 10,000 births.[8] Future epidemiologic surveys in geographically and culturally distinct populations, especially data from developing nations, are needed to determine whether the apparent similarity in rates in European and Japanese studies is indeed universal. As Victor Lotter noted in describing his efforts to conduct an epidemiologic survey of autism in Africa, difficulties in carrying out epidemiological studies of autism (the rarity of the disorder requires large and costly surveys) are exacerbated in developing countries, where referral patterns are irregular and may prohibit meaningful estimation of prevalence rates.[9] Almost all of the epidemiological studies that have been conducted so far have detected higher rates of autism among boys.[10] Male to female ratios in the majority of studies range between 1.4:1 and 3.4:1.[11] Several investigators have observed that the male to female ratio increases as a function of IQ, so there are significantly more autistic boys than girls with an IQ greater than 50.[12] Genetic accounts of autism provide a possible explanation for the lower IQ of females with autism.[13] For instance, females may be more strongly affected by the autism gene. Alternatively, there may be genetic heterogeneity causing milder forms of the disorder to be Y-linked and thus more common in boys.

Although Kanner and Asperger claimed that the parents of their respective patients tended to be intelligent, well-educated, and of high social standing,[14] there is little evidence for this claim. Only one epidemiological study of autism has shown evidence of an association between autism and social class.[15] Moreover, such an association may be a result of better access to treatment; parents of middle and upper socioeconomic groups are simply more likely to have their children clinically evaluated.

In the end, while systems for identifying autism are clinically and scientifically useful, they often enshrine a diagnostic profile rather than advance understanding of the disorder. Understanding autism requires more than documenting peculiar behaviors and expanding or contracting the spectrum of behaviors included in the diagnosis. To solve the mystery of autism, the behaviors we refer to in using diagnostic phrases such as "abnormal social relationships" must be located within the broader profile of abilities and disabilities displayed by persons with autism, and also within the context of normal development. Likewise, we must begin to relate the features of autism to underlying mechanisms. The question "What is autism?" cannot be answered by simply defining a series of characteristics. Indeed, it cannot be answered completely at this time. The point of this book is to outline the information we *do* have, and to consider the questions that remain.

The Developmental Perspective

We view autism through the lens of developmental psychopathology, a discipline devoted to the investigation of psychological problems from a developmental perspective—that is, over time. Such investigations are grounded in the dual notion that studies of normal and abnormal development enhance each other, and that we can only see typical and atypical development clearly when the two perspectives are combined. Thus, while the first aim of this book is to provide information about autism, the second is to show how knowledge of normal development and knowledge of disordered development inform each other. Toward these ends, we draw on the three main approaches used in studies of developmental psychopathology: use of a developmental framework, longitudinal studies, and studies of children at risk. They provide an organizational structure for this book.

Most developmental psychopathology research focuses on a specific disorder within a conceptual framework of what is expected of children at particular ages. For example, the most significant relationships in the lives of infants are those with individuals who provide care and interaction—parents, older siblings, or daycare workers; peer relationships are less important at a very early age. In contrast, in adolescence peer relationships are critical. Hence studying a disorder in infancy would focus on the relationships of the disturbed young child with caregivers, while studies of disturbed adolescents would also examine relationships with peers.

In addition to focusing attention on areas of social and cognitive development that are of significance at particular ages, conceptualizations of normal development generate age-specific expectations. For example, while children's attachments to peers become more important as they grow older, parent-child attachment relationships are significant at every age. However, attachment security in early childhood, when the primary objective is to establish a secure base, is expressed differently than in adolescence, when the goal is to develop an autonomous, open orientation to the world.

The notion of reciprocal influence is crucial to the use of a developmental framework: information gleaned from investigations of abnormal development enhances the conceptualizations of normal development upon which those investigations were based. Studies of children who display insecure or disorganized attachments to their parents, for example, also teach us about the development of attachment security. By examining what happens when adaptive developmental processes go awry, we gain insight into normal development.

Use of this approach requires setting up a conceptual framework for normal development. We articulate such a framework in Chapters 2–6, as we outline what is known about autistic children at different age periods and point out at the same time what the study of autism teaches us about normal development.

A less common approach to research in developmental psychopathology is to study children with a particular disturbance as they develop over time. This line of research illuminates the long-range picture: how the developmental challenges children face at various ages affect the manifestations of a particular disturbance. For example, mild mental retardation may present the greatest challenge during the school years, when children are required to learn in settings where their cognitive and social abilities are publicly evaluated by teachers, peers, and themselves. The years before and after school may be less difficult because scrutiny and social comparison are less pervasive and there are greater opportunities to meld into community life unnoticed. As we will show in relation to autism, each phase of life brings new challenges to children and their families.

It is useful to think of psychological conditions as we would of chronic medical illnesses—something that sufferers must cope with, in varying ways and degrees, for the rest of their lives. The analogy applies to disorders like schizophrenia and depression, in which symptoms may disappear temporarily, and it is particularly relevant to autism. While autistic persons, particularly those with normal intellectual abilities, may develop ways to adapt to the world and even compensate for their limitations, living with autism is an ongoing struggle. From this perspective it is essential to follow individuals suffering from psychological disorders over time to understand the disruption they experience at various ages.

Because of the difficulties involved, few longitudinal studies of disturbed children have been carried out. In the first place, research on psychopathology in children began relatively recently. Because it was necessary to document the existence and define the characteristics of various childhood disorders before examining their developmental trajectories, initial studies focused on establishing the age of onset, identifying particular features, and delineating criteria for differential diagnosis. These objectives could be addressed most expediently by studying different children at different ages, rather than following the same child over time.

Longitudinal research is also more difficult and expensive than cross-sectional research. By definition, this method requires keeping track of individuals over a number of years, and demands a long-term commitment from participants as well as considerable planning on the part of the researcher, who must be able to track and revisit the same subjects year after year. This process is more arduous in countries like the United States, which do not have centralized health care systems, than in Scandinavia and Great Britain, for example, where researchers have access to records that provide health-related information and help locate individuals for follow-up study. As will be discussed in Chapter 7, the few longitudinal studies that exist greatly contribute to our knowledge of autism, allowing us to observe and compare the various obstacles faced by autistic persons and their families in early childhood, adolescence, and early adulthood.

The third approach used in developmental psychopathology research is to observe children who may or may not be symptomatic but are at risk for developing a disorder. Circumstances that render children at risk include medical complications at birth, poverty, or parental mental illness. By studying those who are vulnerable, rather than those known to have a particular problem, these studies cast a wide net; while some participants emerge without signs of distress, others ultimately develop severe disturbances. The broad objective of these studies is to identify a wide spectrum of responses to adverse circumstances rather than to single out a typical normative response. This approach allows researchers to address questions concerning the sequelae of risk conditions and to identify factors that either mitigate or augment their potentially negative consequences, enabling some children to thrive while others experience difficulties.

This approach—studying individual differences in

children at risk—cannot be applied to autism because we do not know whether there *are* risks for autism from which some children escape. Because the majority of children diagnosed with autism suffer from the disorder throughout their lives, it is not possible to identify factors that relieve the symptoms. We do know, however, that autistic children who develop fairly good language skills before five or six years of age remain more intellectually and socially competent later in life. Given this positive association between language ability and adjustment, it seems important to figure out what promotes language abilities in childhood and to further delineate the consequences of adequate language acquisition.

In Chapter 7 we discuss individual differences in autistic children's life adjustment within the context of early risk and mediating factors. Chapter 8 focuses on current conceptualizations of the core deficits and causes of autism, and Chapter 9 on interventions with autistic children. But before we begin to describe what is known about autistic children at various stages in development, it is important to note the problems encountered in viewing autism from a developmental perspective: (1) autism emerges relatively late in development, and (2) there is a high incidence of mental retardation among autistic children.

Lack of Information about the First Two Years

The diagnosis of autism is currently not made until children are between two and a half and three years of age, because symptoms are generally not recognized by parents or by pediatricians before that time. As a result, autistic children are usually not referred for assessment or study until the end of the third year, and we are therefore unable to draw conclusions about autism in infancy. In the absence of direct observation, some crucial questions remain unaddressed, such as whether autistic children lack the earliest kinds of social responsiveness—those that precede social understanding—or whether they show such social responsiveness but then fail to develop more sophisticated forms. The only sources available are parents' retrospective accounts and, more recently, home videotapes of children before they were diagnosed.

So far, neither of these sources have produced compelling evidence of autism in the first 12 to 14 months of life. While we might expect hindsight to illuminate early signs of trouble, many parents report that they did not suspect anything was wrong during their child's first year. Some do describe their children as having been "too good" in that they were happy to remain in their cribs, did not lift their arms to be picked up, and cried very little. But in general, parents did not notice anything unusual about their infants until they were 15 to 20 months of age. Even seasoned parents of several children do not describe their autistic children as having been different in any way before the age of two and a half or three. In most cases parents report that they began to worry during the child's second year of life, when he or she did not start speaking.

Home videotapes seem like an ideal source of information about these early months, but these too have limited usefulness. Videotapes are usually made in special circumstances, like birthday parties, so they may not capture a representative picture of the infant's behavior. For example, a child's affect may appear muted because his emotional expressions are genuinely flat, or merely because the child is overwhelmed by the noise, the presence of people, or seeing other children who are playing with his toys.

Moreover, most autistic children are also mentally retarded and tend not to display behaviors that would be expected of normal children their age. Because the early interpretation of autism hinges on the *absence* of particular behaviors, what appear to be early signs of autism might more properly be ascribed to retardation in general rather than autism in particular. This distinction cannot be made on the basis of videotaped observations. In the absence of direct access to autistic children's first years of life, we can only infer the nature of the early developmental progression from their achievements at ages three to five years.

Autism and Mental Retardation

The complicating factor of mental retardation constitutes a second main source of difficulty in applying a developmental framework to the study of autistic children. Difficulties in applying a normal developmental framework are compounded by the fact that the prevalence of mental retardation changes: specifically, it is higher among autistic children under five years of age than among those who are older. In part due to language delays, almost all autistic children identified between three and five years of age are deemed retarded in their general cognitive development. Only a few among them ultimately develop intellectual skills in the low-average to average range of intelligence.[16]

How can we explain the relatively high prevalence of retardation during the early years, followed by the subsequent emergence of a nonretarded subgroup? It may be the case that almost all young autistic children are genuinely mentally retarded, but the cognitive abilities of a subgroup improve. Alternatively, this pattern may be attributable to difficulties in recognizing autism in young nonretarded children. Nonretarded autistic persons may be identified only later in life, while the retarded autistic children who are so identified remain mentally retarded. Recognizing autism in young nonretarded children may require considerable experience with a variety of children. Before the recent emergence of group daycare settings, in which care providers gain experience from a broad range of children, the vast majority of young children were observed in their homes only by family members and people with limited exposure to children their age. As long as the child did develop language, family, friends, and caregivers may not have detected milder social and cognitive problems. If this hypothesis is true, as anecdotal evidence consistently suggests, the increase in group daycare should reveal larger numbers of young nonretarded autistic children. A third possibility is that nonretarded children are identified, but do not meet enough criteria to be diagnosed as autistic early on. By following children of normal intelligence who display mild symptoms of autism, we may be able to determine whether they appear more clearly autistic as they mature, or whether autistic features diminish over time.

Because autism is often accompanied by mental retardation, most autistic children are developmentally similar to children half their chronological age (although their language development is generally further delayed). As a result, we expect to see achievements in autistic children of three to five years that characterize normal infants of 15 to 24 or 30 months. The only way to attribute a particular characteristic to autism rather than to mental retardation is to contrast the autistic child of a certain mental and chronological age with a mentally retarded nonautistic child of the same mental and chronological age. Throughout this book we will distinguish behaviors that characterize mental retardation in general or autism in particular. By the time autistic children reach five or six years of age, it is possible to identify those who are not retarded and use language functionally. These children act very differently from the majority of autistic children. Given these differences between retarded and nonretarded subgroups, when examining the development of autistic children in middle childhood and adolescence, we consider them independently.

In summary, this volume discusses autism within the framework of developmental psychopathology. We outline the progression seen in normal development and contrast it with the development of individuals with autism. In so doing, we propose that autistic children suffer from a deficit in social understanding, and that this deficit characterizes all autistic children at all age periods. We will show that deficits in social understanding emerge in early infancy, and aim to illuminate how these deficits organize the unfolding pattern of strengths and weaknesses displayed by individuals with autism over the course of their lives.

2 / Physiological Regulation, Perception, and Cognition in the Early Years

Andrew, a five-year-old boy with blue eyes, fair skin, and a slight build lingers in the doorway behind his mother. His eyes are cast down, not focusing on anything in particular. When the examiner greets him he pauses and lifts his head, but the direction of his gaze remains off center. For several minutes Andrew wanders around the periphery of the room, running his fingertips along the wall, over the top of a sofa, and across a cabinet. The examiner encourages him to join her on the floor near a collection of toys. Andrew sits down, but remains still. She hands him a doll and brush, and he bangs them together. She uses the brush to comb the doll's hair and hands them both back to Andrew. He bangs them together again and smells the doll's hair. There is a loud noise outside. Vaulting over the back of a small chair, Andrew races to the window. The examiner beckons several times, but he stays by the window, peering out, until she takes his hand and guides him back to the play area.

In the first three to four years of life, normal children make monumental developmental strides. They learn how to regulate states of arousal, gain physical coordination, develop perceptual skill, and become increasingly knowledgeable about persons and objects in the world. Although individual growth patterns vary, for the most part typically developing children achieve developmental milestones at an even rate. That is, advances in motor development are generally accompanied by advances in cognitive development. Similarly, developmental milestones are typically achieved in an invariant order: for example, crawling precedes walking, walking precedes hopping. Autistic children's development, however, lacks such constancy and invariance.

Normal Development

Regulating States of Arousal

Newborns undergo radical developmental changes to adjust to life outside the womb. The first and most fundamental of these tasks is to regulate states of arousal. At birth, full-term infants—those who are born after a gestational period of 37–40 weeks—fluctuate between sleep, drowsiness, alertness, and crying states. During the first months infants gain the ability to control these fluctuations so they occur with greater regularity. The ability to regulate states of arousal reflects the integration of behavioral, neurological, and physiological systems, all of which operate within a social context.

As infants become better able to regulate states of arousal, they spend longer periods of time awake and alert and sleep less. Although the maturational push that stabilizes states of arousal is universal, sleep cycles vary among individuals and across cultures.[1] Cross-cultural variation suggests that baby sleep patterns are influenced by environmental factors such as employment practices and the organization of living space. In the United States there is a push toward establishing a diurnal schedule with longer stretches of sleep during the night, because parents work during the day.[2] Caregivers influence the timing and smoothness of transitions from sleep to wakefulness by the way they respond to infants' behaviors. In comparison to babies in America, Kipsigis babies in rural Kenya have shorter cycles of sleep and wakefulness. These infants are almost always with their mothers, spending much of the day on their mothers' chests and backs, eating and sleeping at will; they also sleep with their mothers at night, nursing on demand. The response patterns that develop between infants and their caregivers are an early form of dialogue. From the start, this dialogue is embedded in a cultural context, reflecting societal expectations of adult members.

Physical Coordination, Movement, and Perception

Infants' growth in physical size is accompanied by equally striking increases in movement and coordination. With each passing day infants become better able to hold their heads erect, focus their eyes on specific locations, support the weight of their bodies, and move deliberately through space. Over the first two to three years they acquire the ability to sit, to pull themselves up into a standing position, to walk, to run back and forth with smooth changes in speed and direction, and to climb up and down stairs without assistance.[3]

Developments in fine-motor control are also remarkable. In the early months infants struggle to get their hands into their mouths. But as they mature they learn to reach for objects and grasp them, first with their fists and eventually with precision, between thumb and index finger. Soon their repertoire of behaviors expands from mouthing objects to banging and dropping them, transferring them from hand to hand, placing them in containers, stacking them, fitting them through small openings, and piecing them together in puzzles. During the transition from newborn to toddler, infants acquire the skills and sensibilities which enable them to navigate and manipulate the environments they inhabit.

Development of perception is equally essential. At birth, infants are very nearsighted and have blurry vision.[4] Nevertheless, they actively scan their surroundings from the earliest days of life and are able to see objects one or two feet away. This allows infants to make eye contact with their caregivers while feeding, which is important in establishing intimate social relationships. Newborns' visual acuity develops extremely rapidly. By the third month infants appear to perceive and distinguish colors. By seven or eight months of age, as they begin to move independently by crawling, infants' vision resembles that of adults.[5]

Humans' earliest exposure to life outside the womb may be through hearing. Infants in utero are able to hear sounds from the outside world, and their hearing develops rapidly after birth.[6] Newborns appear to be able to distinguish the sound of the human voice from other sounds, and seem to prefer it. In one study of the first week of life, babies learned to turn on recorded speech or vocal music by sucking on an artificial nipple. They ceased sucking, however, when they got rhythmic non-speech or instrumental sounds instead.[7] Because infants are highly responsive to the messages communicated through the sounds of the human voice, caregivers use their voices to influence their states of arousal, soothing their passage into sleep or raising their levels of interest and excitement. Young infants also have the capacity to distinguish between different tastes and odors.[8] They discriminate sweet from sour and salty tastes, preferring the former to the latter, and turn away from pungent odors, often wrinkling their noses in apparent disgust.

Learning about Objects

During the first year infants demonstrate interest in objects by turning their heads and eyes toward them. They look closely at pictures and mobiles, staring and breathing hard. They are captivated by objects that make sounds, and often reach for them and squeal with delight. Some evidence suggests that by three to four months they have a beginning understanding of object constancy, that is, that two objects cannot take up the same space at the same time.[9] While during the first months of life objects cannot compete with the human face for an infant's attention, after six months this is no longer the case.

By the second year infants can manipulate objects quite skillfully. They use objects as tools, employing one to obtain another, and look for objects that are placed inside or beneath one another. They follow the movement of things through space, and surmise the location of moving objects from their trajectory even when movement is hidden, as when a child waits for a toy car to emerge from the end of a tunnel. Toddlers close to two years of age know that objects exist even when out of view, a cognitive achievement that Piaget referred to as "object permanence."[10] During the second and third years of life normal toddlers discover the form, color, and function of objects.

Researchers have learned about the infant's early perception of shape and color in a number of ingenious ways. One test, referred to as habituation or preferential looking, was devised following the notion that infants look more at novel objects that are introduced into their field of vision than at objects previously presented which they have grown accustomed to seeing. This approach has been used to demonstrate young infants' perception of color and shape. For instance, an experimenter repeatedly showed the child pictures of the same shape until the baby became bored and looked at them less and less (i.e., habituated to them). The experimenter then introduced a new shape, taking the child's interest and excitement as an index of shape differentiation.[11]

Another way to examine preverbal children's knowledge of categories is to administer sorting tasks using small replicas of various objects. In the second year of life children sort objects not only by color and form but by functional categories such as vehicles and fruit, thus demonstrating the ability to make finer distinctions between categories and to recognize key similarities and differences in objects of greater complexity.[12] At this time children even begin to generate categories of their own.[13]

Pretend Play

Sometime between 12 and 24 months of age, infants' use of objects undergoes a radical transformation as they begin to engage in pretend play.[14] Though it might appear to be a frivolous distraction from serious learning, play in general and pretense in particular provides a foundation for cognitive and social development.[15] Different forms of pretense emerge at different developmental stages. Children may initially display functional or conventional acts; for example, the child pretends a toy car is a real car. They may also make one object stand for another, by treating a wooden block as a truck, for example. Slightly older children may create imaginary objects with no props at all. For example, the "truck" might stop at a make-believe gas station for refueling. Children may also attribute properties to imagined objects, for instance, if, having pulled up to the gas station, the child declares that it is closed, or sold out of gasoline.

The ability to engage in pretend play with objects requires considerable cognitive and social understanding. Pretend play is the first clear indication of infants' ability to represent people and objects symbolically. In pretending children also draw on knowledge about objects in the world, such as the fact that cars need fuel to run, and an awareness of people and the activities they engage in. Often, before they can talk very well, children play out little stories enacting scripts from their daily lives. The ability to do so demonstrates considerable understanding of cultural conventions. In this way, the pretend scenarios children create provide insights into their knowledge and experience of the world.

Children's capacity for make-believe quickly moves beyond the realm of physical objects. They do not limit themselves to substituting one object for another nor to creating imaginary objects and properties; they begin to conjure up animate beings. On the basis of their observations of children's doll play at various ages, Dennie Wolf and her colleagues have shown that at 18 months children treat dolls as representations of human beings but do not credit them with the power to act and feel independently.[16] Dolls are passive recipients of the children's care: they are fed, washed, and put to bed.

Between two and two and a half years of age, children begin to endow dolls with the capacity for emotion and action: dolls are made to talk and act independently and are credited with sensations, desires, and emotions. They get tired and hungry; they want to go outside to play with their friends; they become afraid, angry, or happy. Later still, at three or four years, children imbue dolls with more explicit and elaborate thought processes and emotional states. A doll might voice a plan to hide from a robber, wonder where a friend has gone, or worry about her baby. This sophisticated variety of make-believe gives us insights into children's emotions, identities, relationships, and world views.[17]

Pretend play often becomes a highly social activity, as

children join siblings and peers in constructing imaginary worlds. Although, according to Piaget, pretend play shifts from a solitary symbolic activity to a social one during the third year of life, naturalistic observations suggest that children engage in pretend play with their mothers much earlier, at 24–28 months.[18] Joint pretend play is highly complex. It requires carrying out coordinated actions within an imagined framework, and often enacting the part of another person or thing. In this sense joint pretend play involves the mutual exploration of social rules and roles. Thus infants' growing knowledge of objects and expanded repertoire of behaviors becomes increasingly significant as they grow older, when objects gradually assume more salient roles in mediating their interactions and relationships with other people.

Development of Young Children with Autism

Regulating States of Arousal

At least during the first two years, autistic and mentally retarded children develop control over states of arousal in much the same way as do normal infants. Parents report that their autistic infants established increasingly integrated and regular cycles of sleep and wakefulness.[19] In fact, many parents have reported that during the first year their autistic children shifted smoothly between sleep and wakefulness, slept soundly for long stretches of time, and were content to lie alone in their cribs.

After the second year, however, some autistic children appear to be overaroused and overactive. At the age when children are diagnosed with autism (usually about two and a half to four years), many parents complain that their autistic children are difficult to calm before bedtime and sleep very little. Some psychophysiological studies have found higher basal arousal levels, indicated by heart rate and respiration, among autistic children.[20]

Physical Coordination, Movement, and Perception

Most young autistic children display well-developed physical and motor coordination and may maintain advanced physical skills through adolescence, a characteristic that differentiates children with autism from those with Asperger Syndrome. In fact, many autistic children are precocious, displaying agility and strength beyond what is expected of normally developing children their age. Autistic children's physical prowess is particularly striking in comparison to the abilities of nonautistic retarded children, who tend to lack physical coordination. Autistic children of all ages are carefully monitored during visits to our research laboratory; as we saw with Andrew, they can jump up on sofas and climb book shelves seemingly without effort or awareness of risk. This is dramatized in the movie "What's Eating Gilbert Grape," in which an autistic boy, Arnie, escapes his brother's surveillance and scales a 150-foot-tall water tower. Horror mounts as Arnie reaches the top, and, seemingly oblivious both to danger and to the reaction of onlookers, hangs on precariously with one hand and waves to his brother who is standing below. Because autistic children's gross motor skills often far outstrip their evaluation of potential danger, parents of autistic children describe the need for constant vigilance.

Similarly, the perceptual and sensory capacities of young autistic children seem to be intact. There have been a few reports of visual acuity problems, although specific deficits have not been identified. In talking about their autistic children in retrospect, parents tend *not* to describe them as having been disinterested or unresponsive to the human voice during the first year, but many recall that at some point prior to diagnosis they suspected that their children were deaf. This suspicion seems to be tied to an emerging awareness of their children's limited social responsiveness rather than to any sensory impairment.

Smell and taste appear to develop normally in children with autism, although many seem to have particularly strong negative reactions to certain smells and foods. Parents of autistic children who participate in our research often mention their children's peculiar food preferences and aversions, including extreme sensitivity to texture and fastidious concern about separating different foods on their plates and refusing, for example, to eat potatoes that have had contact with peas. While these behaviors are also observed in nonautistic children, among persons with autism they often persist into adolescence and adulthood.

Although their perceptual and sensory development is unimpaired, individuals with autism of all ages and intellectual abilities often use their senses in ways that are unusual. For example, persons with autism may habitually smell nonedible objects, or smell food in idiosyncratic, often dramatic ways, as Oliver Sacks described in an account of his picnic with Steven Wiltshire, a high-functioning autistic man noted for his drawing talents. Sacks notes that as they unpacked their food, Steven "half-convulsively swooped his head and sniffed everything as it came out."[21] Children with autism also may have aversive reactions to sounds which are not commonly distressing to others. In our research, for example, an autistic child whose family moved to a coastal town was upset by the sound of fog horns. For more than a month he flinched and ran to the window after each tone, and required assistance learning to tolerate the sound.

Autistic children's way of using their eyes is often

strikingly idiosyncratic. Like Andrew, many autistic children employ peripheral rather than direct perception. That is, they tend to look out of the corner of their eyes or to look at the edge rather than the center of an object. While the difference is subtle, such visual behavior has a dramatic effect on social interactions. In addition, many young autistic children spend long periods repositioning objects along the periphery of their visual fields, both at close and far range, and then squinting and gazing at them out of the corner of their eyes or out of one eye at a time.

While such behavior is unusual, normally developing children sometimes use peripheral perception in attending to certain stimuli, particularly stimuli that are threatening, ambiguous, or otherwise distressing—for instance, seeing one's mother come into view with a still, unexpressive face.[22] Among normal infants, this visual orientation appears to provide a way to monitor a disturbing situation while diminishing its psychological impact. But it is not clear whether these behaviors serve the same function among autistic children. One of the greatest difficulties we face in attempting to understand autism is that the meaning of autistic persons' idiosyncratic behaviors cannot be inferred directly from knowledge of normally developing persons. Rather than interpreting such behaviors as we would those of a nonautistic person, we must locate them within the puzzling composite of strengths and weaknesses that is autism.

Interest in and Learning about Objects

In tandem with their development of sensory, perceptual, and motor abilities, autistic children develop an understanding of objects that resembles that of normal and mentally retarded children at the same developmental level, but they often use objects idiosyncratically. On the basis of the few studies that have been done, autistic children seem to recognize shape, color, and object functions as well as mentally retarded and normal children of similar mental age.[23] Although autistic children may acquire such abilities at an older chronological age than normal, their skills are no more retarded in this regard than those of nonautistic mentally retarded children.

Autistic children demonstrate awareness that objects continue to exist when they are out of view, and they use objects as tools with considerable skill.[24] In our laboratory we have witnessed how autistic children deftly solve problems that their caregivers, much less children at their developmental level, were unable to master. For example, after observing several normally developing children unsuccessfully attempt to extract an object lodged in a narrow tube, we watched, amazed, as a nonverbal autistic child immediately picked up a small rake, and, using the handle as a tool, skillfully removed the object.

Although their knowledge of objects seems to develop normally, albeit slowly because most are mentally retarded, autistic children often use objects in different ways than do normal or mentally retarded children. As mentioned, autistic children may sniff or stroke objects. They may also manipulate certain aspects of an object over and over again, for example, by twirling the wheels on toy cars around and around and around, repeatedly dialing one number on a rotary phone, or dropping one object into another over and over again. Autistic children frequently arrange objects in rows, preferring to line up blocks side by side rather than erecting elaborate towers. Parents commonly report that their autistic children fastidiously organize objects in their rooms into rows. Children who tend to arrange objects in particular ways often become extremely upset when such arrangements are disturbed, and also are likely to protest to changes in daily routine.

It is not clear why autistic children engage in peculiar behaviors with objects. Young infants generally seem to gaze at their fingers and hands, stroke textured material, sniff, wave, and drop objects repeatedly in the service of exploration and learning. But among autistic children these behaviors persist long after the child achieves a more sophisticated knowledge of objects.

Pretend Play

Autistic children show very impoverished pretend play. Their pretend or symbolic play is extremely limited, not only in comparison to normal children their age but even in comparison to chronologically younger normally developing children and mentally retarded children who have equivalent developmental skills and language abilities.[25] The virtual absence of make-believe is among the most striking differences between autistic and nonautistic children's play with objects; it is a hallmark feature of autism. In fact, clinicians frequently ask parents if their children engage in pretend play as a first step in the process of diagnosing autism.

Most autistic children show deficits in even the simplest forms of functional or conventional play. Andrew's play is typical of children with autism in that he did not use the brush to comb the doll's hair, but banged the objects together. Yet this is not always the case. Autistic children with highly developed language skills, particularly language comprehension, do engage in some functional play. Symbolic play seems to go hand in hand with language comprehension, suggesting that the two systems tap a similar underlying ability, namely the capacity to use representational symbols. The fact that autistic children who have more advanced language skills can understand symbol use in play does not prove, however, that they have equivalent capacities for symbolic play. Their capacity for symbolic play is still underdeveloped relative to that of normal children with the same level of verbal comprehension. Aside from functional play, autistic children rarely engage in more sophisticated forms of pretense, such as imagining objects that do not exist, imbuing objects with properties, or attributing emotions, desires, and beliefs to pretend characters. For example, Simon Baron-Cohen reports that in his study of spontaneous pretense only two autistic children displayed instances of pretend play.[26] One child pointed to a piece of sponge that was green and cube-shaped and said, "Are these potatoes? I don't know. They might be peas." The other child pointed to a toy stove and said, "Don't touch it. It's hot." Neither comment was part of a sustained sequence of pretend activity, nor involved the animation of toy animals or dolls.

The limited play of autistic children corresponds to their lower overall involvement with objects. If left completely to their own devices, autistic children are less likely to play with objects than are both normal and mentally retarded nonautistic children. Andrew's behavior is typical, in that autistic children seem to prefer to wander aimlessly rather than to engage in elaborate interactions with objects and other people. Similarly, it may be that the reason autistic children rarely produce pretend play is not because they completely lack the ability to do so, but because the type of object-directed play that they prefer can be carried out without much call for pretense. Objects can be stacked, spun, and lined up without any need for pretense. A human drama, on the other hand, cannot be staged unless one imagines the actions, goals, perceptions, emotions of actors. It is in this sense that pretense is embedded in a sociocultural, as well as cognitive, matrix.[27]

Autistic children's pretend play can be enhanced somewhat through intervention. Vicky Lewis and Jill Boucher presented autistic children with pairs of objects, such as a toy car and a box, together with the instruction to "make the car go in the garage."[28] Autistic children were just as competent as normal children of the same verbal ability at pretending the box was a garage. However, their play appears more rigid and repetitive, lacking the spirit and spontaneity of that of nonautistic children. As observed in our laboratory, autistic children's pretend play often focused on a specific theme in a highly perseverative manner, and was rarely if ever elicited in response to suggestions such as "The car needs gas." Further, autistic children rarely elaborated on the behaviors that are modeled for them, nor do they seem to generalize what they have learned to novel materials or situations.

Identifying the prerequisites for different forms of make-believe provides insight into the underlying impairment in autism. Similarly, identifying the nature of autistic impairment enriches our awareness of the complexity of normal developmental accomplishments. Both social and cognitive factors may help explain autistic children's impoverished pretend play. Pretend play is fundamentally tied to social activity. One prerequisite for conventional use of objects, which is the foundation for functional play, is that children observe adults and older children. Autistic children may show less functional play because they are less attuned to the actions and interests of others. Furthermore, in observing others, they may be less inclined to interpret behaviors in relation to underlying emotions, attitudes, and beliefs. A second tie to social activity is that functional and symbolic forms of play are generally carried out with dolls or with other people. Autistic children, however, are less inclined to initiate social behavior—with dolls or with people—and may show less functional and symbolic play as a result.

In addition, autistic children may show impoverished symbolic play because it requires a kind of cognitive understanding they lack. Engaging in pretend play involves postulating situations that are counterfactual—foregoing literal interpretation of meaning. Making a block stand for an automobile necessitates setting up a different, additional level of reality. To engage in pretense, children must be able to act as if a block were a car, while keeping in mind that a block is really a block. The capacity to posit make-believe events is particularly impressive given that young children are eagerly and earnestly attempting to learn about the real world. And because young children generally engage in pretend play with other children or adults, they must not only attribute imaginary qualities to objects but understand that other people can do this as well.

Various theories have been put forth to account for the development of pretense in three- to four-year-old children, and the lack thereof in children with autism. One theory, proposed by cognitive psychologist Alan Leslie, holds that the ability to engage in pretend play depends on the child's capacity to separate or "decouple" real and imagined properties, and to attribute thoughts and beliefs ("propositional attitudes") to others.[29] Among autistic children, those who display the capacity for object-based pretense, for instance, using a block to stand for an automobile, appear to have some ability to decouple or disengage from reality and act upon an untruth. Yet they appear unable to engage in more advanced forms of pretense. The second part of Leslie's theory accounts for autistic persons' specific deficits with social pretend play by suggesting that so doing requires the ability to think about one's own thoughts and the thoughts of others. This capacity allows children to construe imaginary situations in which, for example, "Dolly wants to go swimming," and for all participants to understand the imaginary nature of what they are doing. From this perspective, autistic children do not engage in pretend play because they are unable to attribute attitudes to other characters and people.

In summary, during the first years of life, autistic children's development is similar in many respects to that of normal children. They acquire the ability to regulate, and ultimately integrate, different states of arousal. Their motor and perceptual abilities and knowledge of objects develops normally, or at least no more slowly than that of other children who are mentally retarded. Yet signs of autism are visible. Particularly when their activity is not structured by an adult, young autistic children display idiosyncratic behavior, such as aimless wandering and stereotypical movement, and frequently engage with objects in unusual, often repetitive ways. Autistic impairment is perhaps most apparent in the relative absence of pretense, a behavior that seems to require both the beginnings of abstract thought, and an awareness of other people and the cultural conventions that organize their lives.

3 / Development of Social and Emotional Understanding

Julia, a five-year-old autistic girl with deep brown eyes and curly brown hair, bounds into the room four paces ahead of her mother. She flaps her hands near her face and screeches. The examiner asks Julia to join her at a small table. Julia sits down and works on a jigsaw puzzle. She finishes quickly, flashes a smile, and immediately reshuffles the pieces to begin again. She does not look up at her mother or the examiner as they praise and applaud her efforts, but shifts her chair, moving away from them. The examiner rolls a small ball toward Julia and she rolls it back, smiling. The examiner points to various objects in the room, saying "look." Julia does not shift her gaze. Julia's mother joins them at the table and pounds wooden pegs into a peg board. She hits her thumb with the hammer and cries out in pain. Julia does not look at her or offer comfort, but picks up the hammer and begins pounding the pegs herself. Julia's mother leaves the room. Julia looks worried and wanders toward the door. When her mother returns, Julia skips to her side and cuddles up against her chest.

Young children's ability to respond to others is perhaps their most remarkable developmental accomplishment. It is in this area that autistic children's development is most startlingly deviant. As we track the social and emotional development of young normal children in the first three to four years of life and contrast it with that of children with autism in this chapter, it will become clear how the developmental pathways of autistic and normal children inform each other. In particular, the unnerving absence of certain behaviors and responses among children with autism calls attention to behaviors that might otherwise go unnoticed, and their crucial role in the orchestration of human relationships.

Normal Social Development

Infants come into the world predisposed to engage in relationships with people. They are primed to learn about and respond to social stimuli and to form attachments to their caregivers. Able to hear voices in utero, newborns prefer to listen to familiar voices. In the behavioral study mentioned in Chapter 2, infants were taught to suck on a rubber nipple to activate a recorded voice. They were then exposed to two recordings of a story, one told by mother and the other by a stranger. Through their sucking behavior, infants demonstrated a preference for mother's voice over that of the stranger.[1]

Infants also track faces with their eyes soon after birth. In the first month they scan only a small portion of the face and tend to look at the outer edges.[2] During the first weeks of life infants reproduce behaviors they observe in others, for example, sticking out their tongues and turning their heads.[3] Imitation contributes to the development of an understanding of self and others, as infants look at bodies in motion while experiencing such movement themselves. Over the next months infants spend increasing amounts of time looking at faces, and their focus shifts from the periphery to central features, particularly the eyes. Sensitivity to bodily movement and attunement to faces in particular provide a foundation for social interaction.

Newborns gradually learn to distinguish the faces of familiar and unfamiliar persons, and by three months display a preference for a photograph of mother's face over that of a stranger.[4] They differentiate between mother and strangers on the basis of taste and smell. When placed between a cloth soaked with mother's breast milk and a pad soaked with breast milk from an unfamiliar mother, the infant consistently turns toward the scent of his or her mother's milk.[5]

In the first six months, normally developing infants prefer facial stimuli to other visual stimuli, and become visibly distressed when presented with photographs in which facial features have been omitted or rearranged.[6] They sustain eye contact with other people for increasing lengths of time, and soon combine looking with smiling, cooing, and laughing.[7] Young infants are captivated by face-to-face exchanges, and will generally engage with anyone, although they show a slight preference for familiar partners.

After six months of age, however, infants no longer rivet solely on the faces of their social partners, but often attend to interesting objects instead. They are particularly likely to focus on novel objects and persons when they are with familiar people in familiar environments. At about nine months infants begin to focus on objects and people at the same time. In what are known as triadic interactions or joint-attention behaviors, infants attempt to share their experience of an object or event with other people.[8] These behaviors initially involve tracking another person's line of sight toward an object, and glancing from the object to the person and back. In this way infants develop awareness of other people's eye gaze learn to use gaze to direct others' attention to objects of interest.[9] Likewise, infants learn to follow and produce pointing gestures and become increasingly able to influence others' attention by using gaze in concert with gestures of pointing, giving, and showing. Further, just as infants follow adults' visual focus of attention, they imitate the ways in which adults physically manipulate objects. Infants as young as nine months-old mimic accurately both the form and function of object-directed actions after adults have demonstrated them.[10] The increasing precision with which infants display delayed or deferred imitation of novel behavior reflects closer attention, better motor coordination, and growing awareness of the purpose of particular behaviors.

At about nine months of age infants also begin to monitor the emotional responses of other people. A study in which infants were observed playing with toys in the presence of caregivers who were attending to their play, and, alternatively, in the presence of caregivers who were not paying attention demonstrated that ten-month-old infants smiled more at caregivers who were attending to them.[11] Infants' interest or pleasure in their toys, however, was not affected by whether or not caregivers were attentive.

By one year of age normally developing infants are discriminating in expressing emotion. Like adults, they smile when they are sharing experiences, but not when they are attempting to obtain an object or assistance. During the second year, infants continue to refine their awareness of others' attention, seek out emotional cues, and increasingly use them to guide their behavior.

Social Referencing

Infants' inherent interest in other people provides at least part of the motive for learning to share and track gaze.

[handwritten margin note: develop gaze to gain attention]

But infants also look at other people's faces for information. Exhibiting a behavior known as social referencing, infants look at their caregivers when faced with a situation which is ambiguous or mildly threatening.[12] They also look up at an adult's face to make sense of confusing messages, for example if an adult offers and then withdraws an object, seemingly in an effort to determine something about the situation or the adult's intentions. Further, infants respond to the emotional signal conveyed, approaching in response to positive affect and retreating in response to negative affect. While they tend not to reference adults in familiar or clearly defined situations, they do respond to adults who express strong emotions no matter how familiar the setting.

Many behaviors that emerge at approximately nine months and continue to develop through the third year of life are thus grounded in the infant's ability to recognize and assume the perspective of another person.[13] Such behaviors reflect the infant's understanding of persons as intentional agents that are clearly different from inanimate objects. Infants do not attempt to look where their dolls are looking, nor do they use such objects as social reference points. As Michael Tomasello and his colleagues have pointed out, knowledge of the intentions of others serves as the foundation for participating in a given culture.[14] Cultural learning entails more than directing one's attention to the location of another's activity; it involves attempting to see a situation the way the other sees it, through another's perspective. In all cultural learning children internalize or appropriate not just knowledge of the activity being performed, but of the social interaction itself; something of the perspective of the child's interactional partner continues to shape the child's world view long after the interaction has ended.[15]

Emotional Expressiveness and Responsiveness

Infants show a range of emotional expressions and responses from birth. Observing the similarity of facial expressions displayed by children and adults across a variety of cultures, Charles Darwin asserted that emotional expressions are universal and innate.[16] More recently, this claim has been supported by studies showing that young infants spontaneously produce facial expressions denoting happiness, sadness, surprise, interest, fear, contempt, anger, and disgust, and these are appropriate to the corresponding events.[17] Darwin also proposed that humans are endowed with an innate ability to recognize facial expressions. By this he meant not only that young infants can see that one facial expression is different from another, but that perhaps they instinctively know the meaning of different facial expressions. This instinctive recognition produces an emotional reaction in the observing infant; for example, infants become melancholy in the presence of someone who is crying.

It appears that by six months infants differentiate between facial expression of simple emotions such as happiness, sadness, fear, and anger. Because preverbal children cannot talk about their feelings, the endeavor to study emotion recognition in infants inspired methodologies that do not require a verbal response. Investigators have presented infants with a series of pictures of different women, each showing the same facial expression (for example, happiness) and then pictures of women showing an emotion other than happiness.[18] Infants lost interest as pictures of the same emotion were presented, but when shown a different expression, such as surprise, they looked with renewed enthusiasm, thus demonstrating that they differentiated among emotional expressions. Because each emotion was represented by multiple faces, we can assume that they discriminated on the basis of emotional expression rather than the physical characteristics of the persons in the photographs. It is not clear, however, whether infants recognize the expressions as emotions; they may have made distinctions based on differences in the visibility of teeth or shape of the eyes.

Young infants also recognize and respond to the vocal expression of emotion. Voices convey emotion not just through words themselves, but through intonation— rising and falling pitch, variation in rhythm, volume, and intensity. Infants respond to the emotional tone of vocalizations, smiling and laughing in response to happy voices, and quieting or fussing in response to those that are sad or angry. By seven months they appear to connect facial expressions with tones of voice. In a study in which infants were shown two films, one of a smiling face and the other an angry face, while they were played an audiotape of either a happy or an angry voice the infants tended to look at the face that matched the voice.[19]

By the second year children begin to develop an awareness of the conditions or actions that bring about simple emotions such as happiness, sadness, anger, and fear. Later on they comprehend complex emotions, such as pride, shame, and guilt, which involve greater understanding of social and interpersonal situations. Recognizing complex emotions involves taking intentions, responsibility, and social norms into account.[20] These crucial developments in social understanding are tied to the development of empathy.

During the first year, infants generally react to another's smile by smiling, and to another's distress by getting quiet or even crying.[21] By the second year, as they become more adept at identifying conditions that anticipate various emotions, they also become more adept at relieving distress.[22] When two-year-olds encounter someone who is upset, they typically recruit help and offer cheerful suggestions and comforting objects. As children develop, they become better able to adopt the perspective of other people and to share their emotional experiences.

Self-Recognition

Consciousness of self is among the major characteristics said to distinguish human beings from other species and two-year-olds from younger children. Yet questions concerning the definition and development of self-consciousness continue to challenge philosophers and scientists. A crucial aspect, *self-recognition,* has been examined in experimental paradigms involving mirrors.[23] Before the age of three months children held up to a mirror show little interest in their own images or in the image of anyone else. At about five months, if a person is reflected in the mirror babies will smile, reach out, and touch the mirror, suggesting that they do not understand that they are seeing a reflection. Ten-month-olds will reach behind them if a toy is slowly lowered behind their back while they are looking in the mirror, but they will not try to rub off a red spot that has been surreptitiously applied to their nose. By 18 months of age, children reach for their own nose when they see the red spot, demonstrating that they recognize the mirror image as a reflection of themselves.[24] And within a few months, when someone points to the child's mirror image and asks, "Who's that?" the normally developing child is likely to answer without hesitation, "Me!"

Early Social Relationships

During infancy children develop a small set of relationships with significant people in their lives. Initially, such persons provide care and sustenance; safety and stimulation become more important later on. The consistency and sensitivity with which caregivers respond to infants provide a framework for the infant's development. John Bowlby suggested that infants who can depend on having their needs and desires met in a timely and predictable fashion are apt to develop a sense of security in the world, whereas those who cannot are likely to feel less secure.[25] Responding with sensitivity involves appreciating the individual characteristics and needs of the infant as they change over time. For example, when infants are young it may be most important to provide immediate responses to expressed distress, whereas later it becomes more important to allow for separation and autonomy. It is also important to recognize that some children's needs may be easier to read or to satisfy than others, a point that is relevant in discussing the relationships of children with autism.

In order to assess the nature of the infant's relationship with his or her caregiver, Mary Ainsworth and her students developed what they called the "strange situation" and provided empirical support for its validity.[26] In this setting infants' responses are observed when the babies are left by their mothers in an unfamiliar place and again after their mothers return. Secure attachment relationships are manifest by infants' discomfort or distress at separation, which is resolved when the caregiver comes back. (Some secure infants are not troubled by separation but respond warmly to the mother's return.) When the attachment relationship is less secure, infants either show very little response to maternal separation and reunion, or a great deal of distress upon separation from caregivers and little relief when their caregiver returns.

attachment theory

According to attachment theory the nature of early attachment relationships is crucial because it influences the child's relationships with other people, both concurrently and later in life. From this point of view, initial attachment experiences form the basis for the child's "working model" of relationships, which serves as a lens or filter through which the child perceives and experiences other relationships.[27]

Interpersonal Conflict and Self-Control

If one of the major tasks in the first 18 months is creating trusting relationships, by the second year of life resolution of conflicts with caregivers, siblings, and peers takes on greater importance. As infants become more able to move around and to express themselves, they inevitably experience increased frustration. Infants spend much of the second and third year of life exploring and learning about their worlds, but they also face more impediments and prohibitions. Young children rely quite heavily on their caregivers in negotiating and resolving these setbacks.[28] At three years of age, children deal with prohibitions in part by trying to change the situation, but also with a great deal of self-comforting, for example, by sucking their thumbs or hugging themselves. By four years of age, children attempt to talk themselves out of their frustration by trying to convince themselves that they did not want whatever it was they could not have, or, alternatively, attempt to remove the prohibition by persuading others that they should have the object they desire.[29] Thus by three or four years of age children possess an understanding of themselves and others and of the cultural conventions that facilitate pursuing their interests and negotiating relationships, all of which enables them to resolve many conflicts themselves.

Social Development in Autistic Children

For reasons mentioned in the previous chapters, very little is known about the social development of autistic children before three to four years of age. There are only a few studies that shed some light on the social responses of very young autistic children. Two of these examined home videos of one-year-old birthday parties taken of infants who were later diagnosed with autism and compared them with videos taken of normal infants.[30] While the differences are small, infants with autism appeared to engage less often than normal infants in face-to-face interaction with parents and other children. Close examination of the tapes suggested that they were also less likely to follow pointing gestures and to turn or look up in response to their names.

In a second study conducted in Great Britain in an effort to establish a basis for early diagnosis, investigators looked back at the infant health records of children who were later diagnosed with autism and compared them with the records of children who developed normally, or had mild to moderate learning difficulties.[31] At their 12-month screening autistic children showed very few problems in any of the areas assessed (vision, motor skills, hearing, and language). In fact, they manifested fewer impairments than children who developed learning disabilities. At 18 months, however, many of the infants who were subsequently diagnosed with autism showed problems in social development. In comparison with the other children, they rarely initiated social exchanges and were less responsive to efforts to engage them in simple forms of interaction.

Similar results were obtained in a third study, also conducted in Great Britain, in which investigators screened forty-one 18-month-old infants who were at high genetic risk for developing autism and fifty randomly selected 18-month-olds, using the Checklist for Autism in Toddlers (CHAT).[32] The CHAT was developed to facilitate early detection of autism, based on empirical work showing that deficits in specific behaviors are indicative of autism: pretend play, following the gaze of others, pointing to indicate objects of interest rather than to obtain an object, exhibiting social interest, and engaging in social play.[33] Four children in the high-risk group failed to demonstrate two or more of these key behaviors, while none of the randomly selected toddlers failed to show more than one. At a 30-month follow-up visit, the four toddlers who had failed to demonstrate two or more of these behaviors received a diagnosis of autism, whereas the other 87 children continued to develop normally. Taken together, these studies suggest that autistic children manifest aberrant social responses by the second year of life.

Because children who later become autistic have not been studied systematically at three to six months of age, we do not know whether they display the same dyadic interactions as normally developing children. When we examined such dyadic interaction in the laboratory with three- and four-year-olds—rolling a ball back and forth with the child or playing tickling games—most of the autistic children were as engaged and playful as the normal children.[34] In contrast to the stereotype of autistic children as aloof and disengaged, they tend not only to respond by smiling and laughing, but to continue the games by lifting their hands to invite more tickling. Further, autistic children showed pleasure in dyadic interactions both with caregivers and strangers.[35] Similarly, these findings are consistent with parents' reports that their autistic children respond positively to attempts to play social games and like to keep the games going.

While this research suggests that autistic children are capable of dyadic interaction at ages three to four, in these settings adults actively engaged the children. Problems arose when social interaction was not structured.[36] In unstructured situations autistic children are much less likely than normal and mentally retarded children to engage in social interaction, and they play less with objects.[37] Instead, autistic children tend to wander aimlessly, showing little interest in people and toys.

Although the quality of autistic children's dyadic interactions varies depending upon the circumstances, triadic interaction—in which the infant combines attention to another person and an object—is deficient across the board. In contrast to normally developing children, autistic children rarely look up at their caregivers as they play with toys, even new or particularly amusing ones. They appear focused on their play materials and are not inclined to share their experiences with others.[38] Autistic children not only find it difficult to initiate triadic interactions but even to respond to someone else's attempts to engage them. Like Julia, autistic children rarely follow the gaze or the pointing gestures of another person and do not imitate others' actions. Instead of redirecting their eyes or turning their heads, they retain a fixed focus, giving the impression that they fail to notice or to understand the meaning of such gestures. Although these behaviors are momentary, they play an essential role in creating connections between people and a common view of the outside world. Perhaps because we take them for granted, the role and consequences of joint attention are most keenly felt when absent. The ramifications of this lack of joint attention are important both in terms of social relationships and cultural learning. Because human beings develop close relationships in large part by sharing experiences, the absence of joint attention undermines the experience of closeness and connection. In addition, it diminishes autistic children's opportunities to learn how to participate in cultural activities because they miss seeing situations through the eyes of an expert member.

Children with autism do look up at adults, however, when they are attempting to secure an object that is out of reach, or when handing an object to an adult for some sort of assistance, for example to unscrew the lid of a jar. Although they use pointing gestures far less often than do normal or mentally retarded children, autistic children occasionally point to request an object or otherwise obtain help. When children with autism do engage in triadic interaction, then, it is generally to make a request, and very rarely to share an emotion or experience.

Social Referencing

Just as children with autism rarely look at others to share their experiences, they tend not to look at faces for information. Autistic children are much less likely to reference another person to make sense of an ambiguous situation. In a study carried out in our laboratory, we had a small, noisy, blinking robot move toward the child who was seated with his or her mother and an experimenter.[39] As the robot entered, the child's caregiver and the experimenter pretended either to be afraid or amused by the robot by gasping and recoiling, or laughing and leaning forward. All the normally developing children and all but two of 30 mentally retarded children looked at least once at the adults demonstrating fear. However, only 13 of 29 children with autism looked at the adult's face, and they did so very briefly. And while normal and mentally retarded children used the adults' emotional display to guide their behavior, hesitating before approaching the robot if they approached it at all, the autistic children who made reference to the adult's face did not seem to use this information; they approached the robot without delay.

The same pattern emerged when the adults pretended to feel amused. In contrast to normal and mentally retarded children, autistic children largely ignored the adults' emotional display. It seems, then, that the autistic children were less likely to try to read the facial expressions of other people to make sense of novel or ambiguous situations and even less likely to use these expressions to guide their behavior.

Nor did autistic children look at the faces of adults who produced confusing, ambiguous behavior.[40] For example, at the experimenter's request, caregivers inexplicably blocked their child's hand while the child was playing with a toy. Normal and mentally retarded children immediately surveyed their caregiver's face for an explanation. In contrast, autistic children were more apt to ignore the interruption and continue playing. Their behavior suggests that autistic children lack either an interest, ability, or willingness to read the facial expressions of others.

As with deficits in imitation and joint attention behaviors, the effects of insufficient social referencing behavior are far-reaching and cumulative. These deficits restrict access to information that is relevant to a given situation, and—what is more important—they diminish autistic persons' participation in creating shared meaning. Joint attention and social referencing behaviors enable children to learn *through* and from other people how to respond to objects and events, both emotionally and behaviorally. In such interactions individuals get to know themselves and others and develop common understandings of objects and experiences. That is, members of a cultural community cultivate a sense of themselves and others through mutual exploration of objects and experiences.[41] The deficit in joint attention and so-cial referencing not only impoverishes judgment about whether to approach or withdraw from an unfamiliar situation, but also impinges on understanding of emotions, identities, and relationships. Such impairment sets autistic children adrift in a culture that is in many ways impenetrable to them.

Emotional Expressiveness and Responsiveness

Given that autistic children have difficulty displaying many of the behaviors that enable people to experience interpersonal connections, it is perhaps not surprising that clinical and popular accounts of autism often herald emotional flatness as a central feature of the disorder. This emphasis is evident in Bruno Bettleheim's case study of an autistic child, entitled "Joey the Mechanical Boy."[42] Although current metaphors are less extreme, the *Diagnostic and Statistical Manual of Mental Disorders* (DSM-III-R) describes autistic children as having an "apparent absence of emotional reaction."[43] While no one would challenge the notion that autism involves affective impairment, such impairment is not most accurately described as "flatness" or "unresponsiveness."[44]

To reconsider the issue of emotional expressiveness, we asked parents to describe the emotional expressiveness of their autistic, mentally retarded, and normally developing children.[45] On the basis of these reports, autistic children did not appear less emotionally expressive than normally developing or mentally retarded children. According to their parents, they showed more negative emotions, such as fear, sadness, and anger, and fewer positive emotions, such as joy and interest, than did comparison children. However, this study does not tell us whether the emotions expressed were fitting in light of the context in which they arose.

Because only a few studies have directly examined the

emotional expressiveness and responsiveness of young autistic children, current information is limited. While readily observable smiles, laughter, and temper tantrums attest to autistic children's ability to express emotion, it is important to establish the social appropriateness of these behaviors. One way to examine emotional understanding among young children with autism is to observe their reactions to situations that usually elicit particular emotions in normally developing children. Using videotaped observations, we coded children's facial expressions in a variety of laboratory settings and found that children in general—with and without developmental disabilities—show little emotion; for the most part, their faces are affectively neutral.[46] This may be an inherent limitation of laboratory research. Because we do not want young children to become frightened or upset, we design only moderately arousing situations. Even when the parent pretends to be frightened by the robot, young normally developing children show little fear. Their faces appear neutral, and those of autistic children are no different.

When observed in pleasant situations, children with autism also showed emotional expressions that resembled those of children with mental retardation and normal children. In general, children showed positive emotions while engaged in social interactions with their parents and other adults. Young autistic children also showed positive emotions in such situations, but they displayed negative emotions more often than normal and mentally retarded children. They also showed discordant affect somewhat more often, meaning that part of the face expresses a positive emotion and the other part expresses a negative emotion. It may be that children manifest such blends when they are confused about social situations, but this has not been established. Nor can we interpret the behavior of autistic children by inferring from findings in studies of normally developing children.

The emotional expressions of young autistic children do differ dramatically from those of normally developing and retarded children in response to praise. As mentioned, young normal and mentally retarded children look up at their parents and smile when they have accomplished a task, soliciting praise. In our laboratory we videotaped autistic children as they completed a puzzle. Like Julia, most of the autistic children smiled when they mastered the task, but did not look up at observers for acknowledgment of their accomplishments.[47] Further, while normally developing children and children with mental retardation show positive emotional expressions in response to praise, children with autism do not. Instead they seem to avert their gaze, and sometimes shift their bodies away from those who are applauding them.

Another striking feature of the emotional responses of young autistic children is that they did not combine looking with smiling. In face-to-face interactions they looked at caregivers as much as did the normal and mentally retarded children, but did not smile as they looked.[48] Similarly, on the rare occasions when they did look up to share an experience with another person, they rarely showed positive affect.[49] It may be that autistic children wish to share experiences with others, but that others are not aware of this given the absence of emotion that usually accompanies such bids for joint attention.

Methods developed by infancy researchers are often used to assess emotion recognition in young autistic children. We presented autistic children with slides of different faces depicting the same emotional expression and then one showing another emotion. Whereas the normally developing and mentally retarded children looked longer at the novel emotion, autistic children did not.[50] These findings may be interpreted as evidence that autistic children were unable to differentiate between emotions. Yet it is possible, though unlikely, that they recognized the change in emotion but were not inclined to look at the novel expressions. Why this would be the case is not clear.

Autistic children also have difficulty pairing facial and vocal expression of emotion. Peter Hobson presented autistic children with photographs of happy, sad, angry, and fearful faces and asked them to match the photographs with vocalizations conveying these emotions, and again with body gestures.[51] Most of these children were extremely poor at emotion matching, yet were quite adept at parallel matching tasks that did not center on emotion, for example, pairing animals with animal sounds. In contrast, almost all of the normal and mentally retarded children of the same mental age completed both matching tasks with ease.

Similar findings were reported from a study examining high-functioning autistic adolescents' ability to match the prosodic and linguistic expression of sadness, happiness, anger, and surprise with facial expressions of these emotions.[52] Autistic adolescents did not differ from schizophrenic and normally developing comparison adolescents in terms of their ability to label facial expressions of these emotions, but they had considerable difficulty pairing them with emotions expressed in the prosody of speech.

Building on previous studies of emotional understanding, Hobson and Weeks gave children photographs that could be grouped according to sex, age, facial expression, or type of hat.[53] The majority of nonautistic children sorted first on the basis of emotional expression. In contrast, autistic children of the same verbal ability were most inclined to sort by type of hat. In addition, almost half of them were unable to sort by facial expression when explicitly instructed to do so. Thus they may lack not only the inclination but the ability to distinguish and interpret emotional signals. As will be discussed further in Chapter 8, such findings led Hobson to adopt Kanner's original hypothesis, that autism involves a specific and innate inability to understand emotion, which is independent of general intellectual ability.

Given their difficulties with emotion expression and recognition, one might expect autistic children to show little capacity to empathize with the emotional experiences of others. Our research group examined empathy in young autistic, mentally retarded, and normally developing children in several laboratory settings.[54] In one situation parents are asked to lie down and pretend to feel ill, and children's responses are videotaped and analyzed. Normally developing children with mental retardation typically approached their parents and looked into their faces to appraise the situation. They often appeared concerned and attempted to soothe mother by smoothing her hair or holding her hand. In contrast, autistic children seemed uninterested in their parents' displays. They rarely made eye contact, and not one child with autism offered comfort.

In another scene mother pretends to hurt herself with a toy hammer while pounding wooden pegs. Normal and mentally retarded children appeared visibly upset in response, and often gave comfort with a hug or a pat on the hand. Most children with autism, however, generally ignored their parents' cries of pain. They tended not look up or otherwise acknowledge the emotional expression, and continued to play without interruption. The absence of an observable response does not necessarily mean, however, that one feels nothing. And because autistic children pay limited attention to others' emotional responses, they are less likely to develop an understanding of conventional displays. Alternatively, children quickly pick up on social display rules, so they might have learned to display empathy while feeling very little. However, conventional expressions of empathy facilitate a form of social connection by reinforcing a sense of mutual membership in a shared culture. The distress one feels in observing autistic children's lack of responsiveness to their parents, not to mention what one imagines the parents feel, testifies to the social significance of such displays.

Further, we apprehend our emotions as we share them with others. As sociologist Charles Taylor explains, "I can only learn what anger, love, anxiety . . . are through my and others' experience of these being objects for *us*, in some common space."[55] Thus autistic children's limited empathy raises questions about their self-understanding. As mentioned, self-recognition is a preliminary form of self-awareness, and one that has been tested. Autistic children do show signs of self-recognition. Several investigators have surreptitiously applied rouge to the noses of small samples of five- to eleven-year-old autistic children and held them up to a mirror, and have found that the children responded by touching their noses.[56] Yet the autistic children did not show the coy or self-conscious affect displayed by normal individuals in such studies.

Early Social Relationships

Since Kanner's initial description of the syndrome, autistic children have been portrayed as unable to form emotional bonds or attachments to their parents.[57] This portrayal, however, lacks empirical support. Recent research suggests that despite limitations in their responsiveness, many autistic children show warm attachments to their caregivers.

Studies that use the "strange situation" to assess attachment security are usually carried out with children between 18 months and two years of age. Because autism is not diagnosed until later, studies of the attachment relationships of autistic children have been conducted with three- to four-year-olds, most of whom are mentally retarded. The autistic children we studied, and those studied by Sally Rogers, Sally Ozonoff, and Christine Maslin-Cole in Denver, Theodore Shapiro and his colleagues in New York, and Cheryl Dissanayake and Stella Crossley in Australia, showed signs of secure attachment relationships.[58] They displayed a clear preference for interacting with their mothers and fathers over strangers, and appeared more comfortable with parents than with the unfamiliar examiner. When caregivers left their children in an unfamiliar room, many children showed mild distress through worried glances and disorganized play. They also reacted more strongly to the caregiver's departure than to that of a stranger.

When observed in the strange situation, autistic children's responses to separation tend to be less acute than those of younger normal children at the same developmental level. These differences may be attributable to autistic children's increased experience with separation; among normally developing children distress at separation diminishes significantly by three to four years of age. Perhaps the autistic children studied would have shown comparable degrees of fussiness and distraction had they been observed at 18 to 24 months. Alternatively, autistic children's relatively subdued responses to separation may be attributable to mental retardation rather than autism. Indeed, three- to four-year-old autistic children do not display any less distress than mentally retarded children of the same developmental level and chronological age. While early diagnosis of the disorder is crucial to delineating the development of attachment in children with autism, this issue is embedded in broader questions about the respective roles of experience and mental ability in the growth of emotional responses and relationships.

Children with autism also show positive responses to being reunited with their caregivers. They often approach their caregivers, they may smile or even initiate some form of physical contact, and their play becomes more organized and spirited. Again, such behaviors are restrained in comparison to those of younger normal children, who typically rush up to the caregivers and seek a great deal of contact.

Only a few studies have tried to characterize autistic children's relationships with their caregivers as secure or insecure and contrast the degree of security shown by autistic children and nonautistic retarded children.[59] In general, the same proportion (40%) of autistic as of retarded children appear to be securely attached.[60] In our research, we asked an expert in early attachment to code the quality of these attachments using the kind of system that was developed to assess young normal children in Ainsworth's study. Because they display repetitive stereotypical movements, peripheral looking, and other ambiguous behavior, all the autistic children in our sample were classified as showing disorganized attachments.[61] However, these behaviors cannot be interpreted as they would for nonautistic children. Nonautistic children's disorganized play, hand flapping, and gaze aversion may be related to biological and social risk factors such as parental psychopathology or child maltreatment, but these possibilities can be discarded among children with autism.

In spite of autistic children's behavioral disorganization, one-third of the autistic children in our study were found to have underlying secure attachments with their mothers. Thus, contrary to widespread belief, it *does* seem possible for autistic children to develop secure relationships with others.

Like the studies of attachment in normally developing infants, this study shows that the mothers of autistic children with secure attachment relationships appear more sensitive to their needs during a play interaction: for example, responding to the child's cues, elaborating and complimenting the child's behaviors, and not intruding. However, it is important to note that these mothers may have seemed more sensitive because their children were more responsive or easier to read than the children of mothers who appeared less sensitive. Consistent with this interpretation, the children who were classified as having more secure attachment relationships also more frequently initiated social interactions with their mothers during the play observation. The development of secure attachments, then, is attributable to characteristics of both the child and the parent.

Evidence that autistic children form secure attachment relationships contributes to conceptualizations of attachment security in normally developing children. In particular, these findings call for a more differentiated view of working models—that is, the models of relationships individuals derive from early relationships to caregivers which organize perception and experience of other relationships. Although some autistic children have secure relationships with their parents, we cannot assume that they go on to construct a schema or prototype of relationships in general. The nature of autism precludes the development of such models because to do so one must be able to take the perspective of another person. And as we have emphasized, autistic persons suffer impairment in their ability to understand and empathize with another's point of view. Autism informs current theories

of the development of attachment relationships in normal development by suggesting that a secure relationship may be necessary but is certainly not sufficient for
the development of good working models of relationships.

Studies of attachment in autistic children suggest it is
necessary to posit a two-tiered theory of the development of working models of relationships. In addition to
forming a secure early attachment relationship, the individual needs to develop an understanding and appreciation of the perspectives of others in order to have a good
working model of relationships. The normal child's early
psychobiological form of attachment is continuously en-
riched as the child becomes aware of the intentions and
emotional experiences of others. Autism disrupts the
seamless integration of new abilities that occurs when
attachment develops normally, thus revealing separable
elements of the developmental process.

Interpersonal Conflict and Self-Control

The emerging picture of autistic children's social understanding leads one to expect that they have difficulty
dealing with interpersonal conflict and little self-control.
Indeed, the limited ability or inclination to monitor other
people's intentions contributes to diminished awareness
both of social norms and the motivation for attempting
to meet them. The simplest forms of control over behavior may therefore be difficult to establish. Autistic children are slow to develop regular eating, sleeping, and
toilet habits, even in comparison to nonautistic children
with mental retardation.

Similarly, autistic children are less responsive to prohibitions. Our research group conducted a study in
which young children were offered candy by the experimenter, and, using verbal commands, parents would at-

tempt to forbid eating the candy for 30 seconds.[62] In contrast to the mentally retarded and normal children, almost all of whom were able to resist eating the candy, only eight of the 28 autistic children resisted totally, and another seven were able to restrain themselves for 15 seconds. Most of the autistic children did not look at the faces of their mothers or the experimenters, while the normal and mentally retarded children looked at their parents and smiled in what appeared to be an attempt to seduce them into giving up the candy. Autistic children's difficulties with self-control may be due in part to a limited repertoire of alternative strategies for pursuing their goals; this is not surprising, given that powers of persuasion stem from the ability to infer and influence the intentions of others. While normal and mentally retarded children continue to develop self-control as they grow to understand the motives and intentions of others and begin to reflect on their own desires, autistic children struggle to gain self-control for much of their lives.

In summary, research on the social development of young children with autism illuminates surprising strengths and striking limitations. Contrary to stereotypes that portray autistic children as emotionally flat and unable to form attachments to others, they express emotions, engage in and even initiate social interactions, and form strong attachment to caregivers. Young autistic children's most striking difficulties involve behaviors that allow individuals to enter into each other's experience of the world. In comparison to normal and mentally retarded children at the same developmental level, young autistic children appear less attentive to the emotional responses of others and less apt to share their own experiences. They rarely look at others to solicit or share responses to objects, nor reference others' faces to make sense of confusing circumstances, nor offer comfort in response to displayed distress. Deficits in these behaviors contribute to the limited interpersonal and cultural awareness that is the hallmark feature of autism. This awareness is also the foundation for a tool that is vitally important in constructing shared meaning and forming relationships as children grow older: language.

4 / Language Acquisition and Use

Lawrence entered the room wearing his backpack. Upon seeing the examiner, his mother whispered, "Say hello, Lawrence." "Say hello, Lawrence," he echoed, and then, "My name's Lawrence, Lawrence P. What's your name? My name's Lawrence P. I'm ten and a half years old." The examiner introduced herself. Lawrence sat down at the table, his backpack pressed up against the back of his chair. The examiner invited him to take it off, but he declined. "My name's Lawrence, Lawrence P. What's your name? My name's Lawrence P. I'm ten and a half years old." The examiner repeated her name and asked Lawrence what he liked to do after school. Lawrence silently scanned the room and asked "What's your name?" After repeating her name again, the examiner said she used to play basketball after school when she was his age and asked Lawrence if he liked sports. "Yeah, I like sports. I like sports. My name's Lawrence, Lawrence P. I'm ten and a half years old. What's your name?"

The emergence of language marks a biological, social-behavioral shift that separates infants from young children. Children's mental and social lives are utterly transformed by their ability to learn and use language. They learn first to distinguish and vocalize the sounds of their native language and to combine these sounds to produce words. As children master the relations between words and their referents and the grammatical rules for linking words together to create meaning, they learn how to use language to achieve particular communicative goals.[1]

Speaking can be thought of as communicative action designed to achieve any number of goals, ranging from securing an object to saying a prayer to expressing sympathy. How such goals are achieved varies across cultures, but learning the language is an integral part of being socialized into a particular community. Thus language develops at the intersection between cognitive, emotional, and social understanding; forms of understanding that are impaired in children with autism.

Language Development among Normal Children

Although normally developing children do not speak during the first year of life, their interactions with others lay the groundwork for developing language. From birth children are predisposed to communicate with the people around them. Newborn infants show a preference for language over other kinds of sounds, and within the first month of life they can distinguish the sounds of their native language from those of a foreign language.[2]

Although newborns' repertoire of expressive language is limited, caregivers quickly learn to distinguish various patterns of crying. At about 3 months of age babies begin to engage in give-and-take exchanges in which they augment communication with social smiles. Infants and caregivers take turns while vocalizing, thus establishing the interactive framework for vocal learning and dialogue.[3]

Phonemes

It can take several years to master the separate sounds or phonemes of a language. By four months of age infants begin to babble, a form of vocalizing that includes consonant and vowel sounds akin to those used in speech. Among children 12 months old and younger, babbling sounds the same across the world's language communities, but it gradually assumes culture-specific intonation patterns. Babies begin vocalizing strings of syllables that sound like the speech of those around them, a behavior known as "jargoning."[4]

Infants develop the ability to distinguish and produce recognizable linguistic signals within the context of increasingly complex social interactions. At about 12 months of age infants increasingly combine vocalization with gazing and pointing behavior. The use of such behaviors to establish joint attention and engage in social referencing is an essential precursor to language development.[5] Social referencing and joint attention behaviors evolve together with children's increased awareness of pointing as a means of communication. For example, when 12-month-olds see a remote-controlled car roll past them, first they point and then look to see how their mothers react. But at 18 months children are more likely to look first at their mothers, and then point only if their mothers are looking.[6] Such visual and gestural behavior forms the foundation of linguistic communication. Indeed, when people talk, they are sharing knowledge about objects and experiences that are the focus of their joint attention.

Words and Grammar

Jerome Bruner described the process whereby children learn to label objects as the "dubbing format," in which an experienced speaker labels an object that is the focus of shared attention.[7] Shared gaze and interest are intimately tied to word-learning. Tomasello and Farrar found a correlation between the amount of time spent in joint-attention episodes at 15 months, and the child's expressive vocabulary at 21 months.[8] Reciprocally, infants tend to look longer at objects and actions that have been named than those that have not been named. Nevertheless, learning what words mean is complicated: a single object or event has many parts and features, which can be referred to in any number of ways. For example, one might point to a dog's ear and say "dog," "ear," "brown," and so on. Given this potential for confusion, language learning remains a mystery.

Children's first words often appear to be crude stabs at the right sound pattern; for example, they might leave out certain parts of a word (saying "to" instead of "tooth"). Because of the idiosyncratic nature of these expressions, it is difficult to determine when children first use words. Adults may be so eager to claim that their children can talk that they discover words in early cooing and babbling. As Michael and Sheila Cole have suggested, it is useful to think of the process of word formation as a joint effort. "Neither the adult nor the child really knows what the other is saying. Each tries to gather in a little meaning by supposing that the other's utterance fits a particular sound pattern that corresponds to a particular meaning. This joint effort, or collusion, may eventually result in something common, a word in a language that both can understand."[9]

Two-year-old children are thought to learn several words a day. Initially, children over- and underextend their use of words.[10] For example, a child might say "dog" in referring to all animals, or, alternatively, only in referring to her own dog. Lexical development booms during the preschool years, as children need less and less time and exposure to acquire new words. They develop more complex ways of dealing with words—for example, by establishing and consolidating categories of meaning through using analogy and metaphor—which require perception of relationships within and across words.

As they acquire words, children begin to string them together, vastly increasing their communicative effectiveness.[11] Bringing into action paralinguistic features such as loudness, intonation, and pitch, children are able to use two-word utterances to convey possession ("Joey truck") or to make requests ("truck Joey"). Although adults often readily interpret what the child means in such instances, the ambiguity of many two-word utterances limits effective communication to familiar contexts. Nevertheless, the child's telegraphic utterances display awareness that varying the order of the words creates different meanings, marking the birth of grammar.[12]

Grammar is the sequencing of parts of words and of words in a sentence. Grammatical structures carve up the world in different ways. Like a painter's palette and brush, the grammatical repertoire in a speech community is a resource for constructing actions, emotions, and identities from a particular point of view. The ways in which we use language shape our perception of events. Speakers of different languages, in this sense, see somewhat different worlds, a principle known as linguistic relativity.[13]

During the second year children master the use of grammatical morphemes, units that create meaning by conveying the relations between elements in a sentence—little words and word-parts that are systematically absent in two-word utterances. Consider the difference between "Dog bites" and "Don't touch the dog 'cause dog bites": The article "the" indicates that it is this dog, not dogs in general that should be avoided. The second sentence also exemplifies how children gradually master the rules for putting words together to create certain relationships and meanings. For instance, in the example above "'cause" connects two propositions and indicates a causal relation between them. Mastering the grammar and syntax of a language involves grasping highly abstract rules that even adult speakers are often unable to explain.

Pragmatics

As children participate in interactions that facilitate the expansion of their vocabularies and the acquisition of grammar, they discover that the sounds they make can be used to achieve goals. At the earliest stages of language development, children demonstrate competent use of prosody, intonation, words, and grammatical constructions to express feelings, moods, dispositions, and attitudes.[14] Expressive and referential functions of language are acquired in an integrated fashion. That is, children simultaneously learn how to use language to refer to objects and events and to express their point of view and desires.

Soviet psychologist Lev Vygotsky proposed that even children's initial sounds are communicative acts, mediating their interactions with people and objects in the world.[15] Indeed, language acquisition is fueled by the desire to communicate intentionally about meaningful, often emotional topics. In her naturalistic research on children and families, Judy Dunn found, for example, that the issues that were most upsetting to children at 18 months were those that they communicated about most effectively at three years.[16]

Children's earliest conversational acts fall into two categories, protoimperatives and protodeclaratives, both of which are preceded (and initially accompanied) by gestures.[17] Protoimperatives involve enlisting another to achieve a desired goal. Rather than acting on objects directly, for example, getting a ball out of a toy box, children learn to direct others' attention by pointing and vocalizing. They also learn that utterances such as "milk" may constitute a request for more, particularly when the message is delivered with empty glass in hand.

Akin to the use of pointing to establish joint attention, protodeclaratives refer to an object to establish it as a joint focus of attention and to convey a particular attitude or emotion. A child might, for example, smile, point to a rabbit, and say "bunny," wanting only to show it to his mother. Participating in these conversational acts enables children to learn how to use the language of a particular culture. In all languages and speech communities, certain features of language index something about participants' feelings and beliefs. Language learners use this information to make sense of experience—their own and that of others—and in so doing are socialized into particular forms of linguistic communication.[18] That is, they learn the conventions for expressing various emotions and stances toward persons and objects in the world.

As they acquire the pragmatic aspects of language, children learn that a single sequence of words can accomplish multiple goals. Interpreting a sentence involves understanding more than the words it contains, grammatical markings such as references to persons and place, and logical connections. Comprehension requires going beyond what is stated in the sentence, focusing also on how the sentence is delivered and the context in which it is articulated. Even a parental statement as simple as "Where's your blanket?" made to an irritable two-year-old may carry numerous situational implications: "Go get your blanket"; "Do you want me to help you find your blanket?"; "It's time for your nap"; and "Cheer yourself up." Thus the relationship between sentence and situation is crucial.

Prosody. The prosodic features of language—stress, pitch, and intonation—are powerful resources for conveying meaning. Highly affective in nature, prosodic features are most accessible to newborn infants. In many but not all cultures caregivers use higher pitch and relatively smooth, simple, and highly modulated intonation patterns in communicating to infants. Studies of mother-child interaction in the United States, Europe, and Japan in various situations suggest that mothers use particular patterns of intonation to convey meaning; they use high, rising pitch to engage and arouse, and low, falling contours to soothe and comfort.[19] These prosodic patterns are perceptually and affectively salient to the infant.[20] Further, habitual associations between prosodic features and affective meaning provide a foundation for mastering the abstract relationship between sound and meaning. Children often rely on intonation to increase comprehension when other linguistic abilities are stretched.

Although prosodic development appears in advance of other aspects of language, children's knowledge of the prosodic system does not fully mature until early adolescence.[21] Prosodic features are used in combination with other aspects of language to stress important words, mark grammatical distinctions, convey emotions and attitudes, and distinguish between various speech acts. For example, "Where's *your* blanket?" connotes a different meaning from "Where's your *blanket?*" In the first case, the speaker may stress "your" to differentiate between the child's blanket and, say, that of another child. Alternatively, emphasis on "blanket" suggests that the speaker wants the child to locate his or her blanket as opposed to another object. Or if a speaker elongates the word "blanket" and delivers the phrase in a sing-song voice, it may be taken as a sign to initiate a game.

How utterances are delivered—the melody and context of speech—reveals the speaker's meaning and attitude. Effective use of language requires attending to these aspects of utterances. Language learners gradually develop control over tone, timing, and pitch as they learn to traverse between an utterance as articulated and the situation at hand to communicate or comprehend the intended message.

Conversational Conventions. Learning how to use language to achieve certain goals requires mastering the conversational conventions within a particular community. Conventions that regulate what is to be said and how to say it vary markedly from one culture to another. In the United States, for example, children are expected to say "please" when requesting something and "thank you" when receiving something. In a Colombian mestizo community such phrases are discouraged, however, because they signal the speaker's inferiority; it is obedience rather than politeness that is valued and expected.[22]

Learning to converse in a language includes mastering conventions for taking turns, taking the floor, and inviting others to speak.[23] Children are able to sustain well-timed turn-taking with adults by the age of two, and with peers shortly thereafter. The ability to enter smoothly into ongoing conversation and to introduce new topics or elaborate on existing topics continues to develop during the middle childhood years.

English philosopher H. P. Grice proposed four principles to facilitate effective conversation: speak no more or less than is required (quantity); speak the truth and avoid falsehood (quality); speak in an informative way (relevance); and avoid ambiguity (clarity).[24] Yet speakers often intentionally violate these maxims in pursuit of particular communicative goals. Irony, for example, involves stating the obvious, while sarcasm entails speaking untruths. In addition, speakers often repeat information or deliberately obscure particular details for the sake of argument. Becoming a competent member of a speech community, then, involves being able to understand and produce speech within a particular context, given certain communicative goals—something that requires considerable experience and expertise.[25] As Ludwig Wittgenstein noted, "the use of language in communication is not a matter of the truth or falsity of atomic propositions, but rather a process of transferring information from one mind to another."[26]

Taking the Listener into Account. To communicate effectively, the speaker must take the listener's perspective into account. In addition to assessing listeners' language ability, speakers must identify topics that are of interest and assess listeners' current knowledge to avoid either confusion or redundancy. Children as young as two and a half years of age show an understanding of these requirements. They simplify their speech when talking to younger children, suggesting that they know the younger child's language ability is less sophisticated than their own.[27] In addition, young children modify what they say as a function of listener's knowledge. For example, when speaking to a stranger, two-and-a-half-year-olds are more likely to give an elaborate account of a trip to the zoo than when speaking with someone who was also present.[28] Our renderings of experience, then, are shaped by those in our midst, and every telling provides speakers and listeners with the opportunity to gain new understandings of themselves and others.

Narrative

Narrative is a fundamental form of language; it is universal and emerges early in the communicative development of children.[29] Narratives depict a temporal transition from one situation to another, offering a vehicle for imposing a thematically coherent order on otherwise disconnected experience.[30] The proclivity to organize experience in terms of a plot is uniquely and characteristically human. Story plots build causal connections between circumstances, emotions, thoughts, and actions, constituting the narrator's theory of events.

The stories people tell about past events are intricately linked to concerns about the present and future.[31] In this sense, narrative activity can alleviate the cognitive and emotional upset that may accompany unmet expectations and unexpected events. As Bruner notes, "while a culture must contain a set of norms, it must also contain a set of interpretive procedures for rendering departures from those norms meaningful in terms of established patterns of belief."[32] A primary function of narrative is to make sense of deviation from cultural canons. At the same time that stories recount events that depart from the ordinary, they also serve to articulate and sustain local understandings of what is normal and appropriate.

The uses of storytelling emerge early in children's development. Two-year-old Emmy, after being tucked into her crib for a nap or for the night, lay alone telling herself little stories that made patterns out of the confusing events of the day.[33] The analysis of how Emmy posed puzzles to herself and put them into temporal or problem-solving frames illuminates how narratives determine the meaning of events, creating coherence out of confusion. Likewise, rendering experiences and events in narrative form consolidates expectations about life's prospects.

Narrative activity facilitates children's understanding of themselves, others, and the workings of the world, enabling them to apprehend experiences and conduct relationships. Furthermore, through conversational narrative children learn to organize and communicate information in a way that can be introduced into social interaction. Rendering experience in narrative form makes it more readily accessible in memory and easier to introduce into conversation.[34] Indeed, narratives of personal experience are simultaneously born out of experience and give shape to experience. In the words of Toni Morrison, "Narrative is creating us at the very moment it is being created."[35]

Language Development among Children with Autism

Language impairment is a central feature of autism. Almost half of the population of autistic individuals never acquires functional language. Although verbal ability is strongly associated with severity of mental handicap, language acquisition is significantly delayed relative to overall cognitive level even among nonretarded autistic individuals, generally emerging at four and a half years of age. Moreover, autistic persons have difficulty communicating with others throughout their lives. This is perhaps not surprising, given that language both evolves out of and incorporates the prelinguistic forms of social communication that prove most problematic for individuals with autism: joint attention and social referencing behaviors. Although they may use words and grammatical structures correctly, their speech reflects fundamental deficits in the comprehension and expression of attitudes and intentions. The persistent communicative impairment autistic persons face illuminates the inseparability of language and social understanding.

Phonemes and Words

While it starts later and moves at a slower rate, phonological development among children with autism resembles that of normally developing children with respect to the order and emergence of speech sounds.[36] Bartolucci, Pierce, Steiner, and Eppel, for example, used a picture-naming task to elicit phonemes from autistic, mentally retarded, and normal children matched by nonverbal mental age. The autistic children did not differ from comparison children in terms of the distribution of various phonemes and the distribution of error patterns. Further, they were as apt as comparison children in discriminating speech sounds, again suggesting the absence of phonological deficits. Relative to normally developing children, however, autistic children are slow in acquiring words. This is perhaps not surprising, given that children pick up the meaning of words while interacting with a person who labels an object or topic both are attending to, and that autistic children have significant deficits in joint attention behaviors.

Autism does not appear, however, to interfere with the acquisition of basic conceptual knowledge that underlies word meaning.[37] Although mentally retarded autistic persons who have only a few words may use them idiosyncratically, this is more likely a result of mental retardation in general than of autism. Indeed, nonretarded individuals can organize conceptual categories for concrete objects in representing noun-word meanings and in naming. Helen Tager-Flusberg, a renowned investigator of language in autism, has shown that autistic children were able to indicate whether a pictured object was an instance of a particular word and to select from an array of pictures those that belonged to the category named.[38] But such findings do not tell us whether the children could recognize the range of meaning that even concrete objects such as boats have for nonautistic children—for example, that boats might signify recreation or livelihood. Whether or not an autistic child—or anyone, for that matter—grasps all the various linguistic meanings depends upon the extent to which he shares or can imagine the perspective of those with whom he speaks.

Moreover, studies of verbal understanding have focused on a narrow range of words limited to concrete objects. Acquiring the meanings of nouns that fit simple perceptual categories is different from acquiring the meaning of multiple words that relate in a particular way: for example, "The boy has a dog." Research on autistic children's comprehension of phrases and sentences suggests that they have more trouble tapping relational meaning than normally developing and mentally retarded controls matched on nonverbal mental age.[39] Similarly, examination of relational terms in the spontaneous speech of a sample of high-functioning autistic children suggests that while they used relational words correctly, they were less apt to use such words than were children with Down Syndrome.

Grammar

While rates of development vary, studies of autistic children who acquire some functional language suggest that their grammar and syntax resemble that of normal children, and that they use a rule-governed grammatical system.[40] Like mentally retarded and normally developing controls, autistic individuals used sequences of words in sentences or anomalous word strings to infer basic semantic relationships, for example, between subject and object or agent and recipient. Autistic individuals may generally rely more heavily on less sophisticated rules. Tager-Flusberg has proposed that there are two classes of syntactic rules.[41] Those in the first set are robust, develop early, and are not contingent upon contextual factors or environmental input. In English, word order exemplifies this category as it conveys relationships between parts of a sentence such as subject and object. The rules in the second set develop later and are sensitive to context. Examples include rules concerning morphemes and auxiliaries such as pronouns ("he," "she," "we," "they") and deictic references ("this," "that," "here," and "there") that are defined by the perspectives of the speakers in the situation at hand. Acquisition of certain grammatical forms also appears to vary according to environmental input. Children who are regularly exposed to yes-no questions (in which they hear auxiliaries in the salient initial position of the sentence), for example, appear to learn auxiliaries at a faster rate than those with more limited exposure to such questions.[42]

Highlighting evidence that autistic individuals have some difficulty with past-tense marking and pronominal and deictic references,[43] Tager-Flusberg has proposed that verbal autistic children resemble normal children in their acquisition of grammatical rules of the first type, but not of the second. Consistent with deficits in social referencing behavior, this assumption is grounded in the notion that autistic persons have difficulty tracking speakers' verbal references.

Pronoun reversals, in particular the substitution of "you" for "I" and "I" for "you," have been interpreted as a sign of autistic persons' deep confusion about identity. Particularly in view of evidence that verbal autistic persons have the ability to use names correctly,[44] such errors point to a specific weakness in using deictics, the proper use of which requires monitoring both the point of view of the speaker and of the hearer. Autistic individuals are likely to have problems appreciating whose perspective should be taken in a particular situation. Alternatively, pronoun reversals may constitute immediate or delayed echoing of particular utterances, or "echolalia," a topic we shall get to shortly.

Autistic individuals may also overuse the robust grammatical rules under circumstances in which normally developing children would be more flexible.[45] This may lead to their having difficulty producing and interpreting syntactic constructions such as questions and passive sentences, which deviate from normative word order. Furthermore, individuals with autism appear not to avail themselves of the range of grammatical resources that can be used to communicate meaning.

As with phonological and lexical levels, understanding autistic persons' language development at the grammatical level is limited by the narrowness of range and variety of grammatical structures that have been studied over time. Beyond identifying grammatical errors or correctness, ongoing longitudinal research will enhance our knowledge of the ways that individuals with autism use grammar, semantics, and syntax to build portraits of themselves and others in the world.

Pragmatics

While autistic individuals' phonological, semantic, and grammatical development follows a fairly normal course, their *use* of linguistic forms proves problematic.[46] These difficulties in acquiring and using language are likely to be part of a more general problem with communication. Autistic individuals' problems in this area may stem from limited participation in reciprocal interactions in which attention, attitudes, and emotions are shared. These deficits contribute to pragmatic difficulties in interpreting subtle meanings of utterances and words, observing social rules, knowing when to switch from one register to another, observing conversational conventions, and taking the listeners' perspective into account.

In parallel with findings from studies of gesture, observations of autistic children in the early stages of language development revealed frequent use of language to obtain a desired object, but less frequent to serve social functions such as gaining or sharing attention. Whereas normal children acquire social and nonsocial communicative functions simultaneously, autistic children may acquire such functions sequentially, with social functions being a relatively late achievement. This possibility is supported by careful naturalistic observations of spontaneous communication.[47] Consistent with this perspective, another line of research suggests that autistic and mentally retarded children are similar with respect to the forms they use to express negation, but that there are significant differences in pragmatic function: autistic children did not use negative speech to inform others nor to manipulate behavior. These pragmatic verbal tools did finally appear in older, more advanced children, but it seems that in general certain types of social functions of language are less accessible to autistic persons than others. The common element in the communicative functions least used and last to develop among autistic persons is that they hinge on the ability to share another's perspective and on knowledge of conventional methods for influencing other people.

Although individuals with autism produce and comprehend a wide range of speech acts, they often do so in an idiosyncratic manner. For example, in response to a question on the Wechsler Intelligence Test, "What do you do when you cut your finger?" autistic children commonly say "bleed."[48] This answer implies an unusual interpretation of what the questioner has in mind. Similarly, the autistic person's pragmatic difficulties may stem from a failure to grasp connotations or affective attitudes that words convey, such as the difference between telling someone they look "skinny," "slender," "slim," or "petite." Although all three words may accurately represent the person's aspect, "skinny" has negative connotations. This sort of insensitivity to shades of meaning reveals, by contrast, the powerful role of language in constructing shared understanding.

Prosody. With individual variations, autistic persons at all ages and levels of language ability show limited competence with prosody—perhaps the first resource infants and caregivers rely on to construct shared meaning.[49] Prosodic deficits are among the most striking and consistently noted features of autism.

Studies carried out in the United States, England, Germany, and Czechoslovakia have found that autistic individuals' speech is characterized by improperly modulated intonation, loudness, pitch, stress, and rhythm. Autistic persons' speech is commonly described as "arhythmic," "hollow," 'dull,' and "wooden," as well as "excessively sing-song" and "over-precise in articulation."[50]

Laboratory studies also suggest that autistic individuals appear to have trouble imitating patterns of intonation. Baltaxe asked a group of autistic individuals to imitate utterances which are known to have distinctive patterns of intonation in English, for example yes-no questions and commands.[51] In comparison to normally developing children whose speech displayed characteristic prosodic patterns, children with autism were less systematic in their use of intonation. Further, whereas normally developing children's articulation varied within different contexts, among children with autism this was not the case. It appears, then, that normally developing children follow rhythmic structure or relative timing in their speech, making each element part of a prosodically organized whole; whereas autistic children follow a serial or chain model—linearly chaining or connecting individual elements.

Complementarily, autistic children do not appear to use intonation to convey meaning in universally recognizable ways. Derek Ricks recorded the voices of young, prelinguistic autistic and normal children in four situations which usually evoke a response in normally developing infants: seeing mother in the morning; watching food being prepared; having food offered and withdrawn; being introduced to a captivating object.[52] Parents were asked to listen to these vocalizations. All of the parents could identify the situations that elicited normally developing infants' vocalizations. However, each autistic child's vocalizations were identified only by his or her own parent. Moreover, whereas parents of normal children could not distinguish their child's voice, parents of autistic children recognized their own child with ease. It seems, then that there are universal vocal expressions that can be readily interpreted, but the autistic children in this sample did not use them.

Another aspect of prosody, emphatic stress, also presents difficulties. Although autistic children appear to be able to distinguish between stressed and unstressed words, they do not seem to make use of stress assignment to decipher utterances. When presented with yes-no questions accompanied by a contradictory visual display (for example, the question "Is the baby sleeping in the bed?" was accompanied by a picture of a dog in a bed), autistic children performed as well as comparison children.[53] While normally developing children were less prone to error if the critical word was stressed (for example, "Is the *baby* sleeping in the bed?"), this was not the case among individuals with autism, suggesting that they did not make use of prosodic markers. Indeed, even the most highly verbal autistic persons have trouble recognizing prosodic markers of figurative language—sarcasm, for instance—a weakness that produces the impression that they are excessively literal. Limited appreciation of prosodic features, then, contributes significantly to impairment in the use of language to communicate with others.

Conversational Conventions. The conversational flow appears least likely to break down when autistic persons are asked questions; this suggests that they have particular difficulty initiating and maintaining topics of conversation.[54] Autistic persons often fail to use eye contact to signal turn-taking; they interrupt other speakers, have trouble adding new, relevant information to previous comments, and themselves often use questions to initiate and continue conversation—questions that are often unrelated to the topic at hand. Further, like Lawrence, the boy described at the start of this chapter, autistic persons tend to repeat the question when they already have the answer, ask questions they answer themselves, and offer idiosyncratic or bizarre associations. Autistic persons appear to suffer from a limited awareness of where a conversation is going—or that interlocutors can journey together into topics and experiences through conversation.

Individuals with autism also tend to ask embarrassing

or intrusive questions, such as "How old are you?" of adult strangers. This tendency usually reflects a general lack of understanding of social norms about what is acceptable in conversation. Such a lack stems in part from difficulty using and interpreting features of language that index something about social roles and identities, feelings and attitudes. Baltaxe, for example, found that German-speaking autistic adolescents often confused the polite and familiar forms of address (Sie and Du).[55] Appreciating conversational norms, then, hinges on understanding the relationships between participants.

Taking the Listener into Account. Difficulties in communicating may be understood as part of a more pervasive problem of autism: that of taking conversational partners into account, not only with respect to status but knowledge and experience as well. Similarly, idiosyncratic remarks based on unique associations imply limited awareness of understandings that are accessible to listeners, limited monitoring of listeners' needs for contextual information, and failure to gauge comprehension.

Such difficulties were apparent when Katherine Loveland and her colleagues asked high-functioning verbal adolescents with autism to teach a simple board game to someone.[56] In comparison to adolescents with Down Syndrome (matched on verbal ability), those with autism required significantly more prompting to communicate the necessary information. These findings were interpreted as a manifestation of autistic individuals' difficulty in assuming another person's perspective in a given situation: here their knowledge of the rules of the game as well as the information needed to play.

Harking back to earlier deficits in joint attention and social referencing, such difficulty suggests a disinclination or inability to share with others in a wider context of social interactions and relationships. As Bosch noted, "It is in language and through language in particular that the success and failure of the constitution of common worlds is most impressively revealed."[57]

Echolalia

Impairment in the ability to anticipate what listeners need or desire to hear is also thought to inhibit spontaneous speech and contribute to the parrot-like echoing known as echolalia. Echolalia is among the most salient behavioral abnormalities of young autistic children. Approximately 80 percent of all verbal autistic persons produce this stereotyped speech, and those who echo most seem to use little spontaneous language.[58] The more generative language an individual possesses, the less apt he or she will be to use echoed speech. Yet *why* echolalia emerges in persons with autism remains unknown.

Observations of autistic persons suggest that they tend to echo speech addressed directly to them, as when Lawrence repeated the command addressed to him, "Say hello, Lawrence." Echolalic speech highlights the difference between comprehension and transmission. Uta Frith points to echolalia as a glaring manifestation of misconnection between the more peripheral processing systems and a central system that is concerned with meaning.[59] Thus autistic persons and others who do not fully understand speech nevertheless may be able to produce it. In addition, autistic persons who do understand speech may echo utterances apparently without communicative intent. Indeed, a rapidly forthcoming echo may be a sign that a message has failed to register.

Other researchers have suggested that echolalia represents a gestalt or holistic method of language processing, such that echoing the question "Do you want a cookie?" means "Yes." It is impossible to ascertain whether this is really the case. In any event, such responses—like Lawrence's repetitive questioning—-engender an acute sense of communication failure among interlocutors. Echolalia, then, contributes significantly to autistic impairment in developing extended, organized discourse.

Narrative

The host of difficulties autistic persons face in conversing with others may be traced to the lack of an impulse or gift to narrate. For it is through narrative that children develop the capacity to construct shared (that is, nonidiosyncratic) understandings of emotions and events, and to render experiences in ways that are comprehensible to members of the same culture. The ability to narrate—to forge connections between settings, characters' behavioral and emotional responses, and consequences—allows people to share their experiences. While normally developing children begin to narrate from a very early age (recall the narrative monologues of two-year-old Emmy), the proclivity eludes even the most high-functioning individuals with autism.

Researchers have done relatively little work on narrative in autism.[60] A few investigators have asked autistic children and adolescents to make up narratives that portray short sequences of pictures. Relative to normal and mentally retarded comparison children, autistic persons told stories that were shorter and less complex, contained more grammatical and lexical errors, and did not narrate in past tense. While good storytellers often deliberately frame past story events as if they were happening in the here-and-now, individuals with autism do not use the present tense as a rhetorical device; rather, they seem unaware of narrative convention.[61] Other studies using picture sequences have reported that autistic children simply describe the pictures, one after the next, without providing causal and intentional features of a story, and that they were less likely than normal and mentally retarded comparison children to talk about mental states.[62]

Yet narrative difficulty might be attributable not solely to impairment in theory of mind, but also to a more pervasive difficulty: that of identifying meaningful aspects of human activity. Katherine Loveland and her colleagues presented a puppet show or a video to high-functioning adolescents with autism and the same show to another group with Down Syndrome. The story line is that a thief tries to steal a secretary's wallet, and she hits him over the head with her umbrella.[63] After viewing the video, participants were asked to tell the story to a listener. The examiners were most struck by the bizarre and irrelevant speech and idiosyncratic, uninformative gestures of the autistic children. Further, they noted that autistic persons portrayed the puppets as moving objects rather than entities with thoughts and feelings. And their observations did not appear to be organized around a plot that endeavored to make sense of troubling events from a particular point of view. Follow-up questions suggested that the groups were similar in their understanding of the story, implying that group differences did not stem from differences in memory of enacted events but from differences in narrative ability.

Finally, in collaboration with Carol Feldman and Jerome Bruner, we carried out a pilot study in which an investigator told stories of deception to high-functioning adolescents, interrupting the readings with "What do you think is going to happen?" followed by "Why do you think that?" Analyses of data from four subjects suggests that they were quite able to answer questions about acts of deception. However, their tellings did not relate circumstances to characters' points of view, nor were they organized around deception—the betrayal of cultural expectations that gave rise to events. Their retellings resembled descriptive accounts, and while they often repeated sentences verbatim, these were frequently inserted out of sequence and out of the context of a story plot.

Observations of nonretarded, high-functioning individuals with autism as they participate in social situations suggest that they may use their cognitive abilities to compensate for social-affective impairment.[64] One gets the sense that highly intelligent autistic people struggle to understand social-affective matters as if they were solving math problems. While they are often able to come up with adequate, albeit strange, accounts of social and personal situations, the process is laborious, operating outside of intuitive notions about how they and others ordinarily feel and think in various situations. Thus despite diligent, genuine, and often courageous effort, even the most intelligent autistic persons cannot compensate for their limited access to a commonality that is effortlessly entered by most of us as we give conventional narrative form to life experiences.

In summary, autistic persons *do* attempt to communicate and may use language appropriately. Indeed, autistic children resemble normal children in their development of phonological, lexical, and grammatical structures. Yet the pragmatic difficulties displayed by individuals with autism show, by contrast, that people speaking a common language index emotions, attitudes, roles, and identities in a way that lends essential continuity to social interactions. This continuity is central to the construction and instantiation of identities, relationships, and cultural affiliation.

5 / Middle Childhood

Thomas is a nine-year-old boy with short blond hair and pale blue eyes. He walks into the room, sits down at a small table, opens a sketch pad, and begins to draw. With eyes riveted on the page in front of him, Thomas works quickly. His mother explains that he has just walked by a photo of Royce Hall at UCLA and wants to reproduce it for his collection. The examiner asks her about this collection. Without lifting his eyes from the page, Thomas states that he draws pictures of buildings. His mother tells him he can finish later. He closes his notebook without pausing to admire his work. The examiner is struck by Thomas's artistic ability, and by his memory for detail. She gives him several cubes; some sides are red, others white, and others are split diagonally into red and white triangles. She presents him with various red and white geometric patterns and asks him to replicate them using the cubes. Thomas completes even the most intricate designs quickly, with apparent ease. The examiner hands him a peg board on which hang several rings of various colors. She shows Thomas a simple design and asks him to reproduce the pattern, stipulating that he may move one ring one space at a time. Confident that he will finish this elementary task momentarily, she searches for a more difficult design. But Thomas appears perplexed. He moves a blue ring forward two spaces, and then a yellow. Fingering a red ring he stops and stares blankly at the pegboard. Three minutes pass. Thomas looks out the window, not saying a word.

For most of us middle childhood is devoted to mastering skills that enable us to move into the adult world. The skills children learn depend both on the culture in which they live and the capabilities they bring to the tasks they face. Children's cognitive and social development takes place as they participate in routine interactions with other people.[1] Social structure and cultural norms shape the children's roles in their families and communities and the nature of their daily activities, including whether they go to school and/or care for siblings and have employment opportunities.

Across cultures, children are expected to develop competence in several domains. In industrialized countries many necessary skills are taught at school, such as reading, writing, and arithmetic. Because the written word is the principal vehicle for ongoing education, mastering reading skills is essential to educational progress. In other parts of the world children learn the skills they need—carpentry, farming, weaving—while working, as apprentices to more expert members of the community. Research in Recife, Brazil, for example, demonstrates how child street vendors acquire knowledge of mathematics.[2] The demands of formal and informal education intensify as children grow older, as does the expectation that children will be able to carry out tasks on their own.[3] By middle childhood children who have not mastered rudimentary skills fall behind and lack the foundation upon which to build more advanced problem-solving abilities. How well children master the skills they need influences their standing with peers and families and how they see themselves. The next section outlines the cognitive and social practices that engage the typical child in these middle years.

Normal Development

Motor and Physical Skills

Growing children spend a great deal of time and energy developing physical coordination, both in terms of fine and gross motor skills. The development of such skills is tied to increasingly sophisticated participation in academic, economic, and social life. Children are expected to use pencils, pens, musical instruments, and other tools requiring fine motor precision, and to engage in a range of activities requiring gross motor skill, ranging from four-square and basketball to working in the field. As during other developmental stages, children's motor, cognitive, and social accomplishments are intertwined. That is, playing on an athletic team requires not only physical strength and hand-eye coordination, but the ability to plan and execute strategies and to connect and communicate with teammates.

Cognitive and Academic Skills

During middle childhood, besides acquiring a great deal of knowledge, children learn to think in new ways. In the early years they are interested in how things work, and spend hours manipulating and organizing objects. Over time they learn to manipulate, reorganize, and transform objects in their minds. This reflects advances in memory, conceptual understanding, and concentration.

In early childhood children display very good visual

or eidetic memory. They are often able to recall objects and scenarios in exact detail for long periods of time.[4] Gradually, however, children begin to store information according to global categories and schemas, and the capacity for eidetic memory fades. For example, whereas young children precisely store and recall certain characteristics of an orangutan they saw at a zoo, older children's recollections are embedded in categorical knowledge of apes. Similarly, children also acquire generalized event representations, or what Katherine Nelson calls "script knowledge."[5] Script knowledge of a trip to the zoo, for example, includes the content and structure of activities such as buying a ticket, looking at the animals, eating lunch, and so on. Thus while young children might recall various aspects of individual trips, older children incorporate these aspects into knowledge of a category of experience. Categorical, scripted understandings are useful in that they enable persons to process and store information more rapidly and effectively,[6] anticipate sequences of events, adhere to cultural expectations, and coordinate group activity. As Nelson points out, acquiring knowledge of scripts is central to acquiring knowledge of a culture; without shared scripts, every social act would need to be negotiated afresh. Indeed, failure to comply with scripts (for example, barging to the front of the ticket line or attempting to give a soda to a seal) may lead to conflict and/or embarrassment.

While acknowledging that changes in memory contribute to the emergence of new behaviors, Piaget posited that middle childhood was marked by a new form of thought, which he called "concrete operations."[7] Whereas young children rely on trial and error as a problem-solving strategy, older children solve problems in their minds; whereas young children's thinking is bound to appearances, older children can imagine physical materials in an altered state. Children become able to combine, separate, order, and transform objects in their minds, and recognize that certain properties of an object remain the same when the object's appearance is altered in a superficial way, for example, if water in a short, wide cup is poured into a tall, thin one, or if the spacing between eight objects is narrowed in one row and widened in another.[8]

In middle childhood children engage in a great deal of cognitive and social problem-solving. Complex problem-solving requires organized planning, flexible thinking, and rejecting impulsive action directed towards an immediate goal in favor of strategies that maximize the chances for success. Referred to as "executive function," such a cluster of abilities is activated in many video and board games, and also in interactions with other people and objects in the world. In the game of checkers, for example, children learn the advantage of foregoing a single jump—capturing an opponent's piece—to set up for a multiple jumping. Similarly, children learn that negotiating with others and temporarily delaying gratification often brings greater satisfaction, for example, by asking for desirable toys rather than grabbing them or by saving money for items of greater worth than those immediately attainable.

Social Understanding

Middle childhood is a time of heightened curiosity about other people. Children ask questions and tell stories about people they meet or imagine and make profound progress in social understanding. This progress is tied to developments in the ability to conceive of mental states—to think about one's own and others' thoughts and feelings. This ability emerges during the latter half of the third year of life.[9] Crucial to understanding other minds is recognizing that other people possess knowledge and beliefs that are different from one's own. Whereas young children typically interpret events only from their own perspective and assume that others share it, such egocentrism declines later on. Middle childhood is a time when children become interested in and able to consider others' points of view and develop what is known as "a theory of mind," or thinking about thinking. This interest and ability grow out of an appreciation that other people can have likes and desires that are different from their own, which is grounded in awareness that individuals have different emotional reactions to persons and events.

The emergence of theory of mind has been documented through naturalistic observation of children's talk about knowing, remembering, forgetting,[10] and tested with experimental paradigms. In the original paradigm, developed by Heinz Wimmer and Josef Perner, the examiner enacts a scenario with two dolls, Sally and Anne.[11] Sally puts a marble into a basket and then leaves the room. Anne enters the room, plays with the marble, and then puts it in a box. The examiner then asks the child where Sally will look for the marble when she returns. Children over four years of age consistently reply that Sally will look for the marble where she left it, in the basket, since she does not know that Anne subsequently moved it. Children younger than four years typically reply that Sally will look in the new location, the box, since they themselves know that is where the marble is, indicating that they do not understand that Sally does not possess this information. This paradigm has been carried out with different characters, materials, and in story form, each time yielding consistent findings. But when the scenarios focus on what another person *likes* rather than *knows*, children as young as three years old consistently demonstrate an appreciation for others' mental states.

...ind becomes increasingly sophisticated ...l-age children, for instance, display what ...d "second-order belief attribution": pre-...aracter's beliefs about another's beliefs. This has been demonstrated in children's reaction to a story about two characters, John and Mary, who are playing in a park:[12] "Along comes an ice-cream man. John wants to buy an ice cream, but he has left his money at home. John goes home to get his money and Mary stays at the park. But as John is leaving his house to return to the park, he sees the ice-cream truck. The ice-cream man tells him he is going to the church. John goes to the church to get his ice cream. Meanwhile, Mary comes home. Her mother tells her John has gone to buy an ice cream." Study participants are asked where Mary thinks John has gone to buy an ice cream. Those who reply that Mary thinks John has gone to the park (because that's where he thinks the icecream truck is) display second-order theory of mind.

An even more advanced measure was developed from twelve short stories in which one character wished to deceive another by lying, joking, pretending, or double-bluffing.[13] One story, for example, features a prisoner who is being interrogated about the location of his army's tanks. The story states that the interrogators assume the prisoner will lie to save his comrades. The prisoner does indeed wish to save them—and hence tells the truth. Study participants are asked to predict where the interrogators will look for the tanks and to explain why the prisoner acted as he did (i.e., that he knows they expect him to lie). This story is considered to be more difficult than other false-belief tasks because it involves double-bluffing and requires understanding characters' intentions and expectations. Normally developing school-age children are able to handle such tasks.

While theory of mind has been a major focus of research over the last decade, investigators have only recently begun to attend to the association between children's understanding of mental states and their socioemotional relationships.[14] Further, as Judy Dunn's work elegantly demonstrates, there are discrepancies between the powers of understanding attributed to young children on the basis of their responses to experimental situations and those they display in naturalistic settings where they are motivated by social goals.[15] Whether vying with siblings for parental attention and approval or expressing empathy with another's distress, children as young as two demonstrate an appreciation of the mental states of other people. Indeed, social understanding burgeons as children engage in relationships and activities with members of their communities.

Building on the recognition that others have different desires, information, and beliefs, children grasp the motives and intentions of others in complex social situations. Their ability to gauge the emotions and objectives of others enables children to attribute responsibility, and, depending on the situation, to obtain credit or escape blame. Similarly, it facilitates the expression of empathy across a wide range of situations. For example, a child might show compassion for a friend's loss of something the loser values despite the object's lack of significance to the one who offers sympathy. Learning how to be with people in the world is rooted in the ability to differentiate oneself as well as to identify with others on emotional and cognitive planes.

Social Relationships

As children grow older their social world gradually expands, but caregivers still dominate it between ages three and seven. In societies where children attend preschool, their first friendships with peers tend to be largely inter-changeable; children are likely to select playmates who are engaged with a desirable toy.[16] During the middle school years children tend to play with stable clusters of friends, and their conceptions of friendship change. Friendships are now organized according to social norms regarding emotions and behavior, many of which are not explicitly articulated. For the most part boys and girls play separately and adhere to different values and norms.[17] Interviews with girls in elementary school, for example, suggest that they most value intimacy and mu-tual rapport, whereas boys' peer groups tend to be larger and emphasize loyalty and shared activity. Social accep-tance depends upon the ability to comprehend and com-ply with the expectations of one's peer group, and failure to do so may result in rejection, often a source of great pain.[18] Given the value placed on conformity, there is probably less room for social deviation in middle child-hood than at any other time, a fact that makes life difficult for even the most skillful autistic children.

Development of Children with Autism and Mental Retardation

The majority of children with autism are also mentally retarded. Because cognitive, social, and motor develop-ment corresponds to mental age rather than to chrono-logical age, most autistic children do not reach the mile-stones associated with middle childhood in normally developing children. Autistic children who do not de-velop the ability to speak or comprehend language con-tinue to struggle with developmental tasks outlined ear-lier. They are closely supervised at home and at school, and are typically placed in highly structured special education classes with a high ratio of adults to students. Nonverbal mentally retarded autistic children have little contact with peers and spend much of their time engaged with objects. From a practical perspective, the daily activities of severely mentally retarded autistic persons are more strongly influenced by their mental retardation than their autism; their lives are quite similar to those of nonautistic children with severe mental retardation.

Mentally retarded autistic children who *are* able to understand and use language have considerably broader life experiences. These children are usually placed in less restrictive school environments and require less supervision. They learn to care for themselves in practical ways and to control their impulses; they can participate in social activities more and need less intervention. In comparison to nonautistic children at the same general level of mental functioning, autistic children often display remarkably well developed visual-spatial abilities, evident in skills like mastery of intricate jigsaw puzzles. Yet they manifest equally striking difficulties in symbolic play, joint attention, and social referencing. While they do more pointing than they did as young children, they remain less inclined to follow and share others' interests or invite others to share in objects and events that capture their attention. Similarly, they are much less likely to look at others in threatening or ambiguous situations, or at persons displaying intense emotion, than are their nonautistic mentally retarded peers.[19] Overall, when children enter middle childhood they increasingly attend to the reactions of adults and other children to make sense of social situations, particularly those involving the threat of negative social repercussions. Children with autism are both less likely to identify such situations and to look toward others for guidance than are their mentally retarded peers. This places them at a double disadvantage, perpetuating their social isolation, for referencing another cements one's relationship with that person and one's membership in a shared culture.

Development of Nonretarded Autistic Children

In middle childhood children with autism who are not mentally retarded face the same challenges as do normally developing children, although autism continues to influence the nature of these challenges and efforts to overcome them. In thinking about these children, it is important to remember that while they develop language and many other intellectual abilities, their cognitive skills tend to be in the low-normal range. Even those whose IQ scores fall in the average range lack complex verbal and symbolic skills, which undercuts their general level of intellectual functioning.

Cognitive and Academic Development

Like normally developing children, children with autism are able to learn to read, write, and do arithmetic, sometimes at high levels of proficiency. While individuals' areas of expertise vary, autistic persons often display great skill in technical areas, which are less dependent on verbal or social competence.

Children with autism who are not retarded display a characteristic pattern of strengths and weaknesses on cognitive tasks. This shows up on tests of intelligence, where their performance tends to be strongest on scales that tap skills in the spatial and visual areas.[20] For example, on the Revised Wechsler Intelligence Scale for Children (WISC-R) autistic children generally obtain their highest scores on the Block Design and Picture Arrangement subtest. The first involves replicating increasingly complex patterns with colored cubes, and the second calls for assembling pieces of a jigsaw puzzle.

In contrast to the ease and proficiency with which they complete visual-spatial tasks, autistic children typically obtain their lowest scores on tasks of verbal and social understanding: the Vocabulary subtest of the WISC-R, and the Comprehension subtest, which includes questions such as "What should you do if a younger child hits you?" and "What should you do if you find a stamped, addressed envelope lying in the street?" Autistic children's difficulty with these questions reveals limited social judgment and little awareness of cultural conventions for relating to others and actively participating in daily life. Some autistic children also have difficulty with tasks that require abstract verbal reasoning, such as the Similarities subtest of the WISC-R, which asks children to identify how different pairs of objects are alike, for example, that an apple and a banana are both fruits.

Motor and Physical Skills

In contrast to their distinctive profile of cognitive strengths and weaknesses, autistic children typically develop physical skills that are comparable to those of normally developing and mentally retarded peers (though motoric clumsiness is a diagnostic feature of Asperger Syndrome, which until quite recently was identified as high-functioning autism). Some parents report, however, that their mentally retarded autistic children are uncoordinated, have unusual gaits, and need remedial help to participate in team games.

Social factors may also limit athletic performance. In middle childhood and beyond, as physical ability is evaluated in relation to participation in team sports, it becomes increasingly difficult to tease apart social acceptance and physical prowess in sports. The fine motor skills of most autistic children resemble and may surpass those of normally developing children; a slightly disproportionate percentage displays extraordinary skills. For example, Thomas, the autistic child portrayed at the start of this chapter, demonstrated an uncanny ability to produce intricate drawings of cathedrals, monuments, and other buildings.[21]

Abilities, Interests, and Proclivities

As Kanner commented about his patients, some children with autism have certain "islets of ability" such as exceptional memories. Both clinical and popular accounts of autism note some children's ability to recite long lists of words, birth dates, phone numbers, and license plates from memory. Some autistic children appear to maintain the eidetic memory of young childhood, so that they can recall details of a text or scene with almost perfect precision.

Extraordinary feats of memory have been reported. Oliver Sacks described Martin A., an autistic person who could recall the entire nine volumes of the 1954 Grove Dictionary of Music and Musicians.[22] Martin's father read the texts to him, and he recounted them in his father's voice. Similarly, physician J. Langdon Down reported giving one of his patients the *Decline and Fall of the Roman Empire*. The patient read the entire work and in a single reading imprinted it in memory. But he had skipped a line on one page, an error he immediately detected and corrected. According to Down, "Ever after, when reciting from memory the stately periods of Gibbon, he would, on coming to the third page, skip the line and go back and correct the error with as much regularity as if it had been part of the regular text."[23]

While this capacity for memorizing may be helpful as children learn to read and spell, it appears unrelated to understanding. The persistence of eidetic memory in persons with autism—books are recalled verbatim, as might be telephone numbers or license plates—suggests that they do not store information according to meaningful categories and schemas. Indeed, extraordinary memory in autistic persons is often associated with defects of reasoning and comprehension.

Autistic children's capacity for memorization tends to be most remarkable in their areas of interest. Many autistic children who are not retarded develop a particular hobby or preoccupation such as dogs, bus routes, or geography. In pursuing these interests autistic children tend to focus less on social and psychological dynamics and more on statistical information. A child interested in baseball, for instance, might know the batting averages of each player on several teams, but not their nicknames, batting styles, or special off-field hobbies. Whereas normally developing children, particularly boys, often want to wear the same sort of shoes and clothing as their favorite players, autistic children do not seem to be inclined to do so.

Autistic children's interests sometimes become so intense that they border on an obsession, dominating their thoughts and their conversations with others. For example, one autistic child who participated in our research displayed a fascination with an old rock group, the Monkees. He mentioned the Monkees in response to questions ranging in both specificity and topic such as his date of birth, the names and ages of his siblings, his favorite subjects in school, and his plans for summer vacation. Similarly, autistic children often display extraordinary dedication to their areas of interest or skill. Kids interested in basketball, for instance, spend hours calculating various players' scoring and rebound and free-throw averages, often updating their calculations throughout each game.

Other autistic children are reported to have difficulties with attention span and are deemed overactive. This is more frequent among autistic children with low intelligence. Problems with impulsivity are associated with mental retardation in general, although mental retardation may not entirely account for autistic children's difficulties in these areas. Furthermore, persons with autism may suffer from additional problems, for example Attention Deficit/Hyperactivity. Overlap between symptoms of various disorders renders diagnosis difficult.

The capacity for planning or executive functions seems deficient in autistic children regardless of their level of functioning.[24] Deficits in executive function among school-aged children with autism have been demonstrated through tasks requiring them to alternate or shift the cues they get and use to find candy hidden under one of a number of cups. For example, over a series of trials children are presented with a red, blue, and green cup, each time in a different order. The first few times the examiner hides the candy under the blue cup, alternating its position, and then the red cup, again alternating its position. When the child identifies color as the correct cue, the examiner shifts to another cue, such as position, for example, always hiding the candy under the middle cup regardless of color. Autistic children tend to be much slower in identifying the correct cue and in shifting cues than children matched on mental and chronological age.

Similarly, highly able autistic children do less well on tasks requiring strategic planning than normally developing comparison children. One such task is referred to as the Tower of Hanoi or the Tower of London. As described in the account of Thomas at the start of this chapter, this task involves moving colored rings across a pegboard to match a particular pattern. However, movement is constrained by rules: move one ring at a time, one space at a time. Further, at some levels, the task requires moving various rings in the opposite direction of their ultimate destination. This is difficult for autistic children—even those who, like Thomas, are not retarded and have highly developed artistic abilities. Autistic children have even greater difficulty at more advanced levels, where mirroring the pattern requires planning an integrated series of movements.

Autistic persons' difficulty in recognizing others' strategies, adapting to changes, and formulating plans significantly impairs their ability to solve problems in social as well as cognitive domains. The capacity to comprehend an array of social signals, to modify one's behavior in response to new information, and to devise strategies for relating to others is critical to establishing and maintaining social connections. Like securing the candy, becoming a knowledgeable member of a cultural community requires integrating a variety of cues and constantly revising one's understanding of relationships and situations as they unfold over time.

Social Understanding

Although autistic children who are not mentally retarded can master many academic skills, they have great difficulty learning about social situations. One of the first and most fundamental skills that children learn is how to recognize the emotions of others. Verbal autistic children are able to identify various emotions when presented with photographs of persons displaying various facial expressions. In fact, autistic children seem to do this nearly as well as other children with comparable language abilities.[25]

Yet the results of these studies may not capture the difficulties faced in everyday life. For example, while the nonretarded autistic children studied in our laboratory were generally accurate in labeling emotional expressions, they required considerably more time than nonautistic children to do so and occasionally offered labels that were odd or inappropriate.[26] For example, given a picture of a boy shaking his fist, one autistic child said that the boy felt "shy," another described him as "scornful," and yet another as "itchy." Errors of this sort—attributing itchiness to a social partner who is conveying feelings of anger—would forcefully and memorably disrupt a social exchange. Further, because comprehending emotional expressions seems to be a complex and time-consuming task for autistic children, they are likely to experience greater difficulty in the context of social interactions in which an array of cues must be interpreted and synthesized simultaneously.

Indeed, when emotions are conveyed within more complex social situations, even the most intellectually able children have difficulty in reading the characters' emotions correctly. Peter Hobson showed autistic children four videotaped segments, each of which depicts a protagonist in a scenario that evokes an emotional response, including happiness, sadness, fear, and anger.[27] In the first segment the protagonist is presented with a birthday cake; in the next he trips and rubs his knee; in the third a jug is about to fall on his head; and in the fourth he places a pile of books on a chair and another person knocks them to the floor. Autistic children had some difficulty identifying the emotions these protagonists were feeling. They had even greater difficulty matching them with drawings of happy, sad, angry, and fearful faces, and with drawings of gestural representations of the same emotions.

Given the generic nature of these situations, autistic children's uncertainty in recognizing emotion reflects limited understanding not only of emotional expression but of the social situations that elicit various emotions. As children grow older, the ability to relate to the emotional experiences of other people depends ever more on having access to culturally determined meaning. That is, the circumstances that are likely to evoke sadness or pride, for example, vary from culture to culture, and assimilating this cultural knowledge is essential in making sense of one's own and others' emotions and actions.

Autistic children's difficulties attest to the generally cumulative effect of emotional abilities and limitations. It is certainly more difficult to share another's emotional expression if one must struggle to interpret it in the first place. Further, it may be that autistic persons' limited ability to interpret emotional displays, particularly within the stream of social interaction, stems from an early lack of attention to emotional displays. As discussed in Chapter 3, young autistic children are much less inclined than their peers to track visually and respond to the emotional expressions of others.

Among normally developing children, interest in affective displays and the circumstances which give rise to them, and the desire to master cultural conventions for self-expression, are both rewarded and motivated by the desire to form emotional connections with other people. Yet this process is somehow disrupted among children with autism; they seem less able to perceive and express emotions and less strongly compelled to develop these skills.

There is variation along this continuum, however. While in general autistic children may pay little attention to affective displays, a study conducted in our laboratory demonstrated that they differentiated between emotions. They tended to look longer at an adult expressing anger over the telephone than at the same adult talking in a neutral voice.[28] And some of the children looked at the angry adult longer than others. Autistic children who at age two to five had shown more interest in an adult feigning distress and had displayed some empathy were also more attentive to the angry adult some seven or eight years later than were those who had shown less empathic as young children. This pattern suggests that there is continuity in social interest and responsiveness. Further, such continuity was independent of children's cognitive ability. Continuity and stability in children's social and emotional abilities will be considered in more detail in Chapter 7.

Clearly, deficits in the ability to perceive and respond to other people's emotions significantly compromise the social understanding and relationships of persons with autism. We now consider related deficits in an ability that is also crucial to social understanding, namely, awareness of other minds.

Understanding the Theory of Mind

Autistic children have great difficulty evaluating their own and others' mental states—developing what we call a theory of mind. When tested with the Sally-Anne scenario described above, all but the most intelligent autistic children state that Sally will look for the marble in the new location (the box), rather than where she left it and thinks it remains (the basket).[29] These autistic children thus fail to differentiate between Sally's knowledge of the location of the marble and their own.

In another version of this paradigm, children were shown a candy box containing a pencil rather than candies.[30] An adult then walks into the room and the child is told that the adult has never seen this box before. What will the adult think is in the box? Here too autistic children invariably answered that the adult will think the box contains the pencil, thereby attributing to the adult the information they possess.

However, some individuals with autism *are* able to pass the Sally-Anne tasks. In fact, such success led to the development of the complex set of theory-of-mind tasks mentioned earlier, in which study participants must ascertain what one character thinks the other thinks and that one thinks the other thinks he will lie.[31] The study, carried out by Francesca Happé, posed the cases of the prisoner who told his interrogators where his comrades were (rather than lying), and a woman who said that she liked her friend's new dress when she actually thought it was hideous.[32] When asked why these people acted this way, highly able autistic subjects as a group were as likely as comparison subjects to explain such behaviors by referring to mental states. When their responses were examined more closely, however, it was clear that the autistic subjects tended to use mental terms in ways that did not fit the context of the story. For example, they would give the same response to each question: "He thought it was a lie"; "She thought it was a lie." Further, several autistic subjects seemed to lack the ability or inclination to make mental-state attributions, and were very creative in finding a physical cause for a character's false utterance. When he was asked to explain why a character lied about being glad to receive encyclopedias instead of the rabbit he desired, one subject responded, "because the book was all about rabbits." Similarly, another autistic man explained a character's pretending a banana was a telephone by saying, "some cordless telephones are made to look like fruit." Such responses illuminate autistic persons' difficulty in interpreting the mental states of other people and help to explain the consequent emergence of their idiosyncratic world views.

Although some individuals with autism who had passed theory-of-mind tasks offered explanations that were inappropriate to the story context, there is a general, consistent pattern in autistic persons' ability to mentalize. That is, subjects who fail simpler theory-of-mind tasks (as in the Sally-Anne experiment) are least likely to draw on a theory of mind to explain the narrative vignettes, and those who pass more complex theory-of-mind tasks are most likely to interpret characters' actions in this fashion. There appears to be a subgroup of people with autism who display a more highly developed understanding of the human capacity to contemplate and communicatively manipulate their own and others' mental states, and this skill is coupled with a more sophisticated awareness of cultural norms and expectations. Whether this subgroup is comprised of individuals who would now be diagnosed with Asperger Sydrome remains a topic of debate.

It has also been suggested, however, that autistic individuals who pass theory-of-mind tests do not truly have the ability to mentalize but cultivate a strategy which allows them to compute or "hack out" solutions to these tests.[33] From this point of view, performance on experimental paradigms is not likely to generalize to life outside the laboratory. Thus whereas normally developing children are likely to display skills in naturalistic settings that may not be captured in the laboratory, individuals with autism are probably helped by the constraints inherent in experimental settings (the absence of time constraints, limited contextual information, and forced-choice paradigms).

Autistic persons who consistently pass theory-of-mind tasks show more evidence of mentalizing in everyday life (based on parent report) than do those who fail such tasks.[34] But, their level of social understanding is still well below that of normally developing children of the same age. The limited awareness of mental states that characterizes the majority of individuals with autism is striking in naturalistic settings. Here anecdotes prove illuminating. Parents of autistic children we have encountered frequently report that their autistic children have little capacity for taking others' tastes, circumstances, and knowledge into account. One mother recalled that for her birthday her nonretarded autistic son bought her the battery-operated motor car that he himself coveted. Another mother described her frustration when her nonretarded autistic son repeatedly asked that she take him miniature golfing as promised, although his sister had just been hospitalized with a serious illness. And a teacher recounted a situation involving an autistic girl, Andrea, who had to leave school at lunch time for a dental appointment. She returned to class 15 minutes late, without explanation. Her teacher asked if she had been out in the yard. Andrea simply said "no," not recognizing the question as a request for information regarding her whereabouts. Her teacher then asked explicitly where she had been, and Andrea said, "at the dentist's." When reminded to bring a note from her mother, Andrea, without apology, handed the teacher a note she had held in her pocket since the morning. Later that day Andrea's mother asked why she hadn't given the note to her teacher when she got to school. Andrea replied, "She didn't ask."

Autistic persons' difficulty in differentiating their knowledge from that of other people is tied to trouble mastering conventions for participating in social life. Andrea, for example, failed to recognize that her teacher did not know where she was, to appreciate her teacher's need to have this information, and to realize the meaning behind the teacher's question. Autistic persons' limited ability to think about how minds work illuminates the extent to which our actions, thoughts, and feelings are tied to an awareness of others' mental states—their thoughts, attitudes, expectations, and wishes. What we do and how we relate to others is motivated by the desire to paint a particular portrait of ourselves in our own mind and in the minds of those with whom we live.

Not surprisingly, given their deficits in theory of mind and other forms of social understanding, the social skills of even the most intellectually gifted children with autism are severely limited. They lack understanding of the cues on how to enter into and sustain conversations with others. While autistic children recognize when they are being overtly teased, they are not sensitive to subtle forms of feedback. For example, an autistic person is not likely to sense when a social partner has grown tired of a particular topic or activity or when the topic has shifted. Because autistic children lack the repertoire of social skills that enable normally developing children to initiate and sustain contact with peers, social interaction is for them like navigating strange waters without adequate maps or instruments.

Social Relationships

In contrast to the social world of normally developing children, that of autistic children does not expand much in middle childhood. Family relationships continue to be central to their lives, to the extent that relationships are important to them. While autistic children may have friendships, these are generally maintained by parents, who arrange for regular social contacts much the way they make play dates for preschool children. Owing to their limited social skills and circumscribed interests, autistic children are often most successful in forming friendships with younger children or those who are mentally delayed. Even the most socially advanced autistic children, who maintain warm relationships with family members and other adults, have few friendships with peers during middle childhood. A study of friendship asked 22 high-functioning children with autism, "Who are your friends?" The children named two friends on average (although 10% were not able to name a single friend), whereas comparison children named an average of 18 children.[35] In addition, autistic children did not differentiate between "friends" and "best friends" and reported significantly more loneliness than comparison children.

Middle childhood can be a difficult time for many normal children too, as they cope with demands for social conformity and overt competition in academic, athletic, and social arenas. Given the serious limitations faced by even the most intellectually sophisticated autistic children, it is not surprising that they are often isolated from others and spend much of their time on the fringe of social groups or alone.

6 / Adolescence

Thirteen-year-old Eric, a boy with piercing green eyes, enters the room. The red shirt he has on reads "Roosevelt Middle School." Pointing to his chest, the examiner asks, "So how do you like it there?" Eric looks puzzled. "What's it like at Roosevelt?" she repeats. "Oh, it's all right. But on Thursday afternoons I go back to Cleveland Elementary. I tutor kids in the crafts room. I'm real good at building things. Sometimes kids tease me. They call me names and stuff." The examiner asks Eric to sit down and explains that she will be showing him five short video segments, and she would like him to tell her what emotion the boy or girl in the video is feeling. Leaning forward in his chair, Eric rivets his attention on the television screen. He watches as the protagonist discovers her mother is going to buy her a new bike. Eric smiles broadly, and turns first toward the examiner and then toward his mother. Speaking over the sound of the tape, he exclaims, "That's happy. That's happy, right?"

As adolescents reach sexual maturity, alterations in the size, form, and function of their bodies are accompanied by equally profound changes in their social roles, relationships, and identities. While the manner in which individuals attain adult status varies across cultures, all adolescents learn to relate in new ways to peers of both sexes, begin to take primary responsibility for themselves and develop emotional independence from their families, master skills necessary for economic survival, and acquire cultural values. In contrast to their earlier years, adolescents are less apt to adopt conventional standards; they are more interested in forging an autonomous identity and challenging the status quo. Conflict often arises as adolescents assert their independence, using knowledge of cultural norms to rebel rather than conform to the expectations of parents and others in authority.

Normal Adolescents

Cognitive Processes

The thinking of adolescents is qualitatively different from that of younger children.[1] Whereas middle school-aged children generally refer to observable properties of objects and follow hard-and-fast rules, adolescents tend to engage in abstract reasoning. Whether contemplating the physical world or attempting to make sense of social and moral situations, adolescents focus on concepts and possibilities. In a laboratory experiment comparing schoolchildren's and adolescents' assessments of misleading statements, the experimenter showed children poker chips of various colors and asked them whether what he said about the chips is true, false, or impossible to tell.[2] He then concealed a chip in his hand and said, "The chip in my hand is green and it is not green." The most common reply among children in elementary school was "impossible to tell," reflecting their tendency to evaluate on the basis of visual evidence rather than assess the logical properties of the experimenter's question. Adolescents, on the other hand, are more likely to focus on the validity of verbal assertions and typically respond that the chip could not be both green and not green.

Adolescents also differ from children in their conceptions of the relation between the actual and the possible. Whereas elementary school children approach problems by burrowing into their immediate perception of reality and speculating about other possibilities as a last resort, adolescents use the opposite tack, beginning with possibility and only subsequently proceeding to reality. They may examine the problem situation carefully to try to determine what all the potential solutions might be, viewing reality as a particular portion of the much wider world of possibility. In making sense of a situation, adolescents construct hypothetical accounts of what might be going on, test their theories against reality, and accept, reject, or revise them accordingly. While adolescents frequently generate unique responses to a given set of circumstances, the ability to consider a wide range of relevant possibilities—including some against which they rebel—reflects considerable knowledge of the culture in which they live.

Paralleling their proclivity to contemplate hypothetical realms of existence, adolescents think a great deal about their own thinking and that of other people. More than when they were younger, adolescents are mindful of a diverse audience of observers and take these varying perspectives into account when assessing situations and determining plans of action. Known as metacognition, this capacity to contemplate principles and ideas serves as the bedrock for much of the learning that takes place in adolescence.[3]

In both formal and informal educational settings, adolescents learn more than simply skills, whether computer programming, weaving, or farming. They also master approaches to the task at hand and the givens of the particular sociocultural world view in which these skills are embedded.[4] In most industrialized countries, for example, students learn how to use their time over days and weeks so that they can perform within deadlines. This need for planning requires strategic thinking about how best to approach a goal. Students also learn to fulfill certain conditions of the setting, such as predictable attendance and appropriate behavior. While some such conditions are stated overtly, others are conveyed less directly, requiring sensitivity to subtle forms of communication. These demands may conflict with adolescents' drive to assert their independence. Nevertheless, if they wish to remain in school or vocational settings, adolescents must manage to be sufficiently responsive to the expectations of teachers and others in authority. Balancing the need for autonomy with demands for conformity is among the greatest challenges adolescents face.

Self Awareness, Social Understanding, Relationships

During the second decade of life, puberty ushers in physical maturity: people attain adult size, develop secondary sexual characteristics, and are capable of sexual reproduction. Physical attractiveness plays an increasingly significant role in determining popularity with peers, such that concern about appearance contributes to heightening self-consciousness.[5] But adolescents learn to cope with these dramatic physical and emotional changes and their social implications in ways that are culturally acceptable, which involve reorganizing relationships with family members and peers.

The unparallelled biological and emotional challenges of adolescence are accompanied by increased social sensitivity. Adolescents are particularly inclined to compare themselves to others and are attuned to the interpersonal consequences of particular attributes. For example, while a 6-year-old might describe herself as "a great soccer player," a 13-year-old is likely to rate herself in comparison to other individuals ("the fourth best soccer player on my team") and to monitor her social status among teammates.[6]

Beyond knowing that desires, thoughts, feelings, beliefs, and intentions vary from one person to another and depend on the situation, adolescents are aware of the importance of this knowledge. Adolescents construct metarepresentations in which they contemplate the thoughts and emotions of other people in relation to their own and take this into account in reasoning about social situations.

The ability to think on a metacognitive level significantly enriches social life. It facilitates empathetic responsiveness, for example, through imagining another's emotional reaction in circumstances one has not experienced. Again, in contrast to the more concrete approach of earlier years, which may make it difficult to empathize with another unless one has been in the precise situation oneself, adolescents can more readily comprehend what others are feeling by extrapolating from relevant experiences in their own lives and availing themselves of more sophisticated cultural understanding. Yet the capacity for complex metarepresentation has drawbacks as well. Contemplation of others' attitudes and responses can lead to self-consciousness, self-effacing rumination, and attributing negative opinions of oneself to other people.[7] A number of studies show a marked decline in children's self-esteem in early adolescence, particularly among girls.[8]

While they may continue to desire family approval, adolescents spend more and more time with peers, in fairly stable social groups with distinct identities. Membership in groups plays a critical role in the way individuals see themselves and are perceived by others, and provides the opportunity to form friendships and to negotiate sexual relationships. Most of the time adolescents are more preoccupied with the activities and attitudes of their peers than with family matters, although this varies considerably across cultures and as a function of family dynamics.[9] By late adolescence these preoccupations begin to give way to concerns about developing enduring sexual relationships, as adolescents emulate the social agendas of adults.

The Adolescent with Autism and Mental Retardation

As in childhood so too in adolescence, autistic individuals' mental and language capacities largely determine their developmental course. But autistic adolescents at all levels of intellectual ability often show aggravation of behavioral symptoms and deterioration of social functioning.[10] Those who do not comprehend or use much language tend to continue to live sheltered lives and do not experience many of the cognitive and social developments associated with adolescence among normal children. In most cases autistic adolescents who are mentally retarded remain closely supervised at school and at home, and their social interactions tend to be highly structured by other people. Those who are mentally retarded but are able to use language continue to work in special classes, usually with a goal of preparing them for sheltered employment and semi-independent living. While perhaps not developing robust friendships, they may cultivate relationships with classmates, have hobbies, and participate in athletic activities.

Physical and sexual maturation is a challenge for these

adolescents and often creates conflict in the family. Issues of control are exacerbated as children grow larger and stronger; it becomes increasingly difficult to monitor and modify their behavior at a time when parents may also feel the need to impose additional restrictions. Like adolescents more generally, mentally retarded adolescents with autism experience heightened sexual and emotional feelings. Those who are nonverbal have limited access to socially appropriate avenues of expression and sometimes manifest explosive, aggressive behavior.

Mentally retarded autistic individuals who have some language manifest similar difficulties. Although the capacity for language is an invaluable resource, deficits in social understanding severely undercut opportunities to adjust to psychological and physical changes within the context of interpersonal relationships. In contrast to adolescents with Down Syndrome, for example, who can be markedly flirtatious, autistic adolescents rarely attempt such advances and may appear aloof to invitations to engage in this sort of interaction. This is perhaps not surprising, given their history of limited attempts to initiate social interaction in infancy and difficulty cultivating close friendships in middle childhood.

In addition to intelligence and language ability, personal malleability influences the life course of autistic individuals. While some mentally retarded adolescents with autism can be calm and responsive, others are explosive and aggressive. It is not clear whether such traits are a continuation of earlier patterns of behavior or whether aggressiveness is tied to disruption associated with puberty; we will return to this issue in discussing longitudinal studies of individuals with autism. Needless to say, the capacity of some autistic individuals and their families for flexible adaptation makes the transition into adolescence more manageable.

Nonretarded Adolescents with Autism

Autistic adolescents who are not retarded still have considerable intellectual and verbal limitations. While three quarters of the population of autistic children are mentally retarded, only a small percentage of the nonretarded subgroup has overall IQs above 100, which is the normal mean. Because the vast majority of autistic persons has nonverbal abilities that are markedly superior to their abilities in verbal domains, it may be that the native intelligence of nonretarded autistic individuals is greater than it seems, but their struggle with language and verbal concepts undercuts their opportunities to learn and reason. Whatever the case may be, these adolescents make heroic efforts to use intellectual skills to mask and compensate for social and verbal limitations.[11]

Cognitive Development

As far as we know, the capacity for formal operations or reasoning about abstract principles has not yet been studied in nonretarded autistic adolescents and adults. Current evidence suggests that autistic individuals in the normal range of intelligence reason concretely, not abstractly. It is as if autism precludes the capacity to abide in the realm of ideas, particularly ideas that are more than one step removed from observable objects and events in the world. Not surprisingly, then, the most successful autistic individuals typically develop expertise in technical rather than abstract domains. For example, high-functioning individuals with autism are far more likely to become computer programmers than physicists or mathematicians.

What is surprising, however, is that many nonretarded autistic adolescents develop a limited understanding of the properties of the physical world. In a study comparing a group of nonretarded adolescents with autism with a group of normally developing adolescents of the same age and similar language abilities, only half of the autistic adolescents passed measures of conservation—understanding that changing the shape of a substance, for example, by pouring water from one container into another, does not alter its weight or volume, and that redistributing objects in space does not change quantity. By contrast, all of the comparison adolescents did so.[12] Further, the autistic children who did demonstrate understanding of conservation had great difficulty articulating the principles they had applied. Perhaps the need to consider two dimensions at once, such as height and width, or number and size, overwhelms autistic persons' reasoning abilities. The same problem came up in executive function tasks (see Chapter 5), which require shifting attention from one property of object to another, for example, color and shape. Whatever the cause for limited acquisition of principles of conservation, significant consequences are likely to ensue. Understanding that properties of objects remain constant across transformations is essential to interpreting and predicting the physical world. Further, this knowledge is a prerequisite for developing abstract concepts and logical principles.

Likewise, many of the autistic adolescents in this study had difficulty figuring out the perceptual perspective of another person. The participant sat opposite an experimenter. Placed between them was a rotating turntable or "lazy Susan," which displayed three objects: a toy owl, a cup, and an apple. Participants were asked to rotate the tray around until they saw the objects from the experimenter's initial perspective. In contrast to the seemingly effortless performance of normally developing adolescents, most autistic adolescents labored over the task and erroneously rotated the turntable full circle, to its starting position. Such difficulties have implications for more sophisticated kinds of perspective taking. That is, persons who struggle simply to appreciate the difference between their own and another's view of a physical object, let alone being able to identify that other perspective, are likely to have even greater trouble appreciating differences in their own and others' responses to emotional experiences and imagining themselves in another's situation—a topic we will return to shortly.

While nonretarded adolescents with autism may excel academically, their success is limited by cognitive constraints, trouble with planning, and difficulty comprehending and complying with the requirements of the educational setting. Whether it is because they cannot or will not plan, autistic adolescents often require a great deal of family support in finishing homework and preparing to leave for school in the morning. While nonretarded adolescents *can* dress themselves for school easily (and, sensitive to the dictates of fashion, may try on several outfits before making a final decision), those with autism usually need assistance with keeping track of the time and remembering the fundamentals and materials they need.

The following examples illustrate the magnitude and impact of these planning difficulties. Marian Sigman observed an interview with a young autistic man, "Tom," holder of an MA degree in a technical subject, who displayed considerable social sophistication yet was unemployed. As it turned out, Tom spent over ten hours every day cutting out appropriate job advertisements from the newspaper, collating them, filing them, but never once actually applying for a position.

Lorna Wing, a long-time expert in autism, described a similar case. A young man who was trained as a piano tuner went to his first job, which was to tune the piano of some family friends. He arrived at their home and proceeded to tune their piano for twelve hours, until the friends suggested that he go home. He was oblivious to the notion that when performing a service in another's house, particularly one that is noisy, one generally does not work through the dinner hour, much less until bedtime. Further, the task did not designate an absolute stopping point, since he could keep improving on his work. Coupled with insensitivity to cultural conventions and social cues, difficulty in organizing goals and developing a strategy for pursuing them impedes the adaptation of even the most talented individuals with autism.

Physical and Motor Development

Although nonretarded autistic adolescents undergo the physical and sexual changes experienced by normally developing adolescents, they are much less inclined to express sexual feelings toward other people. Temple Grandin describes the onset of nervousness and anxiety in puberty:[13] "Shortly after my first menstrual period, the anxiety attacks started. The feeling was like a constant feeling of stage fright all the time. . . The 'nerves' were almost like hypersensitivity rather than anxiety. It was like my brain was running at 200 miles an hour, instead of 60 miles an hour."

In her story, which seems to apply to autistic adolescents in general, Grandin described her struggle to cultivate lasting peer relationships. Understandably, this lack of social contact greatly reduces opportunities to grasp norms concerning emotional displays or conventions for pursuing intimate relationships. Further, such conventions are subtle and complex, frequently involving innuendo. As a result, this area of cultural knowledge may elude even the most observant and sophisticated individuals with autism.

Self Awareness, Social Understanding, and Relationships.
One study of social understanding, conducted in our laboratory, compared 18 nonretarded autistic adolescents with 18 normally developing adolescents matched on gender, verbal ability, and overall IQ score. Findings suggest that the adolescents with autism had trouble talking about their own emotional experiences and in identifying and empathizing with the emotions of others. When asked about times when they had experienced various emotions, autistic adolescents were able to describe situations in which they had experienced simple emotions, such as happiness and sadness.[14] Like adolescents in the normally developing comparison group, adolescents with autism frequently mentioned feeling happy about receiving a desirable gift and feeling sad about the death of a pet. But they had difficulty comprehending complex emotions, such as pride and embarrassment. One quarter of the autistic adolescents brought up precisely the same situation as an instance of pride and an instance of happiness, suggesting they may not fully appreciate that while both feelings refer to positive experiences, pride is associated with positive outcomes for which one is responsible.

Autistic adolescents also failed to clearly distinguish embarrassment from sadness. Several described feeling embarrassed "when I got hurt." In contrast to their nonautistic peers, they did not usually describe feeling proud or embarrassed in situations involving an audience, which is crucial to the concept of embarrassment. In contrast, typical responses from normally developing adolescents were: "I was proud when I won the spelling bee in the school auditorium," and "I felt embarrassed when I threw the ball to the wrong team."

Autistic adolescents' limited reference to an audience recalls young autistic children's failure to look to adults for their reaction after mastering a task (see Chapter 3). This pattern provides insight into the cumulative effects of social referencing or the lack thereof, and the manifestation of this behavior over time. Experiencing complex emotions, such as pride, shame, and guilt, hinges upon making reference to other people. As C. H. Cooley, noted for his early twentieth-century work on the social origins of the self, commented: "The thing that moves us to pride and shame is not the merely mechanical reflection of ourselves, but an imputed sentiment, the imagined effect of this reflection upon another's mind."[15] In this sense, the infant's looks to her caregiver forms the basis for the ongoing development of a sense of self and others in the world.

Susan Jaedicke, Sharon Storoschuk, and Catherine Lord reported consistent findings from their study of high-functioning adolescents with autism, in which subjects were asked to describe their subjective experience of various emotions including happiness, sadness, fear, worry, and anger.[16] In comparison to normal and mentally retarded subjects, autistic individuals were much less likely to relate emotions to interpersonal interaction or the attainment of a goal. Typically, they described material circumstances or events as causes for emotions. Positive emotions, for example, were often associated with receiving favorite foods and objects, and negative emotions were linked to the loss of these items. In contrast, normal and mentally retarded adolescents tended to associate emotions with athletic, academic, and social successes and failures. Further, more of the autistic adolescents' responses were peculiar or idiosyncratic than were the responses of comparison children.

Autistic adolescents also manifest limitations in their

ability to empathize with the emotions of others, as indicated by their responses to protagonists in videotaped vignettes.[17] Participants were presented with five videotaped segments which portrayed a child in situations designed by Norma Feshbach to elicit sadness, happiness, pride, fear, and anger.[18] For example, the tape designed to evoke sadness features a boy unsuccessfully looking for his lost dog. According to Feshbach's model, empathy involves the ability to evaluate another person's emotional state, take his or her perspective, and share his or her response. In keeping with this model, after each vignette children were asked to identify the emotion the child in the videotaped segment was feeling and to report what they themselves were feeling. While not as adept as adolescents in the normal comparison group, high-functioning adolescents with autism were quite accurate in labeling the emotional experience of protagonists. Similarly, the majority of autistic adolescents reported feeling emotions resembling those they attributed to the child protagonist.

Individuals with autism are likely to experience greater difficulty interpreting and responding to emotions outside the controlled context of the laboratory, where they must react quickly, within the ongoing stream of human interaction. By adolescence, normally developing children have developed a sophisticated understanding of the kinds of situations that tend to evoke particular responses among members of the culture in which they live, and have mastered conventions for conveying comfort and concern. In contrast, children and adolescents with autism seem to lack the cultural scripts and conventions for interpreting and responding to social situations.[19] Kathryn Loveland and Belgin Tunali devised a situation involving a tea party during which an examiner related having had her wallet stolen.[20] The majority of adolescents with autism did not comment on the examiner's plight, much less offer sympathetic comments or relevant suggestions. But when another examiner began to solicit information and express concern about the unfortunate event, many did produce relevant responses to the story.

Further, as Dunn has pointed out, normal children quickly realize that outward expressions of empathy, whether or not they reflect internal experience, yield positive rewards.[21] By adolescence, empathetic displays are part of a large repertoire of behaviors individuals use to engage attention, ingratiate themselves, or enter into social groups. Knowledge and use of this social mechanism and the social opportunities that ensue remain outside the reach of individuals with autism.

In the empathy study carried out in our laboratory participants were videotaped as they watched the vignettes, so it was possible to code their expressions. It is interesting that autistic adolescents showed far more facial affect while watching than did adolescents in the normal comparison group.[22] In fact, normally developing adolescents showed little if any affect. Furthermore, careful analysis of the points in the tape which evoked particular emotional displays among autistic adolescents indicated that, for the most part, their affect was appropriate to the situation. That is, adolescents with autism appeared happy during portions of the vignettes in which the protagonist was happy and looked sad or distressed during portions of the vignettes that were most upsetting to the protagonist. They rarely, if ever, demonstrated affect that was inconsistent with the prevailing sentiment of the protagonist on the tape.

These observations suggest that the adolescents with autism were accurate in interpreting and empathizing with others' emotions, in contrast to the relative absence of attention and empathy to distress among young children with autism. It is promising that adolescents *do* respond to others' emotions. Perhaps individuals with autism develop empathy as they get older, but have trouble putting their feelings into words.

The contrast between autistic adolescents' emotional displays and the unresponsive faces of normally developing adolescents warrants comment. While it may be that adolescents in the comparison group were less aroused by the videos, an alternative interpretation is that they were responding to social display rules which discourage dramatic emotional displays in the presence of others.[23] Such display rules are especially potent among adolescent boys, and are probably magnified by the presence of unfamiliar adults and video cameras. Autistic adolescents' expressiveness, then, may demonstrate a *lack* of social understanding, reflecting limited sensitivity to social channels through which display rules are learned.

At the same time that their faces expressed positive and negative emotion, autistic adolescents appeared confused, both while watching the videotaped vignettes and in talking about their own emotions. They seemed to struggle with the tasks and needed both more time to respond and considerable prompting; several of them turned to their mothers for help and confirmation. For example, Eric, the child portrayed at the start of this chapter, stated, "I felt proud when I did something good," and then turned to his mother and asked, "Right, Mom?"

In reviewing videotapes of these interactions, one gets the sense that persons with autism approach situations involving emotion as if they were computational problems, and apply their cognitive capabilities to compensate for deficits in social understanding.[24] Consistent with this observation, many individuals with autism, like Eric, approached the measure of empathy as a problem-solving task, trying to figure out how to determine "that's happy."

In contrast to the reserved stance of their normally developing peers, autistic adolescents' unabashed emotional expressiveness and their often desperate pleas for information make them look rather childlike or naive. The eager attempts of these intelligent adolescents with autism are painful to observe. Such efforts attest to the strides they have made, the energy they expended, and, sadly, the extent to which the complexity of norms for interaction outstrips their advances in social understanding.

Older autistic individuals, whether mentally retarded or not, seem to want social contact a great deal. Their interest in social interaction is the reverse of the social aloofness that many autistic children show in the earlier years. Yet despite great desire and effort, autistic adolescents and adults often seem almost totally unable to read social cues. As illustrated by displays of utter confusion, coupled with overt questioning, they seem to find themselves without an internal guide.

Sir Michael Rutter described a highly intelligent, autistic young man who articulated this experience when he asked his psychiatrist to teach him how to read other people's minds. Lamenting his inability to do so, this young man explained that "other people seemed to have a special sense by which they could read other people's thoughts and could anticipate their responses and feelings; he knew this because they managed to avoid upsetting people whereas he . . . did not realize that he was doing or saying the wrong thing until after the other person became angry or upset."[25] This young man's request reflects some appreciation of the fact that, particularly in adolescence, normal people spend much of their time anticipating and reflecting on their own and others' thoughts and feelings. The ability to engage in such mental activity facilitates effective participation in social interaction with others, and a deep, perhaps ineffable awareness of what it means to belong to a cultural community.

In the absence of this capacity, adolescents with autism develop very restricted friendships and remain in close proximity to family members. The pressure to individuate seems less strong and the conflicts over independence appear to be less marked than those of normal or mildly retarded adolescents. Whereas among normally developing adolescents the desire for autonomy and independence from family members is paralleled by newfound intimacy with peers, this is less often the case among individuals with autism. And for the most intellectually gifted autistic individuals, adolescence is a time when their isolation is most apparent, not only to the observer but to themselves, as they become painfully aware of their circumscribed participation in social life.

In Western cultures normally developing adolescents tend to be highly preoccupied with themselves and how they are perceived by others. Yet little attention has been given to how autistic persons see themselves.[26] While autistic persons' peculiarities and limitations are striking to observers inside and outside of the laboratory, we have little knowledge—and almost no empirical information—about their own awareness of these shortcomings. Such awareness may be a crucial part of adjustment. As Kanner initially pointed out, "[his] most successful autistic patients, unlike most other autistic children, became uneasily aware of their peculiarities, and began to make a conscious effort to do something about them."[27] Kanner did not, however, account for the development of such awareness, nor of his patients' efforts to alter idiosyncratic characteristics and behaviors.

It is not clear how far autistic children, adolescents, or adults can go in making the social comparisons that are so crucial to developing a sense of self. The only information we are aware of was obtained in our study of nonretarded adolescents, in which participants completed the Perceived Self Competence Scale.[28] This scale presents a series of statements, such as: "Some people find it hard to make friends, but for others it's pretty easy." Respondents then indicate what kind of person he or she is most like, and then decides whether the description is "sort of true" or "really true." Based on their responses to these items, adolescents with autism perceived themselves to be less competent than other kids their age in all but the cognitive domain.[29] That is, they perceived themselves to be less competent socially and physically, and reported lower estimates of their overall self-worth than did adolescents in the comparison group. These findings suggest that at the very least, nonretarded autistic adolescents are aware of their social isolation and awkwardness. Whether this is true of retarded individuals with autism remains an open question.

We were also interested in the relationship between intellectual ability, emotional understanding, and perceived self-competence. In particular, we wondered whether the most intellectually gifted individuals were better able to express and comprehend emotions, and whether they perceived themselves as more socially competent than autistic persons with less intellectual ability. To answer these questions, we correlated IQ scores with participants' performance on various aspects of this study. Interestingly, the most highly intelligent individuals with autism perceived themselves as *least* socially competent. In addition, those with the highest

IQ scores were also most accurate in labeling the emotions of others, and had the least difficulty talking about their own emotional experiences.

This investigation also elicited information on parents' perceptions of their children's adjustment and emotional life. Parents of adolescents with autism reported significant deficits in their children's social adaptive behaviors relative to those of their nonautistic peers, suggesting that even this high-functioning group has extreme difficulty maintaining social relationships and functioning independently.[30] However, parents' assessment of their children's social functioning was positively correlated with children's IQ scores. That is, as seen through the eyes of their parents, the most highly intelligent autistic adolescents are best able to function in the social world. In summary, adolescents who perceive themselves as least socially competent appear most skilled in measures of emotional understanding and are described by their parents as better adjusted socially than those who perceive themselves as more socially competent. One interpretation of this contradiction is that autistic persons who are more intelligent and better able to read the emotions of others may be more sensitive to others' negative appraisals of them. They may see themselves more accurately than autistic persons who are less intellectually capable. In Kanner's terms, they may be "more aware of their peculiarities."

What are the consequences of this awareness? Kanner suggests that for some, awareness of peculiarities leads to "a conscious effort to do something about them." Alternatively, might such awareness involve depression and hopelessness? While depression in autism has been the object of little inquiry, a review of existing case studies suggest that it is most common in adolescence, may be more common among nonretarded autistic persons, and is underidentified and undertreated.[31] This supports the possibility that the challenges faced by individuals with autism are exacerbated in adolescence. The incidence of depression and other problems compels consideration of additional forms of intervention, and obliges us to investigate and take seriously the self-understanding of individuals with autism, particularly during adolescence, when issues of identity and social acceptance are most salient.

7 / Stability of Individual Differences and Prediction over Time

Hazel, a soft-spoken woman in her mid-thirties, closes the door behind her, introduces herself, and sits down. "I called earlier this week. My son Ethan has just been diagnosed with autism. What does this mean for him and for our family? What is Ethan going to be like?" As Hazel begins to describe her son, she continues asking questions that probe the future: "He'll be three next month and he's not yet talking. Will he ever speak? Will he have friends? Will he be able to go to school? Do you think Ethan will ever get a job or leave home? Will he marry? What kind of services will he need?"

In describing how autism is manifest at different stages of development, we have drawn primarily from cross-sectional research that involved several samples of children, each at different ages. While this research tells us what might be expected of autistic persons as a group, individuals vary considerably. The ability to predict the later functioning of a given child with autism requires longitudinal research—research that tracks a group over time. Because the same children are observed at different ages, it is more certain that observations reflect changing manifestations of a risk condition rather than variation in the samples studied at different ages. For example, an examiner who observed considerably more joint attention behavior in a group of nine-year-olds than in a group of three-year-olds might conclude that autistic children develop joint attention by middle childhood. Yet this may not be so. The groups may have differed in other respects besides age, for example intellectual ability, which accounted for the appearance of joint attention in the older children. To chart the true developmental course of particular behaviors requires evaluating the same group of children over time.

Moreover, tracking the development of individuals with disabilities greatly enhances understanding of normal development. When development proceeds normally, we are less likely, and perhaps less able, to consider the precursors of specific behaviors and abilities. We are also more likely to attribute false underlying connections to abilities that develop and change in temporal synchrony. Autism compels us to reconsider developmental sequences and associations, and longitudinal research is a crucial part of this endeavor.

It is essential to be able to document the characteristics of individuals and groups during various stages of development when attempting to predict later life adjustment. The information that is gathered in longitudinal studies can be used to identify associations between certain behaviors and abilities. It ought to be possible to discern, for example, whether children who display strong cognitive skills at age two are more likely to display strong cognitive skills in adolescence relative to those who had less well developed cognitive abilities as young children.[1]

In addition, abilities in one domain may be cues to predicting abilities in another domain or envisaging a more general outcome. Language ability, for example, might predict popularity with peers. The advantage of this approach is that it affords consideration of processes that contribute to variations in an individual's development. Investigators can develop and test different models of how developmental advances build on each other. The relationship between language ability and peer relationships could be tested systematically, for example, by examining whether children with superior language skills as preschoolers were more likely to receive positive ratings from peers in elementary school.

Longitudinal research also affords comparisons between different models of development. The strength of the link between early language abilities and peer relationships in elementary school could thus be compared with the strength of the link between early motor abilities and later peer relationships. Such comparisons may clarify the relative importance of early language and motor abilities in the child's subsequent ability to make friends. In these ways, longitudinal research provides crucial information on developmental continuities and how particular behaviors and abilities relate to various aspects of adjustment. This information can ultimately be used to mitigate the negative outcomes of a given syndrome.

Longitudinal Studies of Autistic Children

Because longitudinal research is time-consuming and costly, few such studies have been carried out with autistic children. Most of these studies have examined the general outcome of a group of autistic individuals who had previously participated in a research study or clinical program. They tend to focus on general indices of outcome, such as severity of symptoms, intellectual functioning, language ability, educational attainment, employability, and social adaptation.

Before delving into the longitudinal research on autism, a few caveats bear mention. First, prior to the mid-1970s, investigators did not explain the criteria they used to diagnose autism—whether they included persons with mild or partial symptoms as well as those with more pervasive developmental disabilities.[2] Even now there is variability in the breadth of the diagnostic criteria used, making it difficult to compare or consolidate results across studies. Existing longitudinal research also varies with respect to the ages of subjects when they were initially recruited and when seen at follow-up, and the particular behaviors and abilities measured. While we hope and believe that eventually it will be possible to delineate developmental trajectories of individuals with autism with enough precision to provide a foundation for accurate predictions, the information presently available is incomplete.

Developmental Course of Autism from Childhood to Adolescence

Several investigators have examined a group of autistic children in early childhood and followed them into early or late adolescence, generally with only one follow-up visit, therefore affording comparison of abilities at just two points in time.[3] In general, these studies suggest that individuals with autism remain as severely affected by the disorder in adolescence as in childhood.

With the exception of a few members of Kanner's original sample who appeared to improve during their teen-age years[4], the majority of studies suggest that adolescence may be a time of deterioration in social adjustment.[5] Just over half the adolescents studied in Sweden,[6] for example, and approximately one third (32%) of autistic adolescents studied in Hong Kong showed either a temporary or sustained aggravation of symptoms and degeneration in social functioning after puberty.[7] Parents described hyperactivity, explosive anger, aggressiveness, destructiveness—predominantly against the child himself rather than others—and greater insistence on order and predictability. Behavioral disturbances were often preceded by slow intellectual decline and the loss of some language skills. While most children who appeared to deteriorate during adolescence had shown some of these problems in early childhood, they became more conspicuous and difficult to manage in adolescence. Parents' reports of their children's heightened distress during adolescence[8] are confirmed by autistic individuals' autobiographical accounts of overwhelming anxiety and upheaval during puberty.[9]

Most of what we know about the adjustment of persons with autism derives from parents or caregivers' responses in the context of structured interviews. In many cases the limited verbal abilities of individuals with autism preclude conducting interviews with them. Yet while employment and living arrangements are objective indices of social functioning, adjustment cannot be fully assessed without considering an individual's own assessment of his or her circumstances. Particularly given the previously mentioned inverse relationship between children's assessments of their own social competence and parents' evaluations of their children, it seems critical to solicit first-hand accounts of personal experiences when possible. With Temple Grandin's autobiographical writings as the high point, personal accounts lend authenticity and insight to empirical investigations, illuminating the nature of the problems autistic persons face and the resources they draw on in coping with these problems.

We have yet to determine why deterioration occurs among many autistic adolescents during puberty. In some cases the difficulties appear to be the result of severe brain abnormalities, often manifest in seizure disorders.[10] Although seizure disorders tend to appear in older children, brain dysfunction is not necessarily progressive. It is possible that the effects of nerve damage, which may have been suffered pre- or perinatally, become more acute with age due to increasing social and cognitive demands. Various kinds of neurohormonal changes may also play a role. The onset of epilepsy, whether associated with underlying progressive brain abnormalities or not, also may trigger aggravation of autistic symptoms.[11]

Autistic adolescents' problems are compounded by growth in size and strength, coupled with psychophysiological changes associated with puberty. Family and other caregivers often find it difficult to cope with behaviors they could previously handle when they are added to adolescents' responses to new, often overwhelming sensations and emotions. The loss of methods for maintaining control may lead to a decline in the quality of relationships with family members, teachers , and peers. In some cases it becomes necessary to transfer these youths to restrictive educational environments or residential treatment settings.

While their distress is related to brain abnormalities and cognitive and affective deficits, the difficulties many autistic adolescents experience are mediated by the environment in which they live. Disruption associated with adolescence appears to be less debilitating in communities that provide support for families of autistic children. Chung, Luk, and Lee reported that in Hong Kong, for example, where autistic individuals with autism and their families are part of a large social network, a significant number of parents described their autistic children as showing improved functioning during adolescence.[12]

Likewise, distress associated with adolescents is mini-
mized in North Carolina, where autistic persons and
their families have access to extensive intervention and
support services.[13]

Developmental Course of Autism from Childhood to Adulthood

In most longitudinal studies of autism, adult individuals
are evaluated according to general measures of outcome
such as degree of mental retardation, behavioral disturbance, and social independence. Several investigations,
particularly those carried out in the 1970s and 1980s,
made use of a global classification system that Victor
Lotter developed in 1974 which consists of four categories: "good," indicating that the individual is leading
normal or near-normal social life and is functioning sat-
isfactorily at school or work; "fair," indicating social
and educational progress despite significant abnormalities in behavior or interpersonal relationships; "poor,"
indicating severe handicap and the inability to live independently, accompanied by some measure of social adjustment and the potential for social progress; and "very
poor," indicating dysfunction that prohibits any possibility of independent existence.[14]

The percentage of individuals falling into these different categories varies depending on severity of mental
retardation and autistic features when first seen, as well
as the age of the group at follow-up. Nonetheless, reported outcomes are remarkably uniform in the United
States, Britain, Japan, China, Hong Kong, Canada, and
Sweden. Taken together, longitudinal studies suggest
that approximately 10–15 percent of adults with autism
have good outcomes; 15–25 percent have fair outcomes;
15–25 percent have poor outcomes; and approximately
35–50 percent have very poor outcomes. Thus, some

persons with autism hold jobs and live with minimal or no supervision, but a great many are unable to care for themselves.

Longitudinal investigations emphasize the association between intellectual functioning and outcomes pertaining to employment status, educational attainment, and living situation. Population-based studies including both retarded and nonretarded subgroups report that approximately 3 percent of autistic individuals have paying jobs and live entirely independently.[15] However, such estimates are significantly higher (approximately 20%) when sheltered workshops, family businesses, and household chores are included.[16] While autistic persons often receive assistance finding and maintaining jobs, they tend to perform quite well in jobs involving attention to detail and limited social interaction, such as assisting in a library or operating a key punch.

Nonretarded autistic persons rate higher than the retarded subgroup in employment, educational attainment, and residential independence. Judith Rumsey and her colleagues studied a group of 14 autistic men, nine of whom had IQ scores in the normal range.[17] Four individuals in the high-functioning group were employed, three were receiving vocational education or job training, one participated in a sheltered workshop, and one had recently lost his job. Two of the men in this group had attended junior college, four had received high school diplomas or had passed high school equivalency exams, one had completed eighth grade, and two were enrolled in special education programs. Seven of them continued to live with their parents and two resided in supervised apartments. Of the five mentally retarded autistic men studied, two worked in sheltered workshops, one was in a special job program, one attended a day program at a state hospital, and the other was unemployed.

Andre Venter and his colleagues reported similar findings.[18] Of the 22 nonretarded subjects who were age 18 or older at the time of follow-up, 6 were competitively employed, 13 were in sheltered or supervised employment or in special educational programs, and only 2 were neither employed nor in school. Perhaps the most optimistic findings were reported by Szatmari and his colleagues in Canada, who followed 16 nonretarded children with autism into early adulthood.[19] Six were employed as library aides, cashiers, or factory workers; nine worked in sheltered workshops, vocational training centers, or family businesses; and only one was unemployed. Perhaps the most impressive finding in this study is that half of the participants had either obtained or were pursuing college degrees, while the others were in special education programs through high school. In addition, five of the adults studied lived independently without supervision, and 11 lived with their parents or in a group home.

Rates of institutionalization documented in the 1960s and 1970s suggest that 50 percent of all individuals with autism reside in institutional settings.[20] While current rates of institutionalization are thought to be considerably lower, changes may be attributable to restrictions in availability of healthcare services and the trend toward placing individuals in least restrictive environments. Alternatively, such changes may be attributable to efficacious early intervention. Rates of institutionalization also vary considerably depending on community support for families and autistic individuals. In North Carolina, where there is a comprehensive community support system (the Treatment and Evaluation of Autistic and Communication-Handicapped Children Program or TEACCH), for example, only 7 percent of autistic adults are institutionalized, including 4 percent who are placed in group homes. In fact, with regard to high-functioning autistic individuals, Lord and Venter conclude that availability of support services is the greatest predictor of employment and residential placement.[21] Clearly, in evaluating, and for that matter predicting, the adjustment of individuals with autism, social context must be taken into account.

Comparative Studies

One way to appreciate the nature and scope of autistic impairment more fully is by comparing autistic persons with those who have other disabilities. The social and psychological adjustment of individuals with autism has been compared to that of persons with language disorders, developmental delays, or social abnormalities that did not fit diagnostic criteria for autism.[22] In general, individuals in the various comparison groups fared better than did those with autism.[23] Cantwell, Baker, Rutter, and Mawhood, for example, compared adolescents with autism to adolescents with severe receptive language disorders (dysphasia) on indices of language ability, peer relations, stereotypic and repetitive behavior, and conduct in public.[24] Groups were initially matched on age, IQ scores, verbal ability, and demographic characteristics. At follow-up three years later, the adolescents with dysphasia had made marked overall progress; not so the adolescents with autism. As a group they gained semantic and syntactic skills but continued to have difficulty using language effectively in social situations. And while some individuals developed friendships and became more self-assured in public, many had limited peer relationships and manifested stereotypic, repetitive behavior. As is the case among delayed, disturbed, and normally developing children alike, autistic adolescents who had the most effective communication skills were least disruptive and had better relationships with peers.

Continuity in Symptomatology, Intelligence, Language Ability, and Emotional Responsiveness

Few longitudinal studies have conducted formal diagnostic assessment of autistic children both initially and at follow-up. Existing investigations very rarely report change in the diagnostic status: children diagnosed with autism remain autistic through adolescence and adulthood. For this reason recovery from autism is generally considered impossible. Yet there do seem to be a few exceptions.

Although the incidence of recovery has not been studied systematically, it often happens that one member of a large sample of autistic individuals no longer manifests symptoms of autism to an appreciable degree. In our laboratory, for example, one of 51 individuals who were diagnosed with autism in early childhood—now an adolescent boy—no longer appears to have any difficulties. He attends public school, where he excels academically and has several friends; his cognitive abilities are comparable to those of other children his age; and he no longer engages in stereotypic behaviors associated with autism. Another three of the mentally retarded autistic children in the sample no longer meet all of the criteria for autism but do remain significantly handicapped.

In addition to monitoring changes in diagnostic status, some attempts have been made to determine whether the severity of symptoms remains stable over time. In most cases, this is so. The majority of individuals with autism continue to show considerable cognitive delay, language disturbances, stereotypic behaviors and compulsions, and impairment in social understanding. The most severely affected children remain most severely affected as adolescents and adults.

As demonstrated by Lord and Schopler, autistic children's levels of intelligence and language ability stay relatively stable through adolescence, particularly after correcting for the language delay associated with autism.[25] That is, autistic children with strong intellectual and verbal abilities as children retain strong intellectual and verbal abilities as adolescents and young adults, whereas those with weaker skills remain severely compromised as they grow older. Longer-range testing reveals less stability in intelligence for children who were tested in preschool and followed into adolescence and adulthood. Autistic preschoolers who scored in the normal to low-normal range on nonverbal tests of intelligence were likely to remain high-functioning into school age, unless they showed very poor language development by the time they were six years old. Moreover, a significant number of children who scored in the mild to moderately retarded range on IQ tests as preschoolers later performed in the nonretarded range on nonverbal and performance tests. It appears that preschoolers who are more adept at daily living skills are most likely to make such leaps.[26]

Some autistic children's intellectual abilities improve from childhood through adolescence, largely owing to the acquisition of language. Whereas normally developing children develop language during the second and third years of life, autistic children do so up to two years later. (In fact, it is language delay that usually leads parents to suspect that their children are autistic.) Of the autistic adolescents studied in our laboratory, about half of those with IQ scores in the normal range had tested in the retarded range when they were originally seen at three to five years of age, at which time they had little if any verbal ability. Children whose scores progressed from the retarded to nonretarded range made great strides in language development.

Despite delayed onset, most children with autism develop verbal skills at a steady rate. Occasionally, however, parents report their autistic child has lost or no longer uses language abilities he demonstrated earlier. In such cases parents typically recall that their children uttered a few words between 10 and 18 months, after which time they stopped speaking. While known to many clinicians, this pattern has not been explained.

There also appears to be continuity in autistic persons' emotional responsiveness. Among the children followed in our laboratory those who appeared most responsive to the emotional displays of others as young children were most responsive to comparable displays five years later. As we recall (in Chapter 3), during the initial evaluation the examiner observed the three- to five-year-olds' responses when she feigned injury and expressed pain. When seen again between the ages of eight and ten, in the context of a tea party, the children were exposed to two emotional displays: the examiner first bumped her knee on the table and later conversed angrily on the telephone. Those autistic children who had attended most closely and responded most empathetically to the examiner during their first visit to the laboratory acted in the same fashion some five years later.[27]

Sally Ozonoff and Robin McEvoy examined the capacity for executive function and theory of mind in a sample of nonretarded individuals with autism at approximately 12 years of age and again three years later.[28] They found that performance on executive function matched that of theory of mind, and that there was little improvement in either over time. While autistic persons require far greater verbal ability to solve executive function and theory of mind tasks than do normally developing persons, for them verbal ability is a necessary but not sufficient prerequisite.[29]

Prediction of General Outcome from Earlier Evaluations

It is impossible to foretell a child's future with certainty—we have no satisfactory answers for Hazel, the mother who asks the questions at the start of this chapter, and others in her position. The strongest predictors of positive outcome for autistic children are intellectual ability and language skills. The better equipped they are in these areas, the better able they are to interpret the emotions and mental states of others and to communicate their own. They are also most likely to develop executive functions and the ability to infer the mental states of others, however limited.

Nonretarded individuals with autism are less aloof in early childhood and more likely to develop interest in social interaction as they grow older than are retarded autistic persons. Lorna Wing and Judith Gould (1979) carried out a study of approximately 35,000 children from Camberwell, a borough of London, in which they identified 132 children with autism.[30] They then classified these children as aloof, passive, or odd. Aloof children were entirely withdrawn and did not respond to social overtures or to speech; passive children appeared indifferent but accepted others' attempts to engage them in social interaction; odd children seemed to like being with others but tended to behave in ways that were off-putting and inappropriate. The majority of individuals who were deemed aloof were mentally retarded. At follow-up eight years later, many of the children who had been classified as socially aloof but were not retarded were more aptly classified as either passive or odd. Despite their apparent indifference or the awkwardness of their attempts, they had demonstrated the desire to engage with other people.

In the long run, autistic persons who are functioning within the normal range of intelligence and develop language by age six are more likely than the others to progress academically, develop social relationships, and ultimately to find jobs and live semi-independently. Among the autistic adults studied by Szatmari and his colleagues, intelligence scores, language ability, performance on a problem solving task, and an index of socially adaptive behaviors were strongly associated with favorable educational and vocational outcomes, whereas severity of symptoms was not.[31]

Although intellectual and verbal abilities are critical for later life adjustment, they are mediated by environmental factors. A fair proportion of even the most intelligent, verbally gifted autistic adults struggle unsuccessfully to establish enduring connections with others, to maintain employment, and to live on their own. Lacking access to vital sociocultural knowledge, they remain locked out of the society in which they live. Autistic persons do far better when they live in communities that help them develop communication and vocational skills and modify the learning and work environments to accommodate their limitations.

Prediction of Language Skills from Preschool Behaviors and Abilities

Given the importance of verbal skills to autistic children's ongoing adjustment, it is important to identify their precursors. Our research group has attempted to do so. The primary correlate of language acquisition in autistic children is the ability to share attention with others. Autistic children who display joint attention behaviors are likely to have better language skills than those who do not display these behaviors, both at the time and one year later.[32] Grounded in the notion that joint attention behaviors such as pointing are communicative acts,[33] the same association between joint attention and language development exists in normally developing children. Language develops out of the inclination to solicit others' responses to persons and objects in the world and to share one's own. These behaviors provide a foundation for increasingly complex communication, relationships, and cultural knowledge that undergird social life.

Currently, we are attempting to determine whether nonverbal communicative behaviors predict language abilities in later childhood and adolescence. Preliminary results suggest that joint attention is necessary for both language *acquisition*, and for *ongoing* language development. If these findings are replicated, it will also be important to determine whether interventions that seek to heighten joint attention in autistic children lead to the enhancement of language skills. Difficult as it is to introduce verbal skills to nonspeaking individuals, it may be possible to promote language development by cultivating nonverbal communication.

In summary, longitudinal studies identify both differences in the manifestation of autistic impairment over time, and processes linking earlier abilities and events to later achievements. In a sense, the existing body of longitudinal research sketches fundamental features, providing a frame that awaits detailed elaboration through ongoing work. Studies that have been carried out so far show that the majority of autistic children remain autistic and their symptoms remain severe throughout adulthood. In some cases, however, symptoms of the disorder improve to an appreciable degree. Such improvement is tied to individuals' intellectual and language abilities and is influenced by the environment in which an individual lives. The correct identification of the abilities, behaviors, and precursors that promote adaptive functioning both illuminates the nature of autistic impairment and informs intervention with autistic children.

8 / In Search of Core Deficits and Causes of Autism

Lorna Wing's comments on autism, made some twenty years ago, still serve as a good launching point for this chapter:

> It does not take a great deal of experience with autistic children to be struck by the fundamental gaps in their social behavior. This complex disturbance in social behavior often makes the rearing and educating of these children very difficult. Yet the same disturbance in social behavior compels many researchers to attempt to delineate the nature of the disorder that afflicts these children. Scientific curiosity, it seems, is piqued by the notion that to understand what is deviant in the social phenotype of autistic children is to understand an important component of human nature.

Having outlined the general course of development of individuals with autism and compared it with that of normal children, we now shift focus to what autistic persons have in common—to what might be the core deficit of the disorder. Learning about the specific limitations in autistic persons' behavioral repertoire allows us to parse the smooth continuum of everyday behavior displayed by normally developing individuals, and to discriminate between actions and abilities on the basis of cognitive and affective prerequisites.

Identifying the core deficits of a disorder is important for diagnostic purposes. The correctness of any diagnosis depends on establishing which characteristics of the disorder are central and which peripheral. For example, many physical illnesses are accompanied by a fever, but this is never the principal basis for diagnosis. Specifying core deficits thus guides the course of treatment, keeping the focus on the main problems. Although interventions that target secondary effects of a disorder or facilitate compensatory strategies may be useful, these approaches are not likely to alter the course of the illness in a profound way.

In addition, identifying the core deficits of a disorder is often a first step in the search for causes, while specific conceptualizations influence the approaches used to determine etiology. Genetic conceptualizations, for example, lead to studies of how and whether central symptoms of a disorder run in families. Neurological conceptualizations lead to studies of brain abnormalities, and psychological conceptualizations lead to studies of the nature and scope of cognitive and affective impairment. The way a disorder is conceptualized influences what sort of characteristics will be examined and the methods that will be used. Further, different approaches often inform one another. For instance, the characteristics that are examined in genetic studies—studies of the first-degree relatives of individuals with autism—stem from a particular conceptualization of the core psychological deficits. Similarly, delineating core psychological impairment in autism guides inquiry into the brain structures and neural systems that may be damaged. Deficits in social cognition, for example, suggest the need to investigate the limbic system, which is involved in affective responses. In like fashion, the discovery of abnormalities at neurological and genetic levels informs efforts to identify core psychological deficits.

Criteria for Defining a Core Psychological Deficit

Before attempting to identify core psychological deficits, it is necessary to specify what constitutes a deficit and establishes its centrality to a disorder. If an observer notes that autistic individuals are unable to perform certain tasks successfully, she may conclude that they lack the requisite abilities. Yet it is not so simple. A particular ability will remain undisclosed if the person is not willing to perform a given task. Similarly, an individual may adopt an approach to a task that makes no use of abilities which are nevertheless present. Further, measures used in research usually require a variety of abilities, so it is difficult to attribute success or failure to any one ability or deficit. Even when a particular deficit is identified, questions remain as to whether it represents delayed, as opposed to deviant, development.

Specificity, universality, and primacy are often considered criteria for the centrality of a deficit. That is, the deficit should not be found in individuals with other disorders, should appear in all children sharing the same disorder, and should emerge early in development. These criteria are problematic, however, because every syndrome involves a constellation of deficits. It is hard to imagine a deficit that is specific to a single mental disorder. Further, while a core deficit should appear in all individuals with the same condition, the manifestations of a particular deficit are likely to change with development. Finally, it is important to identify the point in development when a disorder becomes apparent, particularly because initial problems are likely to influence ongoing development. Yet some disorders are not immediately apparent; hence core deficits may be impossible to identify until symptoms show up at a crucial developmental stage: for example, when a child acquires language or reaches a maturational point such as puberty.

Any theory of autism must explain the specific pattern of limitations and abilities shown by persons with autism and must be consistent with what is known about normal development. In Chapter 1 we specified deficits that characterize autistic persons of all ages and levels of intellectual ability, namely, impairment in social understanding, communication, and imaginative activity. The following review shows that each area comprises an array of behaviors which are grounded in cognitive and affective abilities that emerge at different points in normal development. Further, as we have shown in the previous chapters, autistic persons do not suffer global deficits in any of these areas. Rather, autistic impairment is specific to contexts that require comprehending, sharing, and influencing the perspective of another person.

Social understanding. Autistic children display some of the behaviors that are central to developing an awareness of themselves and others. They recognize their reflections in mirrors.[1] They are clearly responsive to other people in situations in which adults or peers actively engage them in social interaction.[2] In addition, many children with autism show signs of secure attachment to caregivers, including wanting to be with them.[3]

Yet autistic persons also manifest a particular pattern of impairment in social behaviors that emerges very early in normal development. They rarely initiate social interactions and conversations and pay limited attention to other people. Autistic children and adults have difficulty recognizing and expressing emotions,[4] particularly complex emotions such as pride, shame, and embarrassment, which necessarily take social standards and expectations into account.[5] They have trouble imitating affective displays.[6] They rarely engage in social referencing, that is, looking at another person to gain information about an ambiguous situation and to use such information to regulate their behavior.[7] Autistic persons have limited empathy in response to the feelings of others and little understanding of others' thoughts, beliefs, and attitudes more generally.[8] In many cases these deficits are particularly striking in contrast to autistic persons' comprehension of nonmental representations such as pictures, photographs, and maps, or their reading abilities or memory skills.[9]

Communication. Autistic persons display a wide range of communicative impairment. Although they use gestures to request assistance in obtaining an object, for example, they rarely use gestures to engage someone's attention or to express support or concern.[10] While many autistic individuals remain mute, even those who develop verbal skills in the normal range manifest delayed speech. Verbal autistic persons appear to grasp grammar and syntax with relative ease, but they often display abnormal prosody and stereotyped, repetitive, or idiosyncratic use of words. Yet perhaps most striking are their difficulties with pragmatics and narrative.[11] Limited understanding of how people use language to achieve goals, and how to render experience in narrative form, makes it difficult for autistic individuals to interpret, initiate, and sustain interaction with others.

Imagination. Autistic persons show striking deficits in pretend play, particularly the spontaneous make-believe involving human drama;[12] they are more likely to engage in repetitive, stereotyped actions with objects. Francesca Happé notes that the obsessive functional play of young autistic children may later give way to similarly obsessional interest in, for example, dates of birth, train schedules, and bus routes.[13] Older, more able individuals with autism appear to prefer facts over fantasy, fiction, or speculation.

In addition to explaining the limitations highlighted above, a theory of autism must also account for stereotypical, repetitive or perseverative behavior. At the same time it needs to encompass the phenomenon Kanner called "islets of ability"—rote memory, extraordinary skills in isolated domains, and above-average intelligence—that are sometimes present. Hence we will consider various theories of autism, first focusing on the psychological and then the biological aspects of the disorder.

The Nature of the Core Psychological Deficits in Autism

There are three main lines of thinking about what constitutes the predominant psychological disability in autism. One ascribes autistic impairment to deficits in thinking and information processing; the second to lack of affective contact; and the third to problems in regulating and use of attention. Each approach highlights different characteristics of persons with autism and different aspects of the behaviors that are impaired or disordered. Depending on its emphasis, every theory of autism makes somewhat different assumptions about the associations between various behaviors—the precursors, prerequisites, and correlates—among normally developing children.

Problems in Thinking

Theories that focus on defective cognition as the central problem in autism themselves fall into two groups. The first emphasizes deficits in concepts that seem to emerge naturally and effortlessly among normal children, in particular the formation of a theory of mind (see Chapter 5), while the second group focuses on deviant cognitive processes. In general, theories that stress deficient concepts are grounded in a modular view of the brain, which attributes modes of thinking to specific mechanisms. Theories that emphasize cognitive processes are derived from a computer-based model of mental functioning and center on how information is apprehended and interpreted.

Mentalizing Abilities. Some investigators pinpoint autistic impairment in the inability to mentalize or read minds,[14] or put more broadly, an inability to form metarepresentations of reality.[15] This hypothesis is supported by evidence that autistic persons show deficits in social, communicative, and imaginative behaviors in contexts where they need to consider mental states (but not in other contexts), and are unable to pass tasks requiring a theory of mind. Clearly, an inability to think about one's own thoughts and those of others has far-reaching consequences for social interaction. We must be able to gauge others' knowledge, beliefs, and intentions with some accuracy, or we cannot handle social situations nor grasp culturally designated meanings of events and experiences.

Proponents of this hypothesis believe they have identified cognitive precursors to theory-of-mind deficits. Alan Leslie, for example, has proposed that pretend play is an early manifestation of the capacity for metarepresentation.[16] In his view the mental processes that enable the child to act on representations that he endows with a temporary reality (for example, making a banana be a telephone) are akin to those involved in the ability to adopt another person's perspective.[17] Leslie has proposed that the capacity for metarepresentation is attributable to an innate module—the Theory of Mind Module—that emerges in normally developing children in the second year of life. From his perspective, autistic children suffer dysfunction in the relevant brain structures.[18] Further, Leslie and Happé have suggested that joint attention behavior also relies on the metarepresentational mechanism that promotes pretense and theory of mind. Hence autistic persons' deficits in joint attention are an even earlier manifestation of a malfunctioning theory-of-mind mechanism.[19]

In a related conceptualization, Simon Baron-Cohen emphasizes the role of attention as a critical precursor to mentalizing.[20] He highlights autistic persons' deficits in joint-attention behaviors, in view of the importance of eye gaze in comprehending the attention and goals of other people. Baron-Cohen suggests that normally developing children's perceptual systems are hardwired to understand other people's intentions. In particular, he posits the existence of an "eye direction detector," which facilitates awareness of people as goal-directed beings with affective stances toward objects in the world. Baron-Cohen's theory holds that such neurological mechanisms are absent or underdeveloped among individuals with autism, thus accounting for deficits in joint attention and eventually in pretense and theory of mind.

Uta Frith has offered another cognitive conceptualization, which identifies the primary problem in autism as a deficit in the "drive for central coherence."[21] Her view is grounded in the belief that normally developing persons are compelled to integrate disparate bits of information into coherent patterns by making inferences about the causes and effects of behavior. Autistic persons suffer from a fundamental, pervasive problem in constructing comprehensive interpretations of situations by reading the intentions of participants from the movements of their eyes and hands and in contextual cues. For example, looking at a picture of some people playing cards around a table, normal persons infer that the player with cards in his back pocket is cheating, that a second player knows this (because he is pointing at the cheat), and that a third, whose face is buried in his cards, does not. In contrast, while autistic persons may note that one player is holding two cards behind his back, they are not likely to see this behavior in the broader context of a card game involving a player who endeavors to win by cheating. Frith provides numerous examples of autistic persons' decontextualized interpretations, only some of which involve a theory of mind. This suggests a problem preceding mentalizing: integrating aspects of a situation into a coherent whole. For instance, when presented with a picture of a bedroom and asked to identify the rectangular object at the head of the bed, one autistic child replied, "It's a ravioli."

Attributing the psychological impairment in autism to a deficient drive for central coherence not only accounts for behaviors and abilities that are lacking, such as joint attention and theory of mind. It also accounts for the visible symptoms, including the obsessive desire for sameness, repetitive and stereotypical movements, restricted range of interest, and fragmented sensations.[22] Along with Leslie, Baron-Cohen, and others whose models of the core cognitive deficits in autism specify modules in the brain that are missing or underdeveloped, Frith and her colleagues are working to identify the brain structures that might account for the drive for central coherence and its impairment in autism.[23]

Executive Function. According to the second set of cognitive theories, the core psychological impairment in autism is better understood in terms of deviant cognitive processes. These theories highlight autistic persons' difficulties with executive function, which is associated with the frontal lobes of the brain.[24] Executive function involves planning strategies to attain future goals: for example, inhibiting direct action when a more roundabout approach is required, and identifying and flexibly switching categories. The notion that executive dysfunction is the core impairment in autism accounts for features of the disorder that are not readily explained in terms of a theory-of-mind deficit, such as narrow range of interests, obsessive desire for sameness, and islets of ability. From this perspective, theory-of-mind deficits may be part of or parallel to a broader problem in processing information.[25] Ozonoff and her colleagues, for example, have suggested that autism-specific difficulties in planning may underlie impairments in theory of mind. Russell and his colleagues argue, from another angle, that autistic people have trouble putting an observable state of reality aside and imagining or invoking an alternative.[26] Thus in the theory-of-mind task they cannot grasp the notion that Sally thinks the marble is where she left it (in the basket), because they cannot free their attention from where the marble is (in the box). Other researchers have conceptualized deficits in cognitive processes apart from executive function. Paul Harris, for example, has argued that difficulties in hypothetical reasoning are at the core of impairments in pretense and theory of mind.[27]

Proponents of the view that flawed executive function or defective information processing constitutes the core impairment in autism often cite a study that found that the deficit in executive function among a high-functioning group of autistic adolescents was more pervasive than their deficits in emotional understanding and expression and theory of mind.[28] Yet this finding is not necessarily specific to autism; executive function impairments are characteristic of other clinical disorders such as Attention Deficit Disorder, Obsessive Compulsive Disorder, Tourette Syndrome, and schizophrenia.[29] Sally Ozonoff and her colleagues, among others, are currently attempting to identify precisely which executive functions are impaired among individuals with autism.[30] They are also exploring possible connections between deficits in these abilities and in theory of mind on the biological level, in particular from damage to the prefrontal cortex.

Problems in Feeling

In his original formulation, Leo Kanner described the problem of autism as a lack of affective contact. Some current theorists, most notably Peter Hobson, hold to this conceptualization, suggesting that autistic children suffer primary deficits in the capacity for personal relatedness, particularly affective relatedness.[31] Following the work of G. H. Mead, Daniel Stern, and Colwyn Trevarthen, among others, Hobson argues that reciprocal, highly affective exchanges provide a foundation for differentiating persons from things and mark the beginning of a path toward more explicit understanding of one's own and others' mental lives.[32] The capacity for understanding mental states, then, is seen as inherently *interpersonal* in that children develop self-awareness and reflection by recognizing others as persons with whom they can identify.

From Hobson's perspective, innate impairment in the ability to perceive and respond to affect in others is what prevents autistic persons from participating in social interactions that are necessary for developing more sophisticated forms of social understanding, including theory of mind. In support of this theory, Hobson cites autistic persons' difficulty in assessing facial expressions, as well as their lack of affective and social contact with others, including disinclination to combine affect and joint attention, and their limited empathetic responsiveness.[33] Within this conceptual framework, autistic persons' repetitive, stereotypic behaviors and restricted interests are thought to be substitutes for the broader interests and directed behaviors that fail to develop as a consequence of limited social involvement.

Other theorists have focused on various social behaviors that facilitate intersubjectivity, affective sharing, and ultimately an understanding of others' minds. Highlighting autistic persons' difficulties with imitation, Andrew Meltzoff and Alison Gopnik have suggested that impairment in the ability to recognize correspondences between their own movements and those of other people disrupts the development of adequate representations of self and other, ultimately precluding the development of a theory of mind.[34] Sally Rogers and Bruce Pennington also identify impairment in the capacity for imitation as a core deficit, but emphasize associated detriments to the development of intersubjectivity, affective sharing, and social and cultural learning.[35]

Problems in Attention and Arousal Regulation

Another group of theorists attributes autistic impairment to difficulty in regulating attention. Some research evidence suggests that autistic children are overselective in attending to the environments they inhabit, concentrating on single dimensions rather than the entire object or the situation as a whole.[36] Cognitive and social problems are also thought to stem from such overselectivity of attention, which contributes to autistic persons' difficulty in developing a comprehensive understanding of social situations and cultural norms.

Some versions of this theory attribute problems with

attention to impaired arousal regulation. Within this framework, autistic individuals are overaroused physiologically; that is, they are overwhelmed by environmental stimuli. Such theories focus on autistic persons' overselectivity, obsessive desire for sameness, restricted interests, and narrowed focus, viewing these behaviors as means of coping with excessive arousal. For some time repetitive and stereotypical behaviors were also thought to serve arousal-controlling functions. However, psychophysiological studies of stereotyped behavior suggest that this is not the case.[37] Theories that focus on attention problems attribute autistic persons' lack of social referencing and associated deficits in emotional understanding and theory of mind to the burden that interactions with people and objects place on the child's limited attentional capacities.

On the Abundance of Theories

Why are there so many different theories when most researchers and clinicians agree on the characteristics of autism? In part it is because researchers emphasize different symptoms in their formulations. Theorists who view autistic persons' problems in *thinking* as fundamental to the disorder emphasize deficient cognitive concepts and processes. Those who focus on *affective* problems stress disturbed social relationships and interactions. And attention theorists most strongly emphasize peculiar behaviors and proclivities.

The features investigators emphasize are often highlighted by the nature of the samples they select to test their theories. Theory of mind, for example, can only be investigated in individuals who are able to speak. Thus researchers who conceptualize autism in terms of theory-of-mind impairment are apt to study older, nonretarded autistic children and adults. Deficits in joint attention and social referencing, which emerge earlier, are likely to be much less salient among such samples. Further, older, nonretarded individuals with autism could well have overcome some of their difficulties with attention regulation and emotional responsiveness—problems that may be more strikingly aberrant in younger, less intelligent children.

Different theories of autism evolve from parallel theories of normal development. For example, theorists who conceptualize normal cognitive development in terms of the formation of representational structures are likely to view the central problem in autism as metarepresentational. In contrast, theorists who use information-processing (computer-like) models of cognitive development are prone to see the central problem in autism as involving deficits in executive function. Similarly, theorists who see imitation as central to normal children's social and emotional development are likely to conceptualize autistic persons' limitations in terms of deficits in imitative behaviors. Yet this goes both ways. That is, inquiry into the nature of autism also shapes theories of normal development. As Lorna Wing commented, "to understand what is deviant in the social phenotype of autistic children is to understand an important component of human nature."[38]

Our Theory: Problems Integrating Affect and Cognition

Our own theoretical perspective reflects the focus of our research program. Although we did study a sample of nonretarded autistic adolescents, the research carried out in our laboratory concentrated mainly on young autistic children, most of them mentally retarded. Our conceptualization of the core impairment in autism is grounded in a particular view of the essential precursors to social understanding that normally develop in the first 12–15 months of life: (1) children attend and react emotionally to social and nonsocial events; (2) they become aware of their reactions; (3) they seek out and interpret others' vocal, facial, and behavioral displays of affect: (4) and they match and compare their own reactions with those of other people.

This early matrix is the foundation for understanding of others' perceptions, desires, and beliefs as distinct from our own, and for interpreting our own and others' emotions and actions within the context of cultural norms, expectations, and conventions—knowledge that is crucial to participating in social life. As reviewed in this book, existing research makes it difficult to delineate precisely the scope of autistic impairment in any of the four areas outlined above. Despite autistic persons' difficulties and idiosyncracies with respect to recognition and expression of emotion, the studies we carried out suggest that autistic children do have emotional reactions that are quite similar to those of normal children. They are not markedly different in their expression of affect during social interactions, and their parents describe them as expressing a comparable range and degree of emotion during daily interactions.[39] Older autistic children attribute emotions to themselves and manifest responses to others in emotionally arousing situations.[40]

Difficulties in clarifying the nature of affective disturbance in autism stem in part from the complex relationship between emotional experiences and their expression. Feelings are private, and feeling states are neither directly observable nor channeled into a single mode of expression. It is thus exceedingly difficult to read and interpret another person's emotional experience, and even more so to penetrate the world of autistic individuals.

Given evidence that autistic persons are hypersensitive to sound and visual stimuli, they may be so flooded with sensations from the outside that they find it difficult to apprehend their own emotional experiences.[41] Preliminary findings from our own studies of autistic children, however, yielded little evidence of strong cardiac responses to emotional stimuli. Further, autistic children manifest at least rudimentary knowledge of their wants and desires through efforts to obtain objects or to regulate the behavior of others. At older ages they are able to describe events that make them happy and sad.[42] Studies based on structured interactions in which adults initiate exchanges have found that three- to five-year-old autistic children were as attentive and showed as much face-to-face interaction as normal children matched on mental age, but they appeared less inclined to combine looking with affective displays.[43] Similarly, in social referencing paradigms, autistic children pay little attention to vocal, facial, and behavioral displays of emotion, even when such displays are explicit and dramatic.[44] They seem to lack the ability and proclivity to solicit another's emotional response and compare (or contrast) it with one's own. But without this give-and-take it seems impossible to appreciate others' feelings or gain a deepening sense of one's own affective experience.

Autistic children may suffer some degree of impairment in any or all of the precursors to sophisticated social and emotional understanding. The trouble could stem from impaired emotional responsiveness or a diminished capacity to apprehend one's own and others' affective states. In other words, the core impairment could be affective or cognitive. But it seems most likely that autistic impairment stems from deficits in *both* areas. Among normally developing children, from infancy onward, cognitive and emotional responses are inextricably linked. Autistic children experience most difficulty in situations that clearly require integrating feeling and thinking—the very situations in which normally developing children acquire the foundation for ongoing participation in social relationships and cultural practices. Lack of the ability or proclivity to share with someone an emotional response to a person or an object drastically limits autistic persons' understanding (including representations) and experience of themselves and others, of their identities, relationships, and of the society in which they live.

Because attention, behavior, and arousal are guided by one's interpretation of a given person or situation, we see difficulties in these areas as secondary rather than primary deficits in autism. Autistic persons' restricted interests and peculiar attention patterns are the result rather than the cause of the cognitive and social deficits.

The Nature of the Core Biological Deficits in Autism

Another way to identify the core deficits in autism is to determine the biological systems that are compromised. Identifying dysfunctions in the central nervous system that parallel psychological impairments in autism will greatly enhance the diagnosis and treatment of the disorder. Neurophysiological studies of autism follow two lines of inquiry: one stressing disturbances of language and cognition, and the other stressing disturbances of sensory modulation and motility. Autistic impairment in language and cognition suggests cortical dysfunction, and impairment in sensory modulation and motility suggests subcortical dysfunction. While successfully identifying central nervous system dysfunction will certainly advance the search for the etiology of autism, it is not sufficient. Because brain structure and function are modified by experiences, dysfunctions in autistic persons' anatomy, physiology, or biochemistry are as likely to *result* from differences in their experiences compared to those of normally developing persons (such as limited or absent capacities for joint attention, social referencing, and pretense and theory of mind) as they are to *cause* such differences. Further, demonstrating that a biological dysfunction is specific to autism does not reveal the origin of the biological dysfunction. Damage to the central nervous system may be genetic or it may occur at any stage of development, beginning in utero with gametogenesis, fertilization, and implantation; when the embryo is maturing; during the birth process; or early in life.

Brain Functioning in Autism

In normal people, the two hemispheres of the cortex specialize in different functions. Language and symbolic functions, for example, are controlled by the left hemisphere, while visual-spatial abilities are controlled by the right hemisphere. Functional and anatomical specialization starts at birth and increases with development. Some studies suggest an imbalance in the hemispheres of persons with autism, such that the right hemisphere is over-activated to the detriment of left hemispheric functions.[45] This hypothesis has been formulated on the basis of electrophysiological and dichotic listening studies. Brain activity is measured using ERPs (event-related potentials), which average an individual's electrophysiological responses to discrete stimuli. By averaging these responses random electrical activity cancels out, and a characteristic wave form results. Investigators have compared autistic and nonautistic persons' ERPs in response to both nonlinguistic (a click or flash) and linguistic (saying "da") stimuli.[46] In each of these studies a disproportionate number of autistic individuals showed either reversed or absent lateralization of brain activity. That is,

stimuli that evoked left hemispheric responses in normally developing individuals evoke right hemispheric
responses or a lack of response among those with autism.

Similar results emerged from research using an alpha-
blocking method in which ongoing electroencepha-
lographic activity is measured during various cognitive
tasks that differentially rely on left and right hemispheric
functions.[47] A significant number of autistic individuals
showed a reversed pattern of brain activity during tasks
involving language or other tasks that were mediated by
the left hemisphere. But autistic individuals' pattern of
hemispheric activity did not differ from that of normal
comparison subjects during visual-spatial tasks.

Dichotic listening studies also confirm that the right
hemisphere is overactive in persons with autism.[48] In
such studies participants are presented with various
auditory stimuli to their left and right ears and are then
asked to report what they hear. For normal individuals,
linguistic stimuli typically showed a left-hemisphere or
right-ear advantage. Individuals with autism, in contrast, exhibited a right-hemisphere or left-ear advantage.
The existing data, then, suggest that autism involves
atypical patterns of hemispheric activity—namely, right-
dominant or symmetric hemispheric activity during linguistic and other tasks associated with the left hemisphere. Yet not all autistic individuals exhibit abnormal
patterns of lateralization. Further, there seems to be some
connection between hemispheric asymmetries and language ability: autistic persons who developed language
before age five tended to exhibit the normal right-ear
advantage during dichotic listening tasks.[49] Shifts toward left-hemispheric dominance associated with the
acquisition of language would not be expected if there
were permanent abnormalities in underlying brain organization.

Another line of research has examined cortical responses to unpredictable, novel stimuli, finding reduced responses—weaker and slower—among individuals with autism.[50] But were autistic persons able to differentiate novel from familiar stimuli? To address this question, Eric Courchesne tested normal and nonretarded autistic persons using a series of background stimuli that included an occasional unpredictable and novel stimulus.[51] He recorded participants' electrophysiological responses to both background and novel stimuli, and found that, although weaker overall in comparison to those of normal subjects, autistic subjects' responses to novel stimuli were significantly stronger than to background stimuli, suggesting that they were capable of detecting and responding to novelty. In fact, autistic subjects tended to have a normal or even heightened response to the first novel stimulus. Yet their subsequent responses were considerably weaker, suggesting that they do not process such information any further. Courchesne concludes from these data that the neural generators involved in detecting novelty have the capacity for normal functioning among individuals with autism, but may be interfered with or hindered by another system.

In addition, several studies of autonomic (cardiovascular) responses to novel stimuli have suggested that autistic individuals have abnormal orienting responses.[52] An orienting response is typically elicited among normally developing persons when they encounter novel, unpredictable stimuli, and is characterized by slowed heart rate and breathing, decreased peripheral blood flow, and lower electrodermal activity. If the stimulus is presented repeatedly, these physiological indices return to baseline as the organism habituates. If the stimulus is intense or noxious, however, the typical response is an initial heart rate increase that fails to habituate or only slightly diminishes when the stimulus is repeated. But among individuals with autism some react to mild novel stimuli as if they were aversive—with heart rate acceleration and less habituation. Studies carried out some years ago have shown that in comparison to normal children, autistic children have elevated heart rates, increased peripheral blood flow, and greater heart rate variability.[53] Such overarousal was thought to interfere with autistic persons' ability to process and interpret information, contributing to deficits in language and social understanding. Although we did not examine orienting responses, preliminary findings from our own research suggest that the basal heart rates of autistic children do not differ from those of mentally retarded comparison children, though they are slightly more variable. The significance of this is yet to be determined.

Brain Structure in Autism

Theories of autism suggest core deficits in functions that are thought to be controlled by cortical structures in the brain. Autopsy studies and studies using computerized tomography have revealed abnormalities in the cerebral cortexes of autistic persons.[54] Because of the interconnections between the cerebellum, other parts of the brain stem, and the cerebral cortex, it has been proposed that the neurophysiological dysfunction in autism involves a cascading series of interacting neuronal loops in the brain stem's reticular formation, the substantia nigra, thalamic nuclei, and the rostral projections from these structures to neostriatal and cortical structures.[55] Speculation about where malformations would be expected have been guided by knowledge of normal brain function coupled with the distinct pattern of abilities and disabilities displayed by persons with autism. Dysfunction of reticular brain stem mechanisms and their projection to higher centers, for instance, could account for autistic persons' inability to modulate sensory input, resulting in under- and overresponsiveness to sensory stimuli and impairment in the ability to direct and sustain attention.

Additional evidence has associated autism with damage to the cerebellum.[56] Magnetic resonance imaging (MRI) revealed that the majority in a group of individuals with autism—varying in levels of intellectual ability—had significantly diminished development ("hypoplasia") of neocerebellar vermal lobules VI and VII. This form of hypoplasia was not seen in patients with various other neurological disorders. Further, the scan showed that the other vermal lobules (I-V and VIII) tended to be normal in size. These findings indicate a specific neuroanatomical pathology in autism that appears to have resulted from damage early in brain development.

Many factors, including malnourishment, viruses, toxic agents, drugs, and genetic mutations, can cause abnormal cerebellar development. Maternal and postnatal histories of autistic individuals have yet to reveal a consistent pattern of drug exposure, illness, and the like that might account for the selective hypoplasia of vermal lobules VI and VII. Moreover, we do not yet understand the functional significance of these lobules—how their reduction might contribute to autistic impairment. Uncovering such information will yield insights into the cerebellar function of normally developing persons as well as those with autism.

Given autistic impairment in social understanding, the disorder may involve dysfunction in the limbic system, particularly cells in the amygdala that are responsive to social-emotional stimuli.[57] Histopathological studies have revealed fewer than average Purkinje cells in the cerebellum and a larger number of small, densely packed cells in the hippocampus, amygdala, entorhinal cortex, and mamillary bodies.[58] Although specific brain abnormalities in autism have yet to be linked with specific behavioral manifestations of the disorder, experimental lesions in the amygdalohippocampal region in infant macaques lead to the manifestation of many autistic-like features.[59] Stimulation of the amygdala in human patients causes them to experience difficulty in interpreting emotions and responding to social situations.[60] Following stimulation to his left amygdala, one patient described a pervasive feeling of not belonging here.[61] Similarly, amygdala lesions in humans are associated with difficulties in recognizing faces and exhibiting inappropriate social behaviors.[62] Taken together, these findings suggest that dysfunction in the amygdala—or in an interconnected system of which the amygdala is part—may play a crucial role in the social deficits in autism.

Exciting research programs currently under way are applying tomography and related techniques to identify regions of the brain involved in theory of mind tasks. In England, Frith, Frith, and Happé, for example, asked normal human subjects to read stories and think about the character's motives and found that subjects exhibited specific activation of the left medial frontal gyrus (Brodmann's area 8).[63] A similar study carried out at the United States National Institute of Neurological Disorders and Stroke showed prominent activation of the left medial frontal lobe and areas of the left temporal lobes.[64] Currently focusing on nonautistic persons, this research will provide a basis for determining whether autism involves damage to these regions of the brain.

The pervasive nature of autism suggests that dysfunctions must occur in both subcortical and cortical areas of the brain. Efforts to specify the nature of this dysfunction will in turn enhance understanding of normal brain development, illuminating the neurobiology of social relatedness and the interconnections among neuronal systems.

Neurotransmitters in Autism

The mechanism underlying autistic impairment might not lie in neuronal systems themselves but in disturbed patterns of neuronal transmission.[65] This hypothesis has given rise to a considerable number of studies of neurotransmitters in autistic individuals. Before discussing these findings, methodological limitations must be considered. Measuring neurotransmitters in the central nervous system requires very invasive surgical procedures. Because there is a great deal of legitimate resistance to these procedures, studies rely on peripheral sources, such as blood, for the material that is assayed. But the extent to which levels of neurotransmitters in peripheral areas represent those in the central nervous system is not known, so evidence of neurotransmitter abnormalities is difficult to interpret. In addition, most studies involve only a small number of subjects, and potentially confounding effects of developmental level, age, sex, and medication status have not yet been examined.

Among the various biochemical studies, the most robust finding is elevated levels of serotonin in the blood of some autistic subjects.[66] Although serotonergic neurons are known to modulate physiological processes such as sleep, pain, sensory perception, motor functioning, appetite, learning, and memory, the meaning of this finding is unclear.[67] Various lines of research suggest that dopaminergic systems are also involved in the pathogenesis of autism, but the evidence is mixed.[68]

One avenue of inquiry relies on the effects of tranquilizers or neuroleptics that block dopamine receptors, and stimulants such as amphetamines that facilitate dopaminergic activity. The observation that tranquilizers inhibit autistic persons' stereotypic and other maladaptive behaviors, while such behaviors are increased with stimulants, suggests that dopaminergic mechanisms play a role in autism. Additional interest has focused on certain peptides, the enkephalins and endorphins, in light of studies showing that animals treated with exogenous opiate compounds show some of the behaviors associated with autism, for example decreased response to painful stimuli, self-injurious behavior and isolation. Preliminary evidence suggests that opiate antagonists may be useful for treating these behaviors.[69]

A greater appreciation of the biological basis for the social-communicative dysfunctions suffered by persons with autism may suggest which specific neuronal systems might most profitably be studied. Although autistic persons' problems with arousal, attention, and social responsiveness have captured the interest of investigators from a wide range of disciplines, the associations between such deficits and underlying neural systems await delineation.

What Are the Causes of Autism?

While theories about the core psychological deficit vary, and evidence concerning core biological dysfunctions, is scanty, there is even less information about the causes of autism. In fact autism is not a unitary disease with a single etiology. It is a heterogeneous behavioral syndrome found in association with many etiologies.

Originally, Kanner suggested that there was a genetic component to autism: an inborn disorder of affective contact unrelated to other psychiatric disorders and medical conditions. But when psychoanalytic theories were paramount, many clinicians assumed that this idea was incorrect and proposed that children become autistic in response to poor parenting, or what Bruno Bettelheim referred to as "the refrigerator mother."[70] This idea has since been rejected by the vast majority of researchers, clinicians, and parents (although it continues to cause them pain). It is contradicted both by studies of the interaction between autistic children and their parents and by evidence that many children who suffer extreme abuse and neglect do not manifest symptoms of autism. Most investigations of the etiology of autism since then have focused on biological rather than environmental causes. And while Kanner's early insight into the genetic component has proved correct, autism has also been observed in association with a variety of medical conditions.[71]

Complications in any part of the process of fertilization, implantation, embryological development, or childbirth could cause damage that leads to autism. Infections affecting the central nervous system in early life could also have this effect. During the rubella epidemic of 1964, for instance, approximately 8 percent of a group of children whose mothers contracted rubella during pregnancy showed symptoms of autism in early life.[72] Subsequent studies, however, have suggested that not more than 5 percent of autism could be attributed to infectious agents.[73] Prenatal, perinatal, and neonatal complications are somewhat more frequent in autistic than in normal samples, but no factors specific to autism have been identified. Furthermore, even if such factors had been found, they could be attributable to congenital defects in the fetus, since complications during the birth process often arise due to fetal malformations.

Evidence that genetic factors play a significant role in the development of autism is mounting, although the data remain indirect.[74] The most striking findings come from studies of monozygotic and dizygotic twins.[75] If autism were transmitted genetically by a single gene, one would expect the prevalence of autism among monozygotic twin pairs to be twice that of dizygotic twin pairs, since monozygotic twins are twice as closely related as dizygotic twins. Research findings more than confirm this assumption: in about 60 percent of monozygotic twins both suffer from autism, while in less than 5 percent of dyzgotic twins do both suffer from autism.

Family studies also suggest genetic transmission. In siblings of autistic children, the incidence of autism is approximately 50 times greater than in the general population.[76] About 2 percent of the siblings of autistic children suffer from clear-cut autism. Children with more severe forms of autism are more likely to have relatives with autism than those with milder symptoms. A few studies have reported three siblings in the same family, all of whom have autism.[77] In addition, about 3 percent of the siblings of autistic children have somewhat atypical forms of autism, and another 3 to 25 percent have some degree of cognitive, communicative, and social difficulties that characterize autistic children.[78]

On the basis of such findings, Sir Michael Rutter has suggested that some families are genetically predisposed to develop language and cognitive disabilities, of which autism is an extreme manifestation.[79] It is not clear, however, whether all forms of autism are genetically transmitted in the same way. About 10 percent of the cases of autism are caused by a specific diagnosable medical condition, including known genetic disorders such as the fragile X-chromosome anomaly and tuberous sclerosis. Preliminary evidence suggests that autism accompanied by profound mental retardation is inherited differently than when not accompanied by severe mental retardation.[80] Along the same lines, rates of mental retardation are not likely to be higher among families of nonretarded individuals with autism, but may be so among families of autistic persons who are also retarded.

While there is strong support for a genetic component, the mode of transmission is still far from clear. The large fall-off from monozygotic twins to dizygotic twins and siblings and the differences between first-degree and other relatives suggest that multiple genes (rather than a single gene) are involved. The association between severity of autism and genetic loading for features of the disorder also point to multiple genes rather than a single gene.

Finally, genetic studies need to broaden their scope by focusing on transmission of the core psychological deficits outlined at the start of this chapter. A particularly compelling question concerns the extent to which close relatives of autistic persons suffer from problems directing and sharing attention, thinking about their own and others' thoughts, and expressing and comprehending emotions. Finding a greater family similarity in one of these domains would strengthen the definition of a core deficit of autism. Similarly, support for the hypothesis that a particular domain is central to the disorder will also fuel investigation of this deficit in the families of autistic individuals.

9/ Interventions

A variety of interventions have been developed to forge optimal development for autistic children and help them and their families cope with problems that arise. This chapter examines some of the approaches used in such interventions, the evidence for the effectiveness of various approaches, and what might be done to improve them. As a sidelight, our examination illuminates the mutually beneficial relationship between intervention research and theoretical and empirical insights into the nature of autism.

In discussing autism it is useful to distinguish between intervention and treatment. The term "treatment" is usually restricted to methods that provide a cure for an illness or disability. Until recently, only a tiny minority of children with autism seems to recover fully (see chapter 7). Very few interventions aim to cure children with autism or succeed in doing so, Ivar Lovaas's program at UCLA being the most notable exception.[1] To date, his treatment program has not been tested empirically in any other site. For the most part, rather than attempting to provide a cure, interventions seek to enhance development and well-being by addressing particular sets of difficulties.

Available Services

The kinds of intervention programs available to autistic children and their families differ enormously from one place to another. First, cultural and economic factors influence the nature of services that are provided. Differences in the structure of social life, say in Japan and the United States, influence the nature and locus of intervention. Many interventions in the United States feature intensive one-on-one therapy, during which a professional meets with the individual autistic child and one of the parents. Children often work with a behavior therapist in their classroom or home, and it is not uncommon for a parent to travel to a training center to learn how to implement a particular program with his or her individual child. By contrast, training programs in Japan are often carried out in community centers and involve groups of autistic children and their families.[2]

Philosophies of education also shape the services that are provided. For example, autistic children in both Great Britain and the United States participate in school-based intervention; yet in the United States autistic children are increasingly mainstreamed, whereas in Great Britain they attend special schools. Beliefs regarding the value of integrating children with special needs influence not only the location of intervention but also the objectives that are pursued and the participants involved.

Particular conceptualizations of the causes of autism also influence the kinds of services. Broadly speaking, commonly held conceptualizations determine whether interventions will be offered in psychiatric or educational settings. Until recently, for example, the French generally accepted psychogenic theories of autism (which attribute the disorder to disturbed attachment relationships). Consistent with this perspective, interventions were carried out in psychiatric hospitals using psychoanalytic methods. Such theories had lost favor in Britain, Japan, and the United States much earlier, leading to the development of educational, school-based interventions. But under this broad category, differing beliefs regarding the value of integrating children with disabilities into mainstream schools contribute to differences in the type of school-based interventions—across countries and across communities within the same country. Interventions implemented in mainstreamed classrooms, for example, may focus more extensively on social adaptation, whereas those carried out in special education facilities may focus to a larger extent on academic or vocational skills.

Economic realities also prevail upon the types of interventions that are carried out. In countries that have socialized medicine, for example, families may avail themselves of interventions that may not be accessible to many in countries like the United States, where individuals pay for services received. Even within the United States, there are great disparities in what schools offer for children with autism, depending on the community. Federal legislation (Public Law 94–142) now guarantees children with disabilities a free public education and special education in the least restrictive environment possible for the child. This law and its successor (Public Law 101–476) have helped to expand the educational options for children with autism, but the quality of programs varies from one school setting to another.

Finally, particular communities may offer especially good services because of an individual or group who have committed themselves to developing a comprehensive intervention. This is the case in North Carolina, for example, where the TEACCH program provides intensive training for parents and their autistic children in modified settings throughout the community.[3] Visual aids, for instance, are used to facilitate autistic persons' understanding of schedules and expectations at school, home, and in the workplace. A similarly comprehensive program has been implemented in the northern region of Spain, where families and professionals participate in an integrated system of education and vocational training for individuals with developmental disabilities, including autism.[4]

Special Education and Other Interventions

In the majority of countries today, the core intervention programs for children with autism are educational. Whether carried out in a regular classroom, a special classroom in a regular school, a special school, or an institution, most of these early education programs concentrate on promoting socialization and communication skills. In addition to practicing simple motor and language skills, young children learn socially appropriate behavior and are taught how to get along in groups. Because it is hard for autistic children to be accepted in social settings in which other children learn such things naturally, they benefit from instruction in smaller groups with more adults around to guide their behavior and make explicit the conventions and expectations that normally developing children may more readily grasp.

In most countries the formal education of children with autism starts at an earlier age than that of normally developing children. Recognizing the benefits of early intervention, U.S. Public Law 99–457 calls for children with autism to be provided with education by three years of age, and some states even offer programs for younger children. Early intervention classrooms usually include children with a variety of disabilities, whereas during the later elementary school years some classes are designed specifically for children with autism.

The educational approach to working with autistic children depends on of the severity of behavioral symptoms and degree of mental retardation. And as with children who have other developmental disabilities, the extensiveness of academic training depends on the child's intellectual capabilities. High-functioning children with autism may pursue advanced academic degrees. However, since the majority are mentally retarded and about half do not use much functional language, the academic education of most autistic children is restricted to basic arithmetic and language skills. Many programs introduce vocational training during adolescence. An essential part of this training incorporates the social skills that are required to function in any given work setting. Indeed, many specialized educational and vocational training programs are supplemented with additional forms of intervention. While numerous therapies have been developed, here we mention some that are most commonly used and have been most rigorously evaluated.

Behavior Therapy

Whether carried out in schools, institutions, or the home, general behavioral techniques form the core of most interventions with autistic children. Behavior therapists— some of whom have devoted their professional lives to improving the behavior of children with autism— have worked to delineate pivotal behaviors that, when changed, generate changes in related behaviors, thus modifying prominent aspects of the syndrome.[5] Behavioral interventions were originally introduced to deal with autistic individuals' self-injurious behaviors, including head-banging, biting, hitting, hair-pulling, and face-scratching. Such behaviors can lead to self-mutilation in extreme cases, and they surely circumvent participation in prosocial activities. The first behavioral interventions used aversive stimulation, such as mild electric shock, to stop the self-abuse and to reduce self-stimulatory and other "bizarre" behaviors.[6] Furthermore, shocks were reduced in the presence of adults, resulting in increased affection and other desirable social behaviors on the part of the child. Since then, less intrusive procedures have been found to manage problem behaviors, rendering such extreme interventions unjustifiable. Currently, behavioral interventions tend to focus on increasing positive communicative and social interactions as much as decreasing negative behaviors.

At the University of California, Los Angeles, Ivar Lovaas and his colleagues developed a very intensive early intervention program which involves the child in one-on-one treatment for approximately 40 hours a week. Follow-up studies of the children in this program show dramatic improvements in their skills and behaviors, with some children showing few remaining signs of autism.[7] These and similar interventions are carried out in a school or clinical setting as well as in the child's home, using instructed parents, teachers, and trained undergraduate and graduate students. The use of several people and variable settings is done to ensure that new skills generalize across persons and environments, a known problem with many behavioral interventions.

The participation of parents is crucial. They spend more time with their child than does anyone else and therefore have the potential to provide an around-the-clock treatment environment. Also, in comparison with clinics and schools, where instructors may focus more heavily on mediating academic deficiencies, in the home environment family members are more likely to focus on additional aspects of the child's behavior, such as tantrums, obsessions and compulsions, or enuresis. Lovaas and his colleagues carried out a follow-up study of 20 autistic children in behavior therapy, and found that those whose parents had been trained to provide treatment either maintained the gains originally established or continued to improve, whereas children whose parents had not been trained, or who had been institutionalized, had lost their previously acquired skills.[8]

In general, behavioral treatment strategies are designed for each child individually, based upon empirical assessment of his or her behavioral excesses and deficits, their frequency, and the situations associated with the appearance and continuation of these behaviors. The assessment is usually formulated in the course of a structured evaluation, in which the child is observed with an adult in a large room containing assorted play materials. At first the adult does not initiate interaction with the child but responds to the child's efforts to initiate interaction. This allows for evaluation of the child's spontaneous social behavior. The adult then attempts to elicit nonverbal and verbal responses from the child by asking questions such as "Can you bring me the blue ball?" or "What's your name?" This affords assessment of receptive and expressive verbal behavior and provides an index of social responsiveness. During the remainder of the time the adult attempts to engage the child in play with toys. Throughout the evaluation, observers document the presence of a variety of prosocial behaviors such as appropriate speech, play, and social interaction, as well as inappropriate behaviors, such as self-injury, tantrums, and noncompliance.

Specific target behaviors are then selected for behavior modification. Traditionally, the procedures used involve systematic strengthening of behaviors that compete with an undesirable behavior targeted to be reduced or eliminated. For example, if a child tends to throw or bang toys, he would be rewarded for playing with toys or holding them. Another procedure, often called "planned ignoring," is to withdraw attention from problem behaviors such as temper tantrums. (Yet because ignoring often results in an initial increase in the intensity and frequency of the target behavior, it may not be advisable for highly aggressive or injurious behavior.) Finally, although severe punishments are no longer thought to be warranted, less drastic alternatives such as "time out" (in which the child is required to sit in a corner of the room, deprived of attention and entertaining objects) are often effective. Similarly, restitution and positive practice may also be helpful. For example, a child who throws food at the wall might be required to clean the wall and to practice appropriate eating behavior.

At the same time, behavioral techniques are used to encourage positive, prosocial behaviors. The most fundamental and common procedure is positive reinforcement, in which desirable behavior is followed immediately by a reward such as a cookie, sticker, or favorite toy. Therapists might also use "chaining," which means that a complex target behavior is broken down into smaller increments. For example, setting the table could be taught step by step: putting mats on the table, folding the napkins, setting the plates on the table, the napkins next to the plates, and so on. Once the first step is mastered, the second step is taught, and reinforcers are provided for completion of both steps. This process continues until the child learns the entire chain of behaviors. Therapists might also gradually shape a response pattern encouraging any approximation to the desired behavior, and over time reward closer and closer approximations. Modeling, or having autistic students observe appropri ate social behaviors, is also an effective technique. In addition to live modeling, some investigators have used video modeling.[9]

High-functioning individuals also benefit from training in self-management, which helps them to monitor, evaluate, and reinforce their own behavior with minimal or no external influence. Initially, self-monitoring is encouraged through positive reinforcement, and then desirable behaviors are self-identified and rewarded. This approach may increase the likelihood of opportunities for spontaneous social interactions with peers, and may be particularly advantageous in environments where it would be intrusive or stigmatizing to have a clinician present.

Despite initial skepticism, many clinicians and investigators have come to use behavioral techniques to enhance social skills and communication. Robert Koegel and his colleagues have shown that when children learn and regularly demonstrate a single social communicative behavior, such as making eye contact in face-to-face interaction, disruptive behavior and inappropriate nonverbal mannerisms decreased without additional intervention.[10] Similarly, cutting down on perseveration in conversation generated collateral improvements in other social communicative behaviors, such as facial expression and voice volume. This research suggests that targeting pivotal classes of social communicative behavior leads to exponential advances in autistic children's social development.

Speech and Language Therapy

Perhaps the most frequent intervention prescribed for children with autism, particularly young children, is speech and language therapy. This is not surprising, considering that difficulty with communication is a central feature of autism, and that language ability is positively associated with later adjustment. Speech and language therapy is usually conducted with the child individually once or twice a week, sometimes for several years. The aims and approach are tailored to the skills and behavioral difficulties of the individual child.

In speakers and nonspeakers alike, idiosyncratic and even self-injurious behaviors may be understood as efforts to communicate, and intervention may focus on replacing such behaviors with more appropriate alternatives. For instance, an individual who appears to use aberrant behavior to obtain attention or disagree may be taught how to secure physical contact by asking or signing, or may learn to protest undesirable proposals by shaking his or her head rather than inflicting harm on self or others.[11] Similarly, erratic flapping or jumping may be replaced by pointing and looking as a means of securing desirable objects.

Again, behavioral techniques are brought in to teach basic speech and language forms. Lovaas and his colleagues devised the first empirically based program for teaching vocal speech.[12] After trying to produce speech by shaping individual vocal responses through the method of successive approximation, these investigators successfully implemented imitation training following a series of systematic steps. The child's vocal responses are reinforced when they match those of the therapist, not when they do not. Once a pattern is established, the method serves as a foundation for beginning more complex language functions, such as semantics and syntax. Once a child has learned to say "apple" through imitation, for example, the same procedures were used to teach the child the meaning of the word through receptive and expressive labeling. To teach receptive labeling, the therapist would hold an apple and one or two additional objects. The therapist says "apple" and guides the child's hand to the apple. This is repeated over many trials in which the therapist gradually fades out the prompt (by providing less guidance) until the child consistently points to the correct object when the therapist says "apple." Similarly, to teach the expressive label, the therapist would point to the apple and ask, "What is this?" and prompt the child by saying "apple," encouraging the child to imitate saying the word. This process is repeated over a series of trials in which the therapist gradually withdraws the prompt, for example by whispering or saying the first part of the word, until the child responds without assistance.

While important, vocabulary, semantic, syntactic, and morphological skills have limited utility in themselves if an individual does not know how to use them to produce or interpret communication spontaneously. The success of interventions designed to improve speech and language therefore hinges on mastering social conventions that organize eye gaze, gesture, and body comportment as well as verbal skills in securing someone's attention, initiating, responding to, and maintaining interactions with others.

Additional Interventions

Pharmacology. Medications are used for certain symptoms suffered by individuals with autism, though they are not a treatment for the condition itself.[13] Further, while there is variation in the response of the population at large to particular medications, these differences are heightened among persons with autism. Medications that generally produce particular effects among nonautistic persons often do not yield the same results among persons with autism, both with respect to benefits and side effects. Thus medications must be monitored carefully. A variety of drugs, including neuroleptics, beta blockers, and opiate blockers, may lessen self-injurious behaviors and aggression. Stimulants are effective for some young children with autism to curb their hyperactive behavior. Antidepression or anti-anxiety medications are sometimes prescribed to treat these illnesses, which occur more often among high-functioning autistic persons. When effective, medications render autistic persons more amenable to and better able to benefit from additional interventions.

Support for Family Members. The presence of an individual with autism in a family significantly affects the daily experiences of other family members. Because of the difficulties of living with children with autism, family members often need other people to talk to about both specific and general problems. Individual and couples therapy can be useful from time to time as can participation in support groups. Support groups are available for siblings of autistic persons as well as for parents. Local chapters of parent organizations such as the Autism Society of America frequently offer educational programs that are useful and circulate newsletters regarding available services and relevant research. Membership in such societies gives the opportunity for families of individuals with autism to form enduring and satisfying connections.

Special Therapies. Although a comprehensive review of the many interventions that have been developed to help children with autism lies beyond the scope of this chapter, a few are considered here.[14] In a unique undertaking, Temple Grandin (the high-functioning autistic woman mentioned in previous chapters) designed her own therapeutic apparatus, the Squeeze Machine. This device provides deep pressure stimulation in an effort to produce a calming effect and increase tolerance for human touch.

Additional interventions have been disseminated

by parents whose children improved significantly while participating. Briefly, these methods include music therapy and Auditory Integration Training, which aim to reduce hypersensitivity to particular sounds. Akin to Grandin's approach, "holding therapy" is also used to reduce stimulation and provide a safe, contained environment. As the name implies, holding therapy involves holding the child for extended periods, particularly when the child is screaming or showing signs of distress. Various forms of vitamin therapy have also been developed, the goal being to normalize body metabolism and improve behavior.[15] Finally, facilitated communication is a method that uses physical touch to help individuals in their efforts at self-expression, for example by holding the person's wrist above a computer keyboard or alphabet board. There is considerable debate about the validity of facilitated communication, and it has caused a great deal of controversy among parents and professionals.[16] Support for the efficacy of most of these programs is anecdotal. Empirical study of the effectiveness of various interventions is sorely needed.

The Effectiveness of Interventions

Many interventions for individuals with autism have not been empirically tested and validated. Further, investigators rarely if ever compare the effectiveness of one program with another or compare the behavior of participants with that of a control sample of subjects that did not receive intervention. The small number of studies of intervention programs reflects, first of all, the pervasive paucity of empirical research on psychological services for children. The relative rarity of autism and the variation individuals show in developmental level and severity of symptoms make it difficult to carry out intervention research.

Another problem in evaluating interventions is that professionals and parents who develop therapeutic methods often advocate enthusiastically for these programs in public arenas before effectiveness has been established for more than one individual or small group. This is not surprising, given the nature of autistic impairment and caregivers' desire to try any intervention that has worked with even a small number of individuals. The unfortunate outcome is that we know almost nothing about what forms of intervention work with what particular groups of individuals, the extent to which these interventions are effective, and factors that enhance positive outcome. For example, while vitamin B6/magnesium therapies appear to be somewhat efficacious for a small percentage of participants, no studies have been carried out that provide a scientific basis for assessing beneficial results.

Nevertheless, recent research has yielded optimistic findings. It seems that highly structured, intensive early intervention does lead to significant developmental progress for children with autism.[17] Many preschool children with autism who participate in intensive behavioral programs for extended periods of time show significant gains in IQ and reductions in stereotypic, antisocial behaviors.

Future Directions

Collaborative multicentered studies also promise to improve intervention research. This approach, currently used to test the effectiveness of services for children with a variety of psychological disorders,[18] may be particularly important for autism because, in any one location, there are probably only a few homogenous individuals suitable for a particular intervention. Multisite studies will generate enough subjects, and therefore enough statistical power, to implement and evaluate specific interventions for individuals of similar age, developmental level, and symptom severity.

Interventions for children and adults with autism will benefit from outcome studies that stem from recent theoretical and empirical insights into the nature of autism. By clarifying associations between early cognitive, social, and emotional abilities and the child's later functioning, longitudinal research turns into an essential guide for determining the aims and methods of intervention, which may then be tested in empirical intervention studies. Existing research consistently highlights the role of joint attention behaviors in language acquisition and expansion.[19] Children with autism who show greater participation in joint attention interactions also appear to be better able to contemplate mental states and relate to the emotional experiences of others than do children who show less joint attention.[20] In our own follow-up study, while measures of the child's sociability were not associated with concurrent level of language skill, we found that young children who are more sociable are more likely to make subsequent gains in language than are less sociable autistic children.

Thus there is considerable evidence that nonverbal social communication skills are a highly consequential—indeed a core—component of autistic impairment; measures of joint attention prove to be among the most powerful early diagnostic indicators of autism.[21] Such evidence points to the importance of targeting these behaviors in intervention and of using them to evaluate early intervention.[22] Existing investigations of interventions are limited by their reliance on global measures of IQ or general measures of social or adaptive functioning.

Applications of a Developmental Perspective. In previous chapters we reviewed what is known about individuals with autism from infancy to adulthood, highlighting the problems autistic individuals experience in understanding other people, particularly in relation to themselves. Such difficulties characterize autistic people regardless of their intellectual ability, and they come up at each stage of development. A central goal of this book is to encourage clinicians, educators, family members, and peers to take these specific difficulties into account. The effectiveness of some language therapies, for example, may depend on teaching autistic persons how to use their newly acquired verbal abilities in particular social settings. Similarly, learning how to relate to fellow workers is essential to the success of vocational training programs. Appreciation of the developmental changes that occur among persons with autism may be eclipsed by emphasis on identifying core deficits and establishing standardized diagnostic criteria that apply to individuals of all ages,[23] yet autism can only be understood within a developmental context. Because social-emotional abilities vary with chronological and mental age, apprehending the nature of autism requires attending to physical, motor, cognitive, and emotional development that occurs throughout the life span.

Notes

References

Index

Notes

1. / WHAT IS AUTISM?

1. Itard (1801).
2. Kanner (1943).
3. See Frith's (1991) translation of Asperger's original account; Klin and Volkmar (1995).
4. Because Asperger Syndrome was not diagnosed until recently, children initially classified as high-functioning autistic who had no history of language delay are now being rediagnosed with Asperger Syndrome.
5. Lorna Wing and Judith Gould (1979) refer to these defining features of autism as "the triad of impairments."
6. Asperger Syndrome appears in the *Diagnostic and Statistical Manual of Mental Disorders-IV* (American Psychiatric Association, 1994).
7. Hoshino, Kumashiro, Yashima, Tachibana, & Watanabe (1982).
8. Epidemiological studies were carried out in Europe by Brask (1972), Ciadella and Mamelle (1989), Gillberg (1984), Lotter (1966), Steinhausen, Gobel, Breinlinger, & Wohleben (1983), Wing, Yeates, Brierly, & Gould (1976); in Japan by Hoshino, Kumashiro, Yashima, Tachibana, & Watanabe (1982); in the United States by Treffert (1970); in Canada by Bryson, Clark, and Smith (1988); and by Lotter (1980) in Africa.
9. Lotter (1980).
10. Two epidemiologic prevalence studies did not detect a

positive relationship between sex ratio and IQ: those conducted by Steinhausen et al. (1983) in West Berlin, and by
Gillberg (1984) in Sweden.

11. The ratios were reported by Ciadella and Mamelle (1989),
Steffenburg and Gillberg (1986), Lotter (1966), and Treffert
(1970). The male to female ratios reported in the
Fukushima prefecture in Japan (Hoshino et al., 1982) and
in Camberwell (Wing, 1981) were considerably higher: 9:1
and 15.2:1, respectively.

12. See Lord and Schopler (1987). In addition, Lord, Schopler,
and Revicki (1982) conducted a study of nearly 400 autistic children in North Carolina—one of the largest samples
of autistic children ever collected. They found that the
girls tended to be more seriously impaired than the boys
on a variety of measures, including language, perceptual
ability, and daily living skills. Girls were not, however,
more severely limited in terms of play, affect, or the
ability to relate to others.

13. Szatmari and Jones (1991).

14. See Kanner (1943) and Frith and Frith (1991) on Asperger.

15. Lotter (1967).

16. In the studies conducted by our research group, only 4 of
the 70 autistic children seen between 3 and 5 years of age
had IQs in the normal range of intelligence (>70). When
we saw these children later, only one showed a decline
in intelligence. Eleven other children showed major increases in intelligence after this period and no longer
tested in the mentally retarded range.

2. / PHYSIOLOGICAL REGULATION, PERCEPTION, AND COGNITION IN THE EARLY YEARS

1. See Emde, Gaensbauer, and Harmon (1976) as well as
Thoman and Whitney (1989) on individual differences in
sleep patterns; see Super and Harkness (1972) on cross-
cultural differences.

2. Kleitman (1963).

3. While individual rates of development vary, infant assessments such as the Bayley Scales of Infant Develop-

ment outline developmental milestones during the first three years of life. See the classic work by Gesell (1929).

4. Researchers estimate that infants have approximately 20/600 vision (Cornell and McDonnell, 1986); that is, objects that appear 20 feet away to adults with normal vision appear approximately 600 feet away to the newborn infant. Blurry vision during the first months is due to the limited power of infants' lenses to accommodate changes in distance and light and the immaturity of their receptors and neural systems (Aslin, 1987).

5. Cornell and McDonnell (1986) and Haith (1990) suggest that infants' visual acuity is close to the adult level by about 7 or 8 months. See Bornstein's (1988) research on color vision.

6. Grimwade, Walker, Bartlett, Gordon, & Wood (1970).

7. Butterfield and Siperstein (1972).

8. Engen, Lipsitt, and Kaye (1963); Lipsitt (1977); and Steiner (1977).

9. Baillargeon, Spelke, and Wasserman (1985).

10. Piaget (1954).

11. Fantz (1961).

12. Nelson (1979).

13. Gopnik and Meltzoff (1987); Sugarman (1983).

14. Piaget (1962); Watson and Fischer (1977).

15. Bruner (1972); Piaget (1962); Vygotsky (1978).

16. Wolf, Rygh, and Altshuler (1984).

17. Because children often project their own experiences onto dolls in play, doll play is often used in psychotherapy with children, both to gain insight into the child's emotional life and to work through upsetting experiences.

18. As Judy Dunn (1988) points out, Piaget's (1962) account may reflect the fact that joint pretend play has been studied almost exclusively in children over three, while they were playing with their peers, rather than in naturalistic contexts over time. See Dunn (1988) and Miller and Garvey (1984) for naturalistic studies of pretense.

19. Children with autism have normal sleep cycles with normal amounts of rapid eye movement (REM) sleep (Ornitz, Ritvo, Tanguay, and Walter, 1969).

20. James and Barry (1984).
21. Sacks (1995).
22. Tronick, Als, Adamsen, Wise, & Brazelton (1978).
23. Ungerer and Sigman (1987).
24. Sigman and Ungerer (1981, 1984a); Sigman, Ungerer, Mundy & Sherman (1986).
25. Frith and Baron-Cohen (1987); Hammes and Langdell (1981); Sigman and Mundy (1987); Sigman and Ungerer (1984a); Ungerer and Sigman (1981); and Wulff (1985).
26. Baron-Cohen (1987).
27. Bruner (1972); Vygotsky (1978). Karin Aronsson (1996) notes that examining children's representations of experience through role-play is a powerful tool for penetrating cultural conventions.
28. Lewis and Boucher (1988).
29. Leslie (1987).

3. / DEVELOPMENT OF SOCIAL AND EMOTIONAL UNDERSTANDING

1. DeCasper and Fifer (1980).
2. Haith, Berman, and Moore (1977).
3. Meltzoff and Moore (1977, 1992).
4. Fantz (1961, 1963). This research is not conclusive (e.g., Haaf, Smith, and Smitely, 1983), and validation from Dannemiller and Stephens (1988).
5. Macfarlane (1975) demonstrated this by presenting newborns with pads soaked with their own mothers' breast milk and that of another mother.
6. Kagan (1971); Kagan, Kearsley, and Zelazo (1978).
7. Bruner (1983), Harmon and Emde (1972), Haith, Berman, and Moore (1977).
8. See Moore and Dunham's (1995) edited volume on joint attention.
  Butterworth and Cochran (1980); Collis and Schaffer
      ife and Bruner (1975).
        38).
        es, Collins, and Hong (1991).

Notes to Pages 38–41 / ⅃

12. Hornik, Risenhoover, and Gunnar (1987), Klinnert, Campos, Sorce, Emde, & Svejda (1983).
13. See classic works by Bruner (1983), Mead (1934), Piaget (1932), and Trevarthen (1979). As Tomasello, Kruger, and Ratner (1993) note, "learning *through* rather than *from* another is possible because human beings are able, depending on one's choice of theory and terminology, to take the role of the other (Mead, 1934), the perspective of the other (Piaget, 1932), to attribute mental states to the other (Premack, 1988), to simulate the mental states of the other (Harris, 1991), to engage in joint attention with the other (Bruner, 1983), to engage in mindreading of the other (Whiten, 1991), to understand the other as a 'person' (Hobson, 1993), or to participate with the other intersubjectively (Trevarthen, 1979)."
14. Tomasello, Kruger, and Ratner (1993).
15. Rogoff (1990).
16. Darwin (1872).
17. Hiatt, Campos, and Emde (1979); Izard, Hembree, Dougherty, & Spizzirri (1983); Izard, Huebner, Risser, McGinnes, & Dougherty (1980).
18. Caron, Caron, and Myers (1985); Horowitz, Paden, Bhana, & Self (1972).
19. Walker-Andrews (1986).
20. Harter and Whitesell (1989), Seidner, Stipek, and Feshbach (1988).
21. See Sagi and Hoffman (1976). Eisenberg and Strayer (1989) distinguish between three reactions, all of which have been termed empathy. The first, "emotional contagion," involves feeling the same emotion as the other person without concern for the welfare of the other. This form is characteristic of children in the first year of life. The second, "sympathetic responding," involves reacting to the emotion of another in a way that conveys concern. And the third denotes the vicarious experiencing of emotion, or "feeling with" another. See also Eisenberg (1992).
22. Dunn (1988); Zahn-Waxler and Radke-Yarrow (1982).
23. Gordon Gallup (1970) designed a series of mirror experi-

ts with chimpanzees that have since been replicated
study self-recognition in children. He showed chim-
nzees their images in a full-length mirror and observed
at after a few days they began to use the mirror to
explore themselves; for example, by picking bits of food
from their faces which they could see only in the mirror.
Gallup tested this by anesthetizing several chimps and
painting dye above their eyes and on one ear. When they
woke up and explored the marked spots with their hands,
Gallup concluded that the chimps had recognized themselves in the mirror.

24. Bertenthal and Fischer (1978); Lewis and Brooks-Gunn
(1979).
25. Bowlby (1973).
26. Ainsworth, Blehar, Waters, & Wall (1978). It is important
to remember that attachment classifications refer to the
security of the attachment *relationship,* not the individual
child.
27. Main (1991).
28. Kopp (1982).
29. Goleman (1995); Kopp (1982).
30. Adrien, Fauer, Perrot, Hameury, Garrau, Barthelemy, &
Savage (1991); Osterling and Dawson (1994).
31. Johnson, Siddons, Frith, & Morton (1992).
32. Baron-Cohen, Allen, and Gillberg (1992).
33. Buitelaar, van Engeland, de Kogel, de Vries, & van Hoof
(1991); Lewy and Dawson (1992); Loveland and Landry
(1986); Mundy (1995); Mundy, Sigman, Ungerer, & Sherman (1986); Sigman, Mundy, Sherman, & Ungerer (1986);
Wetherby (1986).
34. Mundy et al.(1986); Mundy and Sigman (1989); Sigman
et al.(1986).
35. Kasari, Sigman, Mundy, & Yirmiya (1988); Sigman (1989).
See also van Engeland, Bodnar, and Bolhuis (1985) for
further data refuting the hypothesis that autistic children
consistently avoid social interaction.
36. Kasari, Sigman, and Yirmiya (1993).
37. Clark and Rutter (1981); Dawson et al. (1990); Kasari et

al. (1993); Landry and Loveland (1989); Volkmar, Hoder and Cohen (1985).

38. Baron-Cohen (1989); Dawson and Adams (1984); Jones and Prior (1985); Loveland and Landry (1986); Mundy et al. (1986); Mundy, Sigman, and Kasari (1994); Sigman et al. (1986); Stone and Caro-Martinez (1990).
39. Kasari and Sigman (1996); Sigman, Kasari, Kwon, & Yirmiya (1992); Sigman and Kasari (1995).
40. Baron-Cohen (1989).
41. This perspective is consistent with the notion of intersubjectivity discussed by Bruner (1983), Stern (1985), and Trevarthen (1979), among others.
42. Bettelheim (1967).
43. American Psychiatric Association (1987, p. 35).
44. Derek Ricks and Lorna Wing (1975), for example, describe autistic children as displaying extreme, often inappropriate emotional reactions, rather than being unresponsive.
45. Capps, Kasari, Yirmiya, & Sigman (1993).
46. Yirmiya, Kasari, Sigman, & Mundy (1989).
47. Kasari, Sigman, Baumgartner, & Stipek (1993).
48. Dawson et al. (1990); Snow, Hertzig, and Shapiro (1987).
49. Kasari, Sigman, Mundy, & Yirmiya (1990).
50. Sigman, Ungerer, Mundy, & Sherman (1986).
51. Hobson (1986a, 1986b).
52. Van Lancker, Cornelius, and Kreiman (1989).
53. Weeks and Hobson (1987).
54. Sigman, Kasari, Kwon, & Yirmiya (1992).
55. Taylor (1989, p. 35).
56. Dawson and McKissick, (1984); Ferrari and Mathews (1983); Neuman and Hill (1978); Spiker and Ricks (1984).
57. Psychoanalyst Margaret Mahler (1968) suggested that autistic children's development was arrested prior to forming an attachment relationship; consequently, they failed to develop a concept of self and other. Similarly, Michael Rutter (1978, p. 9) described autistic children's "lack of attachment behavior and relative failure of bonding." More recently, Donald Cohen, Rhea Paul, and Fred Volkmar wrote: "Autistic social impairment results in the

child's failure to demonstrate differential attachment to familiar people in contrast with unfamiliar adults or objects" (1987, p. 67).

58. Capps, Sigman, and Mundy (1994); Dissanayake and Crossley (in press); Mundy, Sigman, Ungerer, & Sherman (1986); Rogers, Ozonoff, and Maslin-Cole (1991), Shapiro, Sherman, Calamari, and Koch (1987); Sigman and Mundy (1989); Sigman and Ungerer (1984b).

59. Capps, Sigman, and Mundy (1994); Rogers, Ozonoff, and Maslin-Cole (1991); Shapiro, Sherman, Calamari, & Koch (1987).

60. Rogers, Ozonoff, and Maslin-Cole (1991).

61. See Main and Solomon (1986, 1990) on "Disorganized Attachment" classification.

62. Arbelle, Sigman, and Kasari (1994).

4. / LANGUAGE ACQUISITION AND USE

1. The aspect of language known as "phonology" refers to speech sounds; "syntax" to the rules of grammar; "semantics" to the apprehension of meaning; and "pragmatics" to the use of language to communicate effectively.

2. Eimas (1985); Kuhl, Williams, Lacerda, Stevens, & Lindblom (1992).

3. Berger and Cunningham (1983); Bloom, Russell, and Wassenberg, (1987); Ginsburg and Kilbourne (1988); Tomasello, Mannle, and Kruger (1986).

4. See deVilliers and deVilliers (1978) and Oller (1978) on babbling, and Dore (1978) on jargoning.

5. Bruner (1983); Lewis and Freedle (1973); Snow (1977); Tomasello (1992).

6. Campos and Sternberg (1981); Walden and Baxter (1989). Similarly, at this age infants do not point at novel objects when they are alone in a room.

7. Bruner (1983, p. 122).

8. Tomasello and Farrar (1986). See also Collis and Schaffer (1975); Golinkoff, Hirsh-Paske, Cauley, & Gordon (1987).

9. Cole and Cole (1994, p. 281). There are cross-cultural dif-

ferences in terms of how early and what first words parents attribute to infants. As Elinor Ochs (1982) described, the only word that Samoan parents acknowledge as a child's first word is "tae," a Samoan curse word meaning "shit." They explain this remarkable agreement among their children as confirmation of the notion that once infants begin to talk, they become cheeky and willful.

10. Anglin (1977).
11. Some believe that when children can utter only single words, these words stand for sentences because they are expressing whole ideas; McNeill (1970), for example, calls such utterances "holophrases." Alternatively, Greenfield and Smith (1976) suggest that single-word utterances refer to one element of the situation a child wants to talk about.
12. Brown (1973); Gopnik and Meltzoff (1987).
13. Sapir (1924).
14. Bretherton and Beeghly (1982); Dunn and Kendrick (1982); Miller and Sperry (1987); Ochs (1993); Schieffelin (1990).
15. Vygotsky (1978).
16. Dunn (1988).
17. Bates, Camaioni, and Volterra (1975).
18. Ochs (1993); Ochs and Schieffelin (1989).
19. Fernald (1985); Papousek and Papousek (1981); Stern, Spieker, Barnett, & MacKain (1983). Often referred to as "motherese," exaggerated intonation does not universally characterize the way caregivers speak to infants (Ochs and Schieffelin, 1984).
20. Using nonsense syllables, Morse (1972) found that infants as young as 1 and 2 months of age were able to distinguish between rising and falling intonation. Similarly, Spring and Dale (1977) used the sucking paradigm to show that 1–4 month old infants were able to perceive location of stress on two-syllable sequences like ba'ba-baba'.
21. Atkinson-King (1973).

22. Reichel-Dolmatoff and Reichel-Dolmatoff (1961; in Cole & Cole, 1994).
23. Ervin-Tripp (1973); Sacks (1987); Sacks, Schegloff, and Jefferson (1974); Snow (1977).
24. Grice (1975).
25. Winner (1988). As Talmay Givon (1989, p. 24) has noted, "the relevant context for communication of knowledge (information, belief) from one mind to another is not objective context. . . rather it is itself some knowledge, information or belief held by some interpreter, by some participant in the communication."
26. Wittgenstein (1918).
27. Sachs and Devin (1973); Shatz and Gelman (1973); Tomasello and Mannle (1985).
28. Dunn and Kendrick (1982); Wellman and Lempers (1977). See Duranti and Brenneis (1986); Goodwin and Duranti (1992) on audience as co-author.
29. Applebee (1979); McCabe and Peterson (1991); Miller and Sperry (1988); Nelson (1989); see Ochs and Capps (1996) for review.
30. Bruner (1986, 1990); Burke (1962); Berman and Slobin (1994); Ricoeur (1988); Labov and Waletsky (1968); Propp (1968). On narrative as a theory-building activity see Bruner (1990); Feldman (1989); Ochs, Taylor, Rudolph, & Smith (1992); and White (1980).
31. Goodwin (1990); Heidegger (1962); Ochs (1993b).
32. Bruner (1990, p. 47).
33. Feldman (1989). Pretend play provides similar opportunities for making sense of puzzling events and experiences by putting them into narrative frames.
34. Hudson (1990); Mandler (1984).
35. Morrison (1994, p. 22).
36. Bartolucci and Pierce (1977); Bartolucci, Pierce, Streiner, and Eppel (1976); Boucher (1976); Tager-Flusberg (1981).
37. Tager-Flusberg (1985a, 1986); Ungerer and Sigman (1987).
38. Tager-Flusberg (1985a).
39. Cantwell, Baker and Rutter (1978); Lord (1985); Prior and Hall, 1979; Tager-Flusberg (1981b).

40. See Paul (1987); Pierce and Bartolucci (1977); Swisher and Demetras (1985); and Tager-Flusberg (1981b).
41. Tager-Flusberg (1985b).
42. Newport, Gleitman and Gleitman (1977).
43. Bartolucci, Pierce, and Streiner (1980); Howlin, (1984); Menyuk (1978); Tager-Flusberg, Calkins, Nolin, Anderson, & Chadwick-Dias (1990).
44. Frith (1989b).
45. Bishop (1982); deVilliers and deVilliers (1979).
46. Frith (1989b); Loveland, Landry, Hughes, Hall, and McEvoy (1988); Prizant (1983); Tager-Flusberg (1982, 1993); Tager-Flusberg et al. (1990).
47. Stone and Caro-Martinez (1990); Tager-Flusberg (1989).
48. Lord (1985).
49. See Baltaxe and Simmons (1985) for review. Evidence that the degree of prosodic dysfunction is unrelated to general language ability and is a pervasive problem suggest that prosody may provide important clues into the nature of core deficits in autism. Studies of hemispheric representation of prosodic aspects of speech, for instance, suggest that syntactically relevant aspects of prosody are primarily controlled by the left hemisphere, whereas pragmatic and social emotional aspects of prosody are primarily controlled by the right hemisphere (see Foldi, Cicone, & Gardner, 1983 for review). More research is needed to illuminate how autistic children's prosodic deficits reflect neurological impairments, and how they interact with linguistic, pragmatic, and social-emotional functioning.
50. Fay and Schuler (1980, p. 43).
51. Baltaxe (1977).
52. Ricks (1979). See also Fine, Bartolucci, Ginsberg, & Szatmari (1991).
53. Baltaxe (1984).
54. Baltaxe (1977); Fay and Schuler (1980); Layton and Stutts (1985); Frith (1989b); Hurtig, Ensrud, and Tomblin (1982); Loveland, Landry, Hughes, Hall, & McEvoy (1988).
55. Baltaxe (1977).

56. Loveland, Tunali, McEvoy, & Kelley (1989).
57. Bosch (1970, p. 61).
58. See Schuler and Prizant (1985) for review.
59. Frith (1989a).
60. See Loveland and Tunali (1993) for review.
61. Semiotician Karl Buhler (1934) refers to the framing of past story events as if they were happening in the present: "The mountain comes to Mohammed." Alternatively, storytellers may bring their listeners in to the there-and-then of past events. In this case, "Mohammed comes to the mountain." See also Capps and Ochs (1995a, 1995b).
62. Scopinsky (1986, in Bruner and Feldman, 1993); Baron-Cohen, Leslie, & Frith (1986), respectively.
63. Loveland, McEvoy, Tunali, & Kelley (1990).
64. This perspective is akin to Hermelin and O'Connor's (1985) "logico-affective hypothesis."

5. / MIDDLE CHILDHOOD

1. Lave and Wenger (1991); Leont'ev (1981); Lerner (1991); Rogoff (1990); Valsiner (1988); Vygotsky (1978).
2. Carraher, Carraher, and Schliemann (1985); Saxe (1991).
3. Hareven and Adams (1982); Luria (1961); Miller, Shelton, and Flavell (1970); Tietjen (1989).
4. Pascual-Leone (1988).
5. Nelson (1981, 1986).
6. See DeLoache, Cassidy, and Brown (1985) on early memory strategies; Keeney, Cannizzo, and Flavell (1967) and Weissberg and Paris (1986) on rehearsal, and Hasher and Clifton (1974) on memory organization.
7. Piaget (1952); Piaget and Inhelder (1969). These mental operations are "concrete" because, during middle childhood, children are only able to manipulate objects mentally when the objects are physically present.
8. This form of understanding is known as "conservation" (Piaget and Inhelder, 1969).
9. Astington and Gopnik (1991); Astington and Olson (1995); Flavell (1995); Frye and Moore (1991); Wellman (1990).

10. Bretherton and Beeghly (1982); Shatz, Wellman, and Silber (1983).
11. Wimmer and Perner (1983).
12. Baron-Cohen (1989).
13. Happé (1994). Happé suggests that this task requires a "third order theory of mind": knowing that the prisoner *knows* his interrogators *think* he will *lie*.
14. See special issue of *Cognition and Emotion:* "Connections between emotion and understanding and development," edited by Dunn (1995).
15. Dunn (1988); Dunn and Brown (1993).
16. Hartup (1992), Rubin (1980).
17. Hartup (1992).
18. Howes (1987).
19. Dissanayake, Sigman, and Kasari (1996).
20. Rutter (1978, 1983).
21. See also Oliver Sacks's (1995) profile of Steven Wiltshire, an autistic boy noted for drawing exquisite scenes of cities and streets.
22. Sacks (1995).
23. Down (1887/1990).
24. Hughes and Russell (1993); McEvoy, Rogers, and Pennington (1993); Ozonoff, Pennington, and Rogers (1990); Ozonoff and McEvoy (1994).
25. Braverman, Fein, Lucci, & Waterhouse (1989); Capps, Yirmiya, and Sigman (1992); Hobson, Ouston, and Lee (1989); Ozonoff, Pennington, and Rogers (1990); MacDonald, Rutter, Howlin, Rios, LeConteur, Evered, & Folstein (1989); Yirmiya and Sigman (1991).
26. Capps, Yirmiya, and Sigman (1992).
27. Hobson (1986a, 1986b).
28. Dissanayake, Sigman, and Kasari (1996).
29. Baron-Cohen, Leslie, and Frith (1985).
30. Leslie and Frith (1988); Perner, Frith, Leslie, & Leekam (1989).
31. Baron-Cohen (1989); Happé (1994); Ozonoff and McEvoy (1994).
32. Happé (1994, 1995).
33. Bowler (1992); Frith, Morton, and Leslie (1991).

34. Frith, Happé, and Siddons (1993). Evidence of theory of mind in everyday life was derived from parents' responses to items on the Vineland Adaptive Behavior Scales (Sparrow, Balla, and Cicchetti, 1984) which were deemed to require mentalizing behavior.
35. Kasari (personal communication), on study carried out with Bauminger.

6. / ADOLESCENCE

1. For thorough reviews of adolescent thinking see Feldman and Elliott (1990) and Keating (1990).
2. Osherson and Markman (1975).
3. Piaget (1972); Luria (1976).
4. Barbara Rogoff (1990) applies the notion of apprenticeship to describe the acquisition of skills and knowledge. As Rogoff points out, apprentices acquire knowledge by observing and participating, while their more expert partners support and structure their efforts, passing on skills and knowledge through tacit and explicit communication as they go about their work.
5. Dodge (1983); Langlois (1986).
6. Harter (1982).
7. This comes up in Dunn's work on younger children. Early understanding of others' minds was related to initial negative perceptions of school and sensitivity to the teacher's criticisms (1995).
8. McCarthy and Hoge (1982), Offer, Ostrov, Howard, and Atkinson (1988); Simmons and Blythe (1987).
9. Adolescents who are members of distressed families are frequently preoccupied about issues with parents and siblings that potentially limit their involvement in activities outside the home.
10. Chung, Luk, and Lee (1990); Gillberg and Steffenburg (1987); Rutter and Lockyer (1967); Venter, Lord, and Schopler (1992).
11. Capps and Sigman (1996); Happé (1994); Hermelin and O'Connor (1970); Sigman (1996); Sigman, Yirmiya and Capps (1995).

12. Yirmiya, Sigman, and Zacks (1994).
13. Grandin (1992).
14. Capps, Yirmiya, and Sigman (1992).
15. Cooley (1902, p. 153).
16. Jaedicke, Storoschuk, and Lord (1994).
17. Yirmiya, Sigman, Kasari, and Mundy (1992).
18. This measure of empathy was developed by Feshbach (1982).
19. Loveland (1991).
20. Loveland and Tunali (1991).
21. Dunn (1988).
22. Capps, Kasari, Yirmiya, and Sigman (1993).
23. Cole, 1986; Saarni, 1979. This interpretation is supported by the observation that when sixth graders were alone, they showed more facial affect while viewing emotionally charged slides than when others were present (Yarczower and Daruns, 1982).
24. We credit Carol Feldman with this observation (April, 1990).
25. Rutter (1983, p. 71).
26. Among autistic children early forms of self-perception appear to be intact. They recognize their images and, like normally developing children, touch their rouged noses when they see themselves in the mirror. However, autistic children do not laugh and smile at their reflections, suggesting that they relate to their images somewhat differently than do normally developing children.

    Although we are not aware of studies on self-concept in older individuals with autism, autobiographical accounts provide rich information. See Bemporad (1979), Grandin (1984, 1995b), Grandin and Scariano (1986), Miedzianik (1986), and Williams (1992) as well as analysis by Dewey (1991), Happé (1991), and Volkmar and Cohen (1985).
27. Kanner (1971).
28. Harter (1982).
29. Capps, Sigman, and Yirmiya (1995).
30. On the basis of parents' responses to the Vineland Adaptive Behavior Scale (Sparrow, Balla, and Cicchetti, 1984),

a semi-structured interview designed to assess social adaptation, these adolescents were 3 standard deviations below the normal mean with respect to Socialization Skills, 2 standard deviations below the mean with respect to Daily Living Skills, and 1 standard deviation below the mean in the Communication domain.

31. DeLong (1995), Gillberg (1984), Lainhart and Folstein (1994).

7. / STABILITY OF INDIVIDUAL DIFFERENCES AND PREDICTION OVER TIME

1. Although longitudinal research assesses the same skills and capacities over time, the precise behaviors studied vary with age. One might assess language abilities in a very young child, for example, by the number of words the child can recognize or the mean length of their utterances, whereas in an older child language abilities might be measured by looking at expressive vocabulary and prepositions.

2. See Lotter (1978) for review.

3. Follow-up studies of autistic children from early childhood to middle childhood or adolescence include the following: Cantwell, Baker, Rutter, & Mawhood (1989); Chung, Luk, and Lee (1990); DeMyer, Barton, DeMyer, Norton, Allen, & Steele (1973); Eisenberg (1956); Gillberg and Steffenburg (1987); Goldfarb (1970); Hindley and Owen (1978); Kanner (1971); Lord and Schopler (1989); Lotter (1974); Mittler, Gillies, and Jukes (1966); Venter, Lord, and Schopler (1992).

4. Kanner (1971).

5. Rutter and Lockyer (1967); Venter, Lord, and Schopler (1992). Autistic persons' performance on cognitive measures also appears to decline somewhat in adolescence. Lockyer and Rutter (1970) and Venter et al. (1992) found slight decline in IQ scores as autistic children approach adolescence. However, at least some of this effect may be due to the difference in tests. At follow-up adolescents are often given tests (the WISC-R, for example) that re-

quire a greater variety of behaviors and more attention to verbal instructions than do the nonverbal measures of intelligence used when they were younger, such as the Leiter International Performance Scales (Arthur, 1952).

6. Gillberg and Steffenburg (1987).
7. Chung, Luk, and Lee (1990).
8. Lord and Venter (1992).
9. Grandin (1992, 1995a,b); Williams (1992). See also Happé (1991).
10. Among the longitudinal studies reviewed by Lotter (1978) that reported the onset of epilepsy in adolescence, the mean rate was 11%. It is noteworthy that the overall rate of epilepsy in autism is much higher: approximately 33% of all individuals with autism develop epilepsy in early childhood or adolescence (Deykin and MacMahon, 1979; Gillberg, 1991).
11. Olsson, Gillberg, and Steffenburg (1988); Rutter (1970).
12. Chung, Luk, and Lee (1990).
13. Lord and Venter (1992).
14. Lotter (1974).
15. DeMyer, Barton, DeMyer, Norton, Allen, & Steele (1973); Gillberg and Steffenburg (1987); Lotter (1978); Rutter and Lockyer (1967).
16. Szatmari et al. (1989).
17. Rumsey and Hamburger (1988, 1990), Rumsey, Rapoport, and Sceery (1985).
18. Venter, Lord, and Schopler (1992).
19. Szatmari et al. (1989).
20. Cutler and Kozloff (1987).
21. Lord and Venter (1992).
22. Cantwell, Baker, and Rutter (1978); Cantwell, Baker, Rutter, & Mawhood (1989); DeMyer, Barton, DeMyer, Norton, Allen, & Steele (1973); Gillberg and Steffenburg (1987); Lord and Schopler (1989).
23. Although outcomes have not been compared systematically, prognosis for children with certain syndromes designated as "childhood disintegrative disorders" may be less good than that for children with autism (Hill and

Rosenbloom, 1986; Volkmar and Cohen, 1989). This appears to be the case with respect to disintegrative psychosis (Corbett, Harris, Taylor, & Trimble, 1987; Evans-Jones and Rosenbloom, 1978) in which autistic-like symptoms appear after 2 to 3 years of normal development followed by a brief period of acute regression, confusion, and hyperactivity. Outcomes for children with other syndromes that are grouped among the disintegrative disorders, for example Rett syndrome, tend to be worse than for children with autism.

24. Cantwell, Baker, Rutter, and Mawhood (1989).
25. Lord and Schopler (1989).
26. Lord and Venter (1992). Children's socially adaptive behaviors were identified by parents' responses to the Vineland Adaptive Behavior Scales (Sparrow, Balla, Cicchetti, 1984).
27. Dissanayake, Sigman, and Kasari (1996).
28. Ozonoff and McEvoy (1994).
29. In addition to Ozonoff and McEvoy (1994), see Charman and Baron-Cohen (1992) and Happé (1995).
30. Wing and Gould (1979).
31. Szatmari et al. (1989).
32. Mundy, Sigman, and Kasari (1990, 1994); Mundy, Sigman, Ungerer, & Sherman (1987).
33. Bruner (1983); Franco and Butterworth (1991).

8. / IN SEARCH OF CORE DEFICITS AND CAUSES OF AUTISM

1. Dawson and McKissick (1984); Ferrari and Mathews (1983); Neuman and Hill (1978); Spiker and Ricks (1984).
2. Clark and Rutter (1981); Lord (1984); McHale (1983); Strain, Kerr, and Ragland (1979).
3. Capps, Sigman, and Mundy (1994); Dissanayake and Crossley (in press); Rogers, Ozonoff, and Maslin-Cole (1991); Shapiro, Sherman, Calamari, and Koch (1987); Sigman and Ungerer (1984).

4. Hertzig, Snow, and Sherman (1989); Hobson (1993); Mac-Donald et al. (1989).
5. Capps, Yirmiya, and Sigman (1992).
6. Hertzig, Snow, and Sherman (1989); Loveland et al. (1994); Meltzoff and Gopnik (1993).
7. Sigman, Kasari, Kwon, & Yirmiya (1992).
8. See Sigman et al. (1992), Yirmiya et al. (1992) on empathy.
9. Charman and Baron-Cohen (1992); Leekam and Perner (1991); Leslie and Thaiss (1992).
10. Attwood, Frith, and Hermelin (1988); Buitelaar, van Engeland, de Kogel, de Vries, & van Hooff (1991); BaronCohen (1989); Lewy and Dawson (1992); Loveland and Landry (1986); Mundy, Sigman, Ungerer, & Sherman (1986); Sigman, Mundy, Sherman, & Ungerer (1986); Sigman, Kasari, Kwon, & Yirmiya (1992).
11. For reviews see Baltaxe (1977); Loveland and Tulani (1993); Tager-Flusberg (1993).
12. Baron-Cohen (1987); Hammes and Langdell (1981); Lewis and Boucher (1988); Sigman and Ungerer (1984); Wulff (1985).
13. Happé (1995).
14. Baron-Cohen, Leslie, and Frith (1985).
15. Leslie (1987, 1994).
16. Leslie (1987, 1994).
17. Leslie (1987); Leslie and Frith (1990).
18. Leslie and Thaiss (1992); Leslie and Roth (1993).
19. Leslie and Happé (1989).
20. Baron-Cohen (1993). See also Premack (1990).
21. Frith (1989a); Frith and Happé (1994).
22. Indeed, as Paul Harris (1994) reminds us, research that implements only tasks designed to capture theory of mind may lead investigators to neglect both alternative accounts of the mentalizing deficit and additional difficulties experienced by persons with autism that lie outside this domain.
23. Baron-Cohen, Ring, Moriarty, Schmitz, Costa, & Bell (1994); Fletcher, Happé, Frith, Baker, Dolan, Frackowiak et al. (1995). See review by Lewin (1995).

24. See Duncan (1986) for review.
25. Bishop (1993); McEvoy et al. (1993); Ozonoff and McEvoy (1994); Ozonoff et al. (1994).
26. Hughes and Russell (1993); Hughes, Russell, and Robbins (1994).
27. Harris (1993).
28. Ozonoff, Pennington, and Rogers (1991).
29. See Baron-Cohen and Moriarty (1995) for review.
30. For example, Ozonoff, Strayer, McMahon, & Filloux (1994) found that individuals with autism resembled those with Tourette's Syndrome on tasks requiring inhibition of neutral stimuli, but autistic persons were more severely impaired on measures of cognitive flexibility. Executive function impairments associated with autism may be significantly more severe than in other disorders (see also Rumsey and Hamburger, 1990). The very early onset of executive dysfunction may also distinguish autism from these other conditions (Frith and Frith, 1991; Hughes and Russell, 1993). See related work by Minshew, Goldstein, Muenz, & Payton (1992).
31. Hobson (1990, 1991, 1993).
32. Mead (1934); Stern (1985); Trevarthen (1979).
33. See Hobson (1993); Kasari, Sigman, Yirmiya, & Mundy (1992); Mundy and Sigman (1989); Mundy, Sigman, and Kasari (1993).
34. Meltzoff and Gopnik (1993).
35. Rogers and Pennington (1991); see also Tomasello, Kruger, and Ratner (1993).
36. Frankel, Simmons, Fichter, & Freeman (1984).
37. Frith and Done (1990).
38. Wing (1976).
39. Capps, Kasari, Yirmiya, & Sigman (1993); Dawson, Hill, Spencer, Galpert, & Watson (1990); Kasari, Sigman, Baumgartner, & Stipek (1993).
40. Yirmiya, Sigman, Kasari, & Mundy (1992).
41. James and Barry (1984). This notion is consistent with Temple Grandin's (1984) autobiographical account of her

own experiences, and her successful attempt to resolve this problem by creating a device that limits sensory input.

42. Capps, Yirmiya, and Sigman (1992); Jaedicke, Storoschuk, and Lord (1994).
43. Kasari, Sigman, Mundy, & Yirmiya (1990).
44. Sigman, Kasari, Kwon, & Yirmiya (1992).
45. See Dawson and Lewy (1989) for review.
46. Dawson, Finley, Phillips, & Galpert (1986); Ogawa, Sugiyama, Ishiwa, Suzuki, Ishihara, & Sato (1982); Tanguay (1976).
47. Dawson, Warrenburg, and Fuller (1982, 1983).
48. Blackstock (1978); Hoffman and Prior (1982); Prior and Bradshaw (1979); Wetherby, Koegel, and Mendel (1981). A study by Arnold and Schwartz (1983) did not replicate these results.
49. Dawson (1988); Dawson, Finley, Philips, & Galpert (1986); Prior and Bradshaw (1979); Wetherby, Koegel, and Mendel (1981).
50. Courchesne, Kilman, Galambos, & Lincoln (1984); Dawson, Finley, Phillips, Galpert, & Lewy (1988); Novick, Kurtzberg, and Vaughn (1979).
51. Courchesne (1987).
52. Palkowitz and Wiesenfeld (1980); James and Barry (1980).
53. Cohen and Johnson (1977); Hutt, Forrest, and Richer (1975); Kootz and Cohen (1981).
54. Bauman and Kemper (1985, 1994); Piven, Berthier, Starkstein, Nehme, Pearlson, & Folstein (1990); Williams, Hauser, Purpura, Delong, & Swisher (1980).
55. See Ornitz (1985) for review.
56. Courchesne (1989); Courchesne, Yeung-Courchesne, Press, Hesselink, & Jernigan (1988); Egaas, Courchesne, and Saitoh (1995).
57. Brothers (1990); Brothers and Ring (1992).
58. Bauman and Kemper (1985).
59. Bachevalier (1991).
60. Brothers (1990); Halgren (1992); Gloor (1986).

61. Brothers and Ring (1992).
62. Brothers (1995), citing Aggleton (1992); Jacobson (1986); Tranel and Hyman (1990).
63. Fletcher et al. (1995).
64. Goel, Grafman, Sadato, & Hallett (1995).
65. Ciaranello, VandenBerg, and Anders (1982).
66. Anderson and Hoshino (1987); Yuwiler, Geller, and Ritvo (1985); see Volkmar and Anderson (1989) for review.
67. Young, Kavanagh, Anderson, Shaywitz, & Cohen (1982).
68. Studies in support of the dopaminergic hypothesis include those carried out by Garreau, Barthelemy, Domenech, Sauvage, Num, Lelord, & Callaway (1980); Lelord, Callaway, Muh, Arlot, Sauvage, Garreau, & Domenech (1978); Martineau, Garreau, Barthelemy, Callaway, & Lelord (1981); and Mikkelsen (1982). Contrary findings were reported by Boullin and O'Brien (1972); Minderaa, Anderson, Volkmar, Harcherik, Akkerhuis, & Cohen (1987).
69. Panskepp (1979); Sandman, Patta, Banon, Hoehler, Williams, Williams, & Swanson (1983).
70. Bettelheim (1967).
71. See Coleman and Gillberg (1985) for review.
72. Chess, Fernandez, and Korn (1978).
73. Bauman and Kemper (1994).
74. Smalley (1991).
75. Folstein and Rutter (1977, 1978).
76. Sillman, Campbell, and Mitchell (1989).
77. Ritvo, Ritvo, and Mason-Brothers (1982); Shell, Campion, Minton, Caplan, & Campbell (1984).
78. August, Stewart, and Tsai (1981); Rutter (1978, 1985).
79. Rutter (1985).
80. Waterhouse (1994).

9. / INTERVENTIONS

1. Lovaas (1987); McEachen, Smith and Lovaas (1993). Catherine Maurice's (1993) account of her two sons' struggle with autism suggests that Lovaas's program led to their recovery. In addition, Barry Neil and Samahria Kaufman

(Kaufman, 1976) described an intensive, one-on-one approach that they used with their son, which they claim led to full recovery.

2. Personal communication with M. Tomita, psychologist at group program for autistic children, Matsugaya Welfare Center, Tokyo (Marian Sigman, January 1988).
3. Schopler, Mesibov, and Hearsey (1995).
4. Personal communication with J. Fuentes, Director of Gautena Program, San Sebastián, Spain (Marian Sigman, 1994).
5. Koegel and Frea (1993); Koegel, Koegel, and Schreibman (1991).
6. One of the earliest interventions of this kind was carried out by Ivar Lovaas and his colleagues (Lovaas, Schaeffer, and Simmons, 1965).
7. Lovaas (1987); McEachen, Smith, and Lovaas (1993).
8. Lovaas, Koegel, Simmons, & Long (1973).
9. See, for example, Charlop and Milstein (1989).
10. Koegel, Koegel, Hurley, & Frea (1992). Disruptive/distracting behaviors included perseveration on one topic; inappropriate nonverbal mannerisms included persistent rubbing or manipulation of objects or body parts.
11. Carr (1979) and his colleagues carried out a series of studies of factors that facilitate acquisition of both expressive and receptive sign labels, simple sentences, and abstractions.
12. Lovaas, Berberich, Perloff, & Schaeffer (1991).
13. See Campbell, Cueva, and Hallin (1996) for review.
14. See Gerlach (1993) for elaboration of alternative interventions.
15. Rimland (1988).
16. See Mesibov (1995); Rimland (1994).
17. Birnbrauer and Leach (1993); Bondy and Frost (1995); Harris, Handelman, Gordon, Kristoff, & Fuentes (1991); Koegel and Koegel (1995); Laski, Charlop, and Schreibman (1988); Lovaas (1987).
18. Weiss and Weisz (1995); Weisz, Weiss, Han, Granger, et al. (1995).

19. Loveland and Landry (1986); Mundy, Sigman, and Kasari (1990).
20. Hobson (1993); Leslie (1987); Sigman (1995); Tomasello (1995).
21. Baron-Cohen, Allen, and Gillberg (1992).
22. Mundy and Crowson (in press).
23. While neuropsychological research is extremely helpful in identifying deficits, neuropsychologists tend to make use of cross-sectional research designs rather than multi-age or stage comparisons.

References

Adrien, J. L., Fauer, M., Perrot, A., Hameury, L., Garrau, B., Barthelemy, C., & Savage, D. (1991). Autism and family home movies: Preliminary findings. *Journal of Autism and Developmental Disorders, 21,* 43–51.

Aggleton, J. P. (1992). The functional effects of amygdala lesions in humans: A comparison with findings from monkeys. In J. P. Aggleton (Ed.), *The amygdala: Neurobiological aspects of emotion, memory, and mental dysfunction* (pp. 485–503). New York: Wiley-Liss.

Ainsworth, M. D. S., Blehar, M. C., Waters, E., & Wall, S. (1978). *Patterns of attachment: A psychological study of the strange situation.* Hillsdale, NJ: Erlbaum.

American Psychiatric Association (1987). *Diagnostic and statistical manual of mental disorders.* (3rd rev. ed.). Washington, DC: American Psychiatric Association.

American Psychiatric Association (1994). *Diagnostic and statistical manual of mental disorders.* (4th ed.). Washington, DC: American Psychiatric Association.

Anderson, G. M., & Hoshino, Y. (1987). Neurochemical studies of autism. In D. J. Cohen & A. Donnellan (Eds.), *Handbook of autism and pervasive developmental disorders* (pp. 166–191). New York: Wiley.

Anglin, J. M. (1977). *Word, object, and conceptual development.* New York: W. W. Norton.

Applebee, A. N. (1979). *The child's concept of a story: Ages two to seventeen.* Chicago: University of Chicago Press.

Arbelle, S., Sigman, M. D., & Kasari, C. (1994). Compliance

with parental prohibition in autistic children. *Journal of Autism and Developmental Disorders, 24,* 693–702.

Arnold, G., & Schwartz, G. E. (1983). Hemispheric lateralization of language in autistic and aphasic children. *Journal of Autism and Developmental Disorders, 13,* 129–139.

Aronsson, K. (1996, March). Plenary address. Paper presented at the Annual Meeting of American Association of Applied Linguistics, Chicago, IL.

Arthur, G. (1952). *Leiter International Performance Scale.* Washington, DC: Psychological Services Center.

Aslin, R. N. (1987). *Visual and auditory development in infancy.* (2nd ed.). New York: Wiley.

Astington, J. W., & Gopnik, A. (1991). Theoretical explanations of children's understanding of the mind. *British Journal of Developmental Psychology, 9,* 7–31.

Astington, J. W., & Olson, D. R. (1995). The cognitive revolution in children's understanding of mind. *Human Development, 38* 179–189.

Atkinson-King, K. (1973). Children's acquisition of phonological stress contrasts. *UCLA Working Papers in Phonetics, 25,* 1–28.

Attwood, A. H., Frith, U., & Hermelin, B. (1988). The understanding and use of interpersonal gestures by autistic and Down's syndrome children. *Journal of Autism and Developmental Disorders, 18,* 241–257.

August, G. J., Stewart, M. A., & Tsai, L. (1981). The incidence of cognitive disabilites in the siblings of autistic children. *British Journal of Psychiatry, 138,* 416–422.

Bachevalier, J. (1991). An animal model for childhood autism: Memory loss and socioemotional distubances following neonatal damage to the limbic system in monkeys. In C. A. Tamminga & S. C. Schulz (Eds.), *Schizophrenia research. Advances in neuropsychiatry and psychopharmacology* (vol. 1, pp. 129–140). New York: Raven Press.

Baillargeon, R., Spelke, E. S., & Wasserman, S. (1985). Object permanence in five-month-old infants. *Cognition, 20,* 191–208.

Baltaxe, C. A. M. (1977). Pragmatic deficits in the language of autistic adolescents. *Journal of Pediatric Psychology, 2,* 176–180.

Baltaxe, C. A. M. (1984). The use of contrastive stress in normal, aphasic, and autistic children. *Journal of Speech and Hearing Research, 27,* 97–105.

Baltaxe, C. A. M., & Simmons, J. Q. (1985). *Prosodic development in normal and autistic children.* New York: Plenum Press.

Baron-Cohen, S. (1987). Autism and symbolic play. *British Journal of Developmental Psychology, 5,* 139–148.

Baron-Cohen, S. (1989). The autistic child's theory of mind: A case of specific developmental delay. *Journal of Child Psychology and Psychiatry and Allied Disciplines, 30,* 285–297.

Baron-Cohen, S. (1993). *From attention-goal psychology to belief-desire psychology: The development of a theory of mind and its dysfunction.* Oxford: Oxford University Press.

Baron-Cohen, S., Allen, J., & Gillberg, C. (1992). Can autism be detected at 18 months? The needle, the haystack, and the CHAT. *British Journal of Psychiatry, 161,* 839–843.

Baron-Cohen, S., Leslie, A. M., & Frith, U. (1985). Does the autistic child have a "theory of mind"? *Cognition, 21,* 37–46.

Baron-Cohen, S., Leslie, A. M., & Frith, U. (1986). Mechanical, behavioural and intentional understanding of picture stories in autistic children. *British Journal of Developmental Psychology, 4,* 113–125.

Baron-Cohen, S., & Moriarty, J. (1995). Developmental dysfunction syndrome: Does it exist? In M. Robertson & V. Eapen (Eds.), *Movement and allied disorders* . New York: Wiley.

Baron-Cohen, S., Ring, H., Moriarty, J., Schmitz, J., Costa, D., & Bell, P. (1994). Recognition of mental state terms: Clinical findings in children with autism and a functional neuroimaging study of normal adults. *British Journal of Psychiatry, 165,* 640.

Bartolucci, G., & Pierce, S. J. (1977). A preliminary comparison of phonological development in autistic, normal, and mentally retarded subjects. *British Journal of Disorders of Communication, 12,* 137–147.

Bartolucci, G., Pierce, S. J., Streiner, D., & Eppel, P. T. (1976). Phonological investigation of verbal autistic and mentally retarded subjects. *Journal of Autism and Childhood Schizophrenia, 6,* 303–316.

Bartolucci, G., Pierce, S. J., & Streiner, D. (1980). Cross-sectional studies of grammatical morphemes in autistic and mentally retarded children. *Journal of Autism and Developmental Disorders, 10,* 39–50.

Bates, E., Camaioni, L., & Volterra, V. (1975). The acquisition of performatives prior to speech. *Merrill Palmer Quarterly, 21,* 205–226.

Bauman, M., & Kemper, T. (1985). Histoanatomic observations of the brain in early infantile autism. *Neurology, 35,* 866–874.

Bauman, M., & Kemper, T. (1994). *The neurobiology of autism.* Baltimore: Johns Hopkins University Press.

Bemporad, J. R. (1979). Adult recollections of a formerly autistic child. *Journal of Autism and Developmental Disorders, 9,* 179–197.

Berger, J., & Cunningham, C. C. (1983). Development of early vocal behaviors and interactions in Down's syndrome and nonhandicapped infant-mother pairs. *Developmental Psychology, 19,* 322–331.

Berman, R., & Slobin, D. (1994). *Relating events in narrative: A cross-linguistic developmental study.* Hillsdale, NJ: Erlbaum.

Bertenthal, B. I., & Fischer, K. W. (1978). Development of self-recognition in the infant. *Developmental Psychology, 14,* 44–50.

Bettelheim, B. (1967). *The empty fortress: Infantile autism and the birth of self.* New York: Free Press.

Birnbrauer, J., & Leach, D. (1993). The Murdoch Early Intervention Program after 2 years. *Behaviour Change, 10,* 63–74.

Bishop, D. (1982). Comprehension of spoken, written, and signed sentences in childhood language disorders. *Journal of Child Psychology and Psychiatry and Allied Disciplines, 23,* 1–20.

Bishop, D. (1993). Autism, executive functions and theory of mind: A neuropsychological perspective. *Journal of Child*

Psychology and Psychiatry and Allied Disciplines, 34, 279–293.

Blackstock, E. (1978). Cerebral asymmetry and the development of early infantile autism. *Journal of Autism and Developmental Disorders, 8,* 339–353.

Bloom, K., Russell, A., & Wassenberg, K. (1983). Turn-taking affects the quality of infant vocalizations. *Journal of Child Language, 14,* 211–227.

Bondy, A., & Frost, L. (1995). Educational approaches in preschool. Behavior techniques in a public school setting. In E. Schopler & G. Mesibov (Eds.), *Learning and cognition in autism* (pp. 311–334). New York: Plenum Press.

Bornstein, M. H. (1988). *Perceptual development across the life cycle.* Hillsdale, NJ: Erlbaum.

Bosch, G. (1970). *Infantile autism: A clinical and phenomenological-anthropological investigation taking language as the guide* (D. Jordan and I. Jordan, Trans.). New York: Springer-Verlag.

Boucher, J. (1976). Articulation in early childhood autism. *Journal of Autism and Childhood Schizophrenia, 6,* 297–302.

Boullin, D. J., & O'Brien, R. A. (1972). Uptake and loss of 14-C-dopamine by platelets from children with infantile autism. *Journal of Autism and Childhood Schizophrenia, 2,* 67–74.

Bowlby, J. (1973). *Attachment and loss.* Vol. 2: *Separation anxiety and anger* (pp. 292–312). New York: Basic Books.

Bowler, D. M. (1992). "Theory of mind" in Asperger's syndrome. *Journal of Psychology and Psychiatry, 33,* 877–893.

Brask, B. H. (1972). A prevalence investigation of childhood psychoses. *Nordic Symposium on the Care of Psychotic Children.* Oslo: Barnepsychiatrist Forenin.

Braverman, M., Fein, D., Lucci, D., & Waterhouse, L. (1989). Affect comprehension in children with pervasive developmental disorders. *Journal of Autism and Developmental Disorders, 19,* 301–316.

Bretherton, I., & Beeghly, M. (1982). Talking about internal states: The acquisition of an explicit theory of mind. *Developmental Psychology, 18,* 906–921.

Brothers, L. A. (1990). The social brain: A project for integrating primate behavior and neurophysiology in a new domain. *Concepts in Neuroscience, 1,* 27–51.

Brothers, L. A. (1995). Neurophysiology of the perception of intentions by primates. In M. Gazzaniga (Ed.), *The cognitive neuroscience.* Cambridge: MIT Press.

Brothers, L., & Ring, B. (1992). A neuroethological framework for the representation of minds. *Journal of Cognitive Neuroscience, 4,* 107–118.

Brown, R. (1973). *A first language: The early stages.* Cambridge: Harvard University Press.

Bruner, J. S. (1972). The nature and uses of immaturity. *American Psychologist, 27,* 687–708.

Bruner, J. S. (1983). *Child's talk.* New York: Norton.

Bruner, J. S. (1986). *Actual minds, possible worlds.* Cambridge: Harvard University Press.

Bruner, J. S. (1990). *Acts of meaning.* Cambridge: Harvard University Press.

Bruner, J. S., & Feldman, C. (1993). Theories of mind and the problem of autism. In S. Baron-Cohen, H. Tager-Flusberg, & D. Cohen (Eds.), *Understanding other minds: Perspectives from autism.* Oxford: Oxford University Press.

Bryson, S. E., Clark, B. S., & Smith, I. M. (1988). First report of a Canadian epidemiological study of autistic syndromes. *Journal of Child Psychology and Psychiatry and Allied Disciplines, 29,* 433–445.

Buhler, K. (1934). *Sprachtheorie: Die darstellungsfunktion der Sprache.* Jena: Gustav Fischer.

Buitelaar, J. K., van Engeland, H., de Kogel, K. H., de Vries, H., & van Hoof, J. J. M. (1991). Differences in the structure of social behaviour of autistic children and non-autistic retarded controls. *Journal of Child Psychology and Psychiatry and Allied Disciplines, 32,* 995–1015.

Burke, K. (1962). *A grammar of motives and a rhetoric of motives.* Cleveland: Meridian Books.

Butterfield, E. L., & Siperstein, G. N. (1972). Influence of contingent auditory stimulation upon nonnutritional sucking. In J. Bosma (Ed.), *Oral sensation and perception: The mouth of the infant.* Springfield, IL: Charles Thomas.

Butterworth, G., & Cochran, E. (1980). Towards a mechanism of joint visual attention in human infancy. *International Journal of Behavioral Development, 3,* 253–270.

Campbell, M., Cueva, J. E., & Hallin, A. (1996). Autism and pervasive developmental disorders. In J. M. Wiener (Ed.), *Diagnosis and psychopharmacology of childhood and adolescent disorders* (2nd ed., pp. 151–192). New York: Wiley.

Campos, J. J., & Sternberg, C. R. (1981). *Perception, appraisal, and emotion: The onset of social referencing.* Hillsdale, NJ: Erlbaum.

Cantwell, D. P., Baker, L., & Rutter, M. (1978). A comparative study of infantile autism and specific developmental receptive language disorder. IV. Analysis of syntax and language function. *Journal of Child Psychology and Psychiatry and Allied Disciplines, 19,* 351–363.

Cantwell, D. P., Baker, L., Rutter, M., & Mawhood, L. (1989). Infantile autism and developmental receptive dysphasia: A comparative follow-up into middle childhood. *Journal of Autism and Developmental Disorders, 19,* 19–32.

Capps, L., Kasari, C., Yirmiya, N., & Sigman, M. (1993). Parental perception of emotional expressiveness in children with autism. *Journal of Consulting and Clinical Psychology, 61,* 475–484.

Capps, L., & Ochs, E. (1995a). *Constructing panic: The discourse of agoraphobia.* Cambridge: Harvard University Press.

Capps, L., & Ochs, E. (1995b). Out of place: Narrative insights into agoraphobia. *Discourse Processes, 19,* 407–439.

Capps, L., & Sigman, M. (1996). Autistic aloneness. In R. D. Kavanaugh, B. Zimmerberg, & S. Fein (Eds.), *Emotion: Interdisciplinary Perspectives.* Hillsdale, NJ: Erlbaum.

Capps, L., Sigman, M., & Mundy, P. (1994). Attachment security in children with autism. *Development and Psychopathology, 6,* 249–261.

Capps, L., Sigman, M., & Yirmiya, N. (1995). Self-competence and emotional understanding in high-functioning children with autism. *In Emotions in developmental psychopathology. Special issue of Development and Psychopathology, 7,* 137–149.

Capps, L., Yirmiya, N., & Sigman, M. (1992). Understanding

of simple and complex emotions in non-retarded children with autism. *Journal of Child Psychology and Psychiatry and Allied Disciplines, 33,* 1169–1182.

Caron, R. F., Caron, A. J., & Myers, R. S. (1985). Do infants see emotional expressions in static faces? *Child Development, 56,* 1552–1560.

Carr, E. G. (1979). Teaching autistic children to use sign language: Some research issues. *Journal of Autism and Developmental Disorders, 9,* 345–359.

Carraher, T. N., Carraher, D. W., & Schliemann, A. D. (1985). Mathematics in the streets and in schools. *British Journal of Developmental Psychology, 3,* 21–29.

Charlop, M. H., & Milstein, J. P. (1989). Teaching autistic children conversational speech using video modeling. *Journal of Applied Behavior Analysis, 22,* 275–285.

Charman, T., & Baron-Cohen, S. (1992). Understanding drawings and beliefs: A further test of the metarepresentation theory of autism. *Journal of Child Psychology and Psychiatry and Allied Disciplines, 33,* 1105–1112.

Chess, S., Fernandez, P. B., & Korn, S. J. (1978). Behavioral consequences of congenital rubella. *Journal of Pediatrics, 93,* 699–703.

Chung, S. Y., Luk, S. L., & Lee, P. W. H. (1990). A follow-up study of infantile autism in Hong Kong. *Journal of Autism and Developmental Disorders, 20,* 221–232.

Ciadella, P., & Mamelle, N. (1989). An epidemiological study of infantile autism in the French department of Rhone: A research note. *Journal of Child Psychology and Psychiatry and Allied Disciplines, 30,* 165–175.

Ciaranello, R. D., VandenBerg, S. R., & Anders, T. G. (1982). Intrinsic and extrinsic determinants of neuronal development: Relation to infantile autism. *Journal of Autism and Developmental Disorders, 12,* 115–145.

Clark, P., & Rutter, M. (1981). Autistic children's response to structure and to interpersonal demands. *Journal of Autism and Developmental Disorders, 11,* 201–217.

Cohen, D. J., & Johnson, W. T. (1977). Cardiovascular correlates of attention in normal and psychiatrically disturbed children. *Archives of General Psychiatry, 34,* 561–567.

Cohen, D. J., Paul, M. R., & Volkmar, F. R. (1987). Issues in the classification of pervasive developmental disorders and associated conditions. In D. J. Cohen, A. M. Donellan, & R. Paul (Eds.), *Handbook of autism and pervasive developmental disorders* (pp. 221–243). New York: Wiley.

Cole, P. (1986). Children's spontaneous control of facial expression. *Child Development, 57,* 1309–1321.

Cole, M., & Cole, S. R. (1994). *The development of children.* (2nd ed.). New York: Scientific American Books.

Coleman, M., & Gillberg, C. (1985). *The biology of the autistic syndromes.* New York: Praeger.

Collis, G. M., & Schaffer, H. R. (1975). Synchronization of visual attention in mother-infant pairs. *Journal of Child Psychology and Psychiatry and Allied Disciplines, 16,* 315–320.

Cooley, C. H. (1902). *Human nature and the social order.* New York: Scribner.

Corbett, J., Harris, R., Taylor, E., & Trimble, M. (1987). Progressive disintegrative psychosis of childhood. *Journal of Child Psychology and Psychiatry and Allied Disciplines, 18,* 211–219.

Cornell, E. H., & McDonnell, P. M. (1986). Infants' acuity at twenty feet. *Investigative Ophthamology and Visual Science, 27,* 1417–1420.

Courchesne, E. (1987). *A neurophysiological view of autism.* New York: Plenum Press.

Courchesne, E. (1989). Neuroanatomical systems involved in infantile autism. In G. Dawson (Ed.), *Autism: Nature, diagnosis and treatment* (pp. 119–143). New York: Guilford Press.

Courchesne, E., Kilman, B. A., Galambos, R., & Lincoln, A. J. (1984). Autism: Processing of novel auditory information assessed by event-related brain potentials. *Electroencephalography and Clinical Neurophysiology: Evoked Potentials, 59,* 238–248.

Courchesne, E., Yeung-Couchesne, R., Press, G. A., Hesselink, J. R., & Jernigan, T. L. (1988). Hypoplasia of cerebellar vermal lobules VI and VII in infantile autism. *New England Journal of Medicine, 318,* 1349–1354.

Cutler, B. C., & Kozloff, M. A. (1987). Living with autism:

Effects on families and family needs. In D. J. Cohen, A. M. Donnellan, & R. Paul (Eds.), *Handbook of autism and pervasive developmental disorders.* Silver Spring, MD: V. H. Winston.

Dannemiller, J. L., & Stephens, B. K. (1988). A critical test of infant pattern preference models. *Child Development, 59,* 210–216.

Darwin, C. (1872). *The expression of the emotions in man and animals.* London: Murray.

Dawson, G. (1988). *Cerebral lateralization in autism: Its role in language and affective disorders.* New York: Guilford Press.

Dawson, G., & Adams, A. (1984). Imitation and social responsiveness in autistic children. *Journal of Abnormal Child Psychology, 12,* 209–225.

Dawson, G., Finley, C., Phillips, S., & Galpert, L. (1986). Hemispheric specialization and the language abilities of autistic children. *Child Development, 57,* 1440–1453.

Dawson, G., Finley, C., Phillips, S., Galpert, L., & Lewey, A. (1988). Reduced P3 amplitude of the event-related brain potential: Its relationship to language ability in autism. *Journal of Autism and Developmental Disorders, 18,* 493–504.

Dawson, G., Hill, D., Spencer, A., Galpert, L., & Watson, L. (1990). Affective exchanges between young autistic children and their mothers. *Journal of Abnormal Child Psychology, 18,* 335–345.

Dawson, G., & Lewy, A. (1989). Reciprocal subcortical-cortical influences in autism: The role of attentional mechanisms. In G. Dawson (Ed.), *Autism: Nature, diagnosis and treatment* (pp. 144–173). New York: Guilford Press.

Dawson, G., & McKissick, F. (1984). Self-recognition in autistic children. *Journal of Autism and Developmental Disorders, 14,* 383–394.

Dawson, G., Warrenburg, S., & Fuller, P. (1982). Cerebral lateralization in individuals diagnosed as autistic in early childhood. *Brain and Language, 15,* 353–368.

Dawson, G., Warrenburg, S., & Fuller, P. (1983). Hemisphere functioning and motor imitation in autistic persons. *Brain and Cognition, 2,* 346–354.

DeCasper, A. J., & Fifer, W. P. (1980). Of human bonding: Newborns prefer their mother's voices. *Science, 208,* 1174–1176.

Deloache, J. S., Cassidy, D. J., & Brown, A. L. (1985). Precursors of mnemonic strategies in young children. *Child Development, 56,* 125–137.

DeLong, R. (1995). Medical and pharmacologic treatment of learning disabilities. *Journal of Child Neurology, 10,* S92-S95.

DeMyer, M. K., Barton, S., DeMyer, W. E., Norton, J. A., Allen, J., & Steel, R. (1973). Prognosis in autism: A follow-up study. *Journal of Autism and Childhood Schizophrenia, 3,* 199–245.

DeVilliers, J. G., & DeVilliers, P. A. (1978). *Language Acquisition.* Cambridge: Harvard University Press.

DeVilliers, J. G., & DeVilliers, P. A. (1979). *Early Language.* Cambridge: Harvard University Press.

Dewey, M. (1991). Living with Asperger's syndrome. In U. Frith (Ed.), *Autism and Asperger's syndrome* (pp. 184–206). Cambridge, Eng.: Cambridge University Press.

Deykin, E. Y., & MacMahon, B. (1979). The incidence of seizures among children with autistic symptoms. *American Journal of Psychiatry, 136,* 1310–1312.

Dissanayake, C., & Crossley, S. A. (in press). Proximity and sociable behaviours in autism: Evidence for attachment? *Journal of Child Psychology and Psychiatry and Allied Disciplines.*

Dissanayake, C., Sigman, M., & Kasari, C. (1996). Long-term stability of individual differences in the emotional responsiveness of children with autism. *Journal of Child Psychology and Psychiatry and Allied Disciplines, 37,* 461–467.

Dodge, K. A. (1983). Behavioral antecedents of peer social status. *Child Development, 54,* 1386–1399.

Dore, J. (1978). *Conditions for acquisition of speech acts.* New York: Wiley.

Down, J. L. (1887/1990). *Mental affections of childhood and youth.* Oxford: Blackwell.

Duncan, J. (1986). Disorganisation of behaviour after frontal lobe damage. *Cognitive Neuropsychology, 33,* 271–290.

Dunn, J. (1988). *The beginnings of social understanding.* Oxford: Blackwell.

Dunn, J. (1995). Children as psychologists: The later correlates of individual differences in understanding of emotions and other minds. *Cognition and Emotion, 9,* 187–201.

Dunn, J., & Brown, J. R. (1993). Early conversations about causality: Content, pragmatics and developmental change. *British Journal of Developmental Psychology, 11,* 107–123.

Dunn, J., & Kendrick, C. (1982). The speech of two- and three-year-olds to infant siblings: "Baby talk" and the context of communication. *Journal of Child Language, 9,* 579–595.

Duranti, A., & Brenneis, D. (1986). The audience as co-author. Special issue of *Text, 6,* 239–347.

Egaas, B., Courchesne, E., & Saitoh, O. (1995). Reduced size of corpus callosum in autism. *Archives of Neurology, 52,* 794–801.

Eimas, P. D. (1985). The perception of speech in early infancy. *Scientific American, 204,* 66–72.

Eisenberg, L. (1956). The autistic child in adolescence. *American Journal of Psychiatry, 112,* 607–612.

Eisenberg, N., & Strayer, J. (Eds.) (1989). *Empathy and its development.* New York: Cambridge University Press.

Eisenberg, N. (1992). *The caring child.* Cambridge: Harvard University Press.

Emde, R. N., Gaensbauer, T. J., & Harmon, R. J. (1976). Emotional expression in infancy: A behavioral study. *Psychological Issues Monograph Series, 10*(1, Serial No. 37).

Engen, T., Lipsitt, L. P., & Kaye, H. (1963). Olfactory responses and adaptation in the human neonate. *Journal of Comparative and Physiological Psychology, 56,* 73–77.

Ervin-Tripp, S. M. (1973). Language acquisition and communicative choice. In A. S. Dil (Ed.), *Essays by Susan M. Ervin-Tripp.* Stanford, CA: Stanford University Press.

Evans-Jones, L. G., & Rosenbloom, L. (1978). Disintegrative psychosis in childhood. *Developmental Medicine and Child Neurology, 20,* 462–470.

Fantz, R. L. (1961). The origins of form perception. *Scientific American, 204,* 66–72.

Fantz, R. L. (1963). Pattern vision in newborn infants. *Science, 140,* 296–297.

Fay, W., & Schuler, A. L. (1980). *Emerging language in autistic children.* Baltimore: University Park Press.

Feldman, C. F. (1989). *Monologue as problem-solving narrative.* London: Sage.

Feldman, S. S., & Elliott, G. R. (Eds.) (1990). *At the threshold: The developing adolescent.* Cambridge: Harvard University Press.

Fernald, A. (1985). Four-month-old infants prefer to listen to motherese. *Infant Behavior and Development, 8,* 181–195.

Ferrari, M., & Matthews, W. (1983). Self-recognition deficits in autism: Syndrome-specific or general developmental delay? *Journal of Autism and Developmental Disorders, 10,* 51–57.

Feshbach, N. (1982). Sex differences in empathy and social behavior in children. In N. Eisenberg (Ed.), *The development of prosocial behavior* (pp. 315–338). Cambridge, Eng.: Cambridge University Press.

Fine, J., Bartolucci, G., Ginsberg, G., & Szatmari, P. (1991). The use of intonation to communicate in pervasive developmental disorders. *Journal of Child Psychology and Psychiatry and Allied Disciplines, 32,* 771–782.

Flavell, J. H. (1995). Young children's knowledge about thinking. In J. H. Flavell, F. L. Greene, & E. R. Flavell (Eds.), *Monographs of the Society for Research in Child Development* (Vol. 60). Chicago: Society for Research in Child Development.

Fletcher, P. C., Happé, F., Frith, U., Baker, S. C., Dolan, R. J., Frackowiak, R. S. J., et al., (1995). Other minds in the brain: A functional imaging study of theory of mind in story comprehension. *Cognition, 57,* 2.

Foldi, N. S., Cicone, M., & Gardner, H. (1983). Pragmatic aspects of communication in brain-damaged patients. In S. J. Segalowitz (Ed.), *Language functions and brain organization* (pp. 51–86). New York: Academic Press.

Folstein, S. E., & Rutter, M. (1977). Infantile autism: A genetic study of 21 twin pairs. *Journal of Child Psychology and Psychiatry and Allied Disciplines, 18,* 297–321.

Folstein, S. E., & Rutter, M. (1978). A twin study of individuals with infantile autism. In M. Rutter & E. Schopler (Eds.), *Autism: A reappraisal of concepts and treatment* (pp. 219–241). New York: Plenum Press.

Franco, F., & Butterworth, G. (1991, March). Infant pointing, prelinguistic reference and co-reference. Paper presented at the Meeting of Society for Research in Child Development, Seattle, WA.

Frankel, F., Simmons, J. Q., Fichter, M., & Freeman, B. J. (1984). Stimulus overselectivity in autistic and mentally retarded children: A research note. *Journal of Child Psychology and Psychiatry and Allied Disciplines, 25,* 147–155.

Frith, C. D., & Done, D. J. (1990). Stereotyped behaviour in madness and in health. In S. J. Cooper & C. T. Dourish (Eds.), *Neurobiology of sterotyped behaviour* (pp. 232–259). Oxford: Clarendon Press.

Frith, C. D., & Frith, U. (1991). Elective affinities in schizophrenia and childhood autism. In P. E. Bebbington (Ed.), *Social psychiatry: Theory, methodology and practice* (pp. 65–88). New Brunswick, NJ: Transaction Publishers.

Frith, U. (1989a). *Autism: Explaining the enigma.* Oxford: Blackwell.

Frith, U. (1989b). A new look at language and communication in autism. *In Autism. Special issue of British Journal of Disorders of Communication, 24,* 123–150.

Frith, U. (1991). *Autism and Asperger syndrome.* Cambridge, Eng.: Cambridge University Press.

Frith, U., & Baron-Cohen, S. (1987). Perception in autistic children. In D. J. Cohen, A. Donnellan, & R. Paul (Eds.), *Handbook of autism and pervasive developmental disorders* . New York: Wiley.

Frith, U., Happé, F., & Siddons, F. (1993, March). Theory of mind and social adaptation in autistic, retarded and young normal children. Paper presented at the Biannual Meeting of the Society for Research in Child Development, Seattle, WA.

Frith, U., & Happé, F. (1994). Autism: Beyond theory of mind. *Cognition, 50,* 115.

Frith, U., Morton, J., & Leslie, A. M. (1991). The cognitive basis of a biological disorder: Autism. *Trends in Neuroscience, 14,* 433–438.

Frye, D., & Moore, C. (Eds.). (1991). *Children's theories of mind: Mental states and social understanding.* Hillsdale, NJ: Erlbaum.

Gallup, G. G. J. (1970). Chimpanzees: Self-recognition. *Science, 167,* 86–87.

Garreau, B., Barthelemy, C., Domenech, J., Sauvage, D., Num, J. P., Lelord, G., & Callaway, E. (1980). Disturbances in dopamine metabolism in autistic children: Results of clinical tests and urinary dosages of homovanilic acid (HVA). *Acta Psychiatrica Belgica, 80,* 249–265.

Gerlach, E. K. (1993). *Autism treatment guide.* Eugene, OR: Four Leaf Press.

Gesell, A. (1929). *Infancy and human growth.* New York: Macmillan.

Gillberg, C. (1984a). Autistic children growing up: Problems during puberty and adolescence. *Developmental Medicine and Child Neurology, 26,* 125–129.

Gillberg, C. (1984b). Infantile autism and other childhood psychoses in a Swedish urban region: Epidemiological aspects. *Journal of Child Psychology and Psychiatry and Allied Disciplines, 25,* 35–43.

Gillberg, C. (1991). The treatment of epilepsy in autism. *Journal of Autism and Developmental Disorders, 21,* 61–77.

Gillberg, C., & Steffenburg, S. (1987). Outcome and prognostic factors in infantile autism and similar conditions: A population-based study of 46 cases followed through puberty. *Journal of Autism and Developmental Disorders, 17,* 273–288.

Ginsburg, G. P., & Kilbourne, B. K. (1988). Emergence of vocal alternation in mother-infant interchanges. *Journal of Child Language, 15,* 221–235.

Givon, T. (1989). *Mind, code and context: Essays in pragmatics.* Hillsdale, NJ: Erlbaum.

Gloor, P. (1986). *The role of the human limbic system in perception, memory, and affect: Lessons from temporal lobe epilepsy.* New York: Raven Press.

Goel, V., Grafman, J., Sadato, N., & Hallett, M. (1995). Modeling other minds. *Neuroreport: An International Journal for the Rapid Communication of Research in Neuroscience, 6,* 1741–1746.

Goldfarb, W. (1970). A follow-up investigation of schizophrenic children treated in residence. *Psychosocial Process, 1,* 9–64.

Goleman, D. (1995). *Emotional intelligence.* New York: Bantam Books.

Golinkoff, R. M., Hirsh-Pasek, K., Cauley, K. M., & Gordon, L. (1987). The eyes have it: Lexical and syntactic comprehension in a new paradigm. *Journal of Child Language, 14,* 23–45.

Goodwin, M. H. (1990). *He-said-she-said: Talk as social organization among Black children.* Bloomington, IN: Indiana University Press.

Goodwin, C., & Duranti, A. (1992). Rethinking context: An introduction. In A. Duranti & C. Goodwin (Eds.), *Rethinking context: Language as an interactive phenomenon* (pp. 1–42). Cambridge, Eng.: Cambridge University Press.

Gopnik, A., & Meltzoff, A. N. (1987). The development of categorization in the second year and its relation to other congnitive and linguistic developments. *Child Development, 58,* 1523–1531.

Grandin, T. (1984). My experiences as an autistic child and review of selected literature. *Journal of Orthomolecular Psychiatry, 13,* 144–174.

Grandin, T. (1992). Calming effects of deep touch pressure in patients with autistic disorder, college students, and animals. *Journal of Child and Adolescent Psychopharmacology, 2,* 63–72.

Grandin, T. (1995). How people with autism think. In E. Schopler & G. B. Mesibov (Eds.), *Learning and cognition in autism* (pp. 137–156). New York: Plenum Press.

Grandin, T. (1995b). *Thinking in pictures.* New York: Doubleday.

Grandin, T., & Scariano, M. (1986). *Emergence labelled autistic.* Tunbridge Wells, Eng.: Costello.

Greenfield, P. M., & Smith, J. H. (1976). *The structure of commu-*

nication in early language development. New York: Academic Press.

Grice, H. P. (1975). Logic and conversation. In P. Cole & J. C. Moran (Eds.), *Syntax and semantics III: Speech Acts* (pp. 41–58) New York: Academic Press.

Grimwade, J. C., Walker, D. W., Bartlett, M., Gordon, S., & Wood, C. (1970). Human fetal heartrate change and movement-response to sound and vibration. *American Journal of Obstetrics and Gynecology, 109,* 86–90.

Haaf, R. A., Smith, P. H., & Smitely, S. (1983). Infant response to facelike patterns under fixed-trial and infant control procedures. *Child Development, 54,* 172–177.

Haith, M. M., Berman, T., & Moore, M. J. (1977). Eye contact and face scanning in early infancy. *Science, 198,* 853–855.

Haith, M. M. (1990). Progress in the understanding of sensory and perceptual processes in early infancy. *Merrill Palmer Quarterly, 36,* 1–26.

Halgren, E. (1992). Emotional neurophysiology of the amygdala within the context of human cognition. In J. Aggleton (Ed.), *The amygdala: Neurobiological aspects of emotion, memory, and mental dysfunction* (pp. 191–228). New York: Wiley-Liss.

Hammes, J. G. W., & Langdell, T. (1981). Precursors of symbol formation and childhood autism. *Journal of Autism and Developmental Disorders, 11,* 331–346.

Happé, F. G. E. (1991). The autobiographical writings of three Asperger syndrome adults: Problems of interpretation and implications for theory. In U. Frith (Ed.), *Autism and Asperger syndrome* (pp. 207–242). Cambridge, Eng.: Cambridge University Press.

Happé, F. G. E. (1994). An advanced test of theory of mind: Understanding of story characters' thoughts and feelings by able autistic, mentally handicapped and normal children and adults. *Journal of Autism and Developmental Disorders, 24,* 129–154.

Happé, F. G. E. (1995a). The role of age and verbal ability in the theory of mind task performance of subjects with autism. *Child Development, 66,* 843–855.

234 / References

Happé, F. G. E. (1995b). *Autism: An introduction to psychological theory.* Cambridge: Harvard University Press.

Hareven, T. K., & Adams, K. (Eds.). (1982). *Aging and life course transitions: An interdisciplinary perspective.* New York: Guilford.

Harmon, R. J., & Emde, R. N. (1972). Neonatal muscle tone recorded from eye movement leads. *Psychophysiology, 9,* 458–460.

Harris, P. L. (1991). The work of the imagination. In A. Whiten (Ed.), *Natural theories of mind: Evolution, development and simulation of everyday mindreading* (pp. 283–304). Oxford: Blackwell.

Harris, P. L. (1993). Pretending and planning. In S. Baron-Cohen, H. Tager-Flusberg, & D. Cohen (Eds.), *Understanding other minds: Perspectives from autism.* Oxford: Oxford University Press.

Harris, P. (1994). Understanding pretense. In C. Lewis & P. Mitchell (Eds.), *Origins of a theory of mind* (pp. 235–260). Hillsdale, NJ: Erlbaum.

Harris, S., Handleman, J., Gordon, R., Kristoff, B., & Fuentes, F. (1991). Changes in cognitive and language functioning of preschool children with autism. *Journal of Autism and Developmental Disorders, 21,* 281–290.

Harter, S. (1982). The perceived competence scale for children. *Child Development, 53,* 87–97.

Harter, S., & Whitesell, N. (1989). *Developmental changes in children's emotion concepts.* New York: Cambridge University Press.

Hartup, W. W. (1992). *Friendships and their developmental significance.* Hillsdale, NJ: Erlbaum.

Hasher, L., & Clifton, D. (1974). A developmental study of attribute encoding in free recall. *Journal of Experimental Child Psychology, 17,* 332–346.

Heidegger, M. (1962). *Being and time* (J. Macquarrie & E. Robinson, Trans.). New York: Harper and Row.

Hermelin, B., & O'Connor, N. (1970). *Psychological Experiments with Autistic Children.* Oxford: Pergamon.

Hermelin, B., & O'Connor, N. (1985). The logico-affective disorder in autism. In E. Shopler & G. B. Mesibov (Eds.), *Communication problems in autism* (pp. 283–310). New York: Plenum Press.

Hertzig, M. E., Snow, M. E., & Sherman, M. (1989). Affect and cognition in autism. *Journal of the American Academy of Child and Adolescent Psychiatry, 28,* 195–199.

Hiatt, S. W., Campos, J. J., & Emde, R. N. (1979). Facial patterning and infant emotional expression: Happiness, surprise, and fear. *Child Development, 50,* 1020–1035.

Hill, A. E., & Rosenbloom, L. (1986). Disintegrative psychosis of childhood: Teenage follow-up. *Developmental Medicine and Child Neurology, 28,* 34–40.

Hindley, C. B., & Owen, C. F. (1978). The extent of individual changes in I.Q. for ages between 6 months and 17 years, in a British longitudinal sample. *Journal of Child Psychology and Psychiatry and Allied Disciplines, 19,* 329–350.

Hobson, R. P. (1986a). The autistic child's appraisal of expressions of emotion. *Journal of Child Psychology and Psychiatry and Allied Disciplines, 27,* 321–342.

Hobson, R. P. (1986b). The autistic child's appraisal of expressions of emotion: A further study. *Journal of Child Psychology and Psychiatry and Allied Disciplines, 27,* 671–680.

Hobson, P. R. (1990). On the origins of self and the case of autism. *Development and Psychopathology, 2,* 163–181.

Hobson, R. P. (1991). What is autism? *Psychiatric Clinics of North America, 14,* 1–17.

Hobson, R. P. (1993). Understanding persons: The role of affect. In S. Baron-Cohen, H. Tager-Flusberg, & D. J. Cohen (Eds.), *Understanding other minds: Perspectives from autism* (pp. 204–224). Oxford: Oxford University Press.

Hobson, R. P., Ouston, J., & Lee, A. (1989). Naming emotions in faces and voices: Abilities and disabilities in autism and mental retardation. *British Journal of Developmental Psychology, 7,* 237–250.

Hoffman, W., & Prior, M. (1982). Neuropsychological dimensions of autism in children: A test of the hemispheric hypothesis. *Journal of Clinical Psychology, 4,* 24–41.

Hornik, R., Risenhoover, N., & Gunnar, M. (1987). The effects of maternal positive, neutral, and negative affective communications on infant responses to new toys. *Child Development, 58,* 937–944.

Horowitz, F. D., Paden, L., Bhana, K., & Self, P. (1972). An infant-control procedure for studying infant visual fixations. *Developmental Psychology, 7,* 90.

Hoshino, Y., Kumashiro, H., Yashima, Y., Tachibana, R., & Watanabe, M. (1982). The epidemiological study of autism in Fukushima-ken. *Folia Psychiatrica et Neurologica Japonica, 36,* 115–124.

Howes, C. (1987). Peer interaction of young children. *Monographs of the Society for Research in Child Development, 53*(1, Serial No. 217).

Howlin, P. (1984). The acquisition of grammatical morphemes in autistic children: A critique and replication of the findings of Bartolucci, Pierce, and Streiner, 1980. *Journal of Autism and Developmental Disorders, 14,* 127–136.

Hudson, J. (1990). The emergence of autobiographical memory in mother-child conversation. In R. Fivush & J. Hudson (Eds.), *Knowing and remembering in young children* (pp. 166–196). Cambridge, Eng.: Cambridge University Press.

Hughes, C. H., & Russell, J. (1993). Autistic children's difficulty with mental disengagement from an object: Its implications for theories of autism. *Developmental Psychology, 29,* 498–510.

Hughes, C., Russell, J., & Robbins, T. W. (1994). Evidence for executive dysfunction in autism. *Neuropsychologia, 32,* 477–492.

Hurtig, R., Ensrud, S., & Tomblin, J. (1982). The communicative function of question production in autistic children. *Journal of Autism and Developmental Disorders, 12,* 57–69.

Hutt, S. J., Forrest, S. J., & Richer, J. (1975). Cardiac arrhythmia and behavior in autistic children. *Acta Psychiatrica Scandinavica, 51,* 361–372.

Itard, E. M. (1801). *De l'éducation d'un homme sauvage, ou des premiers developpements physiques et moraux du jeune sauvage de l'Aveyron.* Paris: Imprimeur-Librairie.

Izard, C. E., Huebner, R., Risser, D., McGinnes, G., &

Dougherty, L. (1980). The young infant's ability to produce discrete emotion expressions. *Developmental Psychology, 16,* 132–140.

Izard, C. E., Hembree, E. A., Dougherty, L. M., & Spizzirri, C. (1983). Changes in 2- to 19-month-old infants' responses to acute pain. *Developmental Psychology, 19,* 418–426.

Jacobson, R. (1986). Disorders of facial recognition, social behavior and affect after combined bilateral amygdalotomy and subcaudate tractotomy: A clinical and experimental study. *Psychological Medicine, 16,* 439–450.

Jaedicke, S., Storoschuk, S., & Lord, C. (1994). Subjective experience and causes of affect in high-functioning children and adolescents with autism. *Development and Psychopathology, 6,* 273–284.

James, A., & Barry, R. J. (1980). Repiratory and vascular responses to simple visual stimuli in autistics, retardates, and normals. *Psychophysiology, 17,* 541–547.

James, A. L., & Barry, R. J. (1984). Cardiovascular and electrodermal responses to simple stimuli in autistic, retarded and normal children. *International Journal of Psychophysiology, 1,* 179–193.

Johnson, M. H., Siddons, F., Frith, U., & Morton, J. (1992). Can autism be predicted on the basis of infant screening tests? *Developmental Medicine and Child Neurology, 34,* 316–320.

Jones, V., & Prior, M. R. (1985). Motor imitation abilities and neurological signs in autistic children. *Journal of Autism and Developmental Disorders, 15,* 37–46.

Kagan, J. (1971). *Change and continuity in infancy.* New York: Wiley.

Kagan, J., Kearsley, R. B., & Zelazo, P. (1978). *Infancy: Its place in human development.* Cambridge: Harvard University Press.

Kanner, L. (1943). Autistic disturbances of affective contact. *The Nervous Child, 2,* 217–250.

Kanner, L. (1971). Follow-up study of 11 autistic children originally reported in 1943. *Journal of Autism and Childhood Schizophrenia, 1,* 119–145.

Kanner, L. (1971). Follow up of eleven autistic children, originally reported in 1943. *Journal of Autism and Childhood Schizophrenia, 2,* 119–145.

Karniol, R. (1989). The role of manual manipulative stages in the infant's acquisition of perceived control over object. *Developmental Review, 9,* 205–233.

Kasari, C., & Sigman, M. (1996). Expression and understanding of emotion in atypical development: Autism and Down Syndrome. In M. Lewis & Sullivan (Eds.), *Emotional development in atypical children.* Hillsdale, NJ: Erlbaum.

Kasari, C., Sigman, M., Mundy, P., & Yirmiya, N. (1990). Affective sharing in the context of joint attention interactions of normal, autistic, and mentally retarded children. *Journal of Autism and Developmental Disorders, 20,* 87–100.

Kasari, C., Sigman, M., & Yirmiya, N. (1993). Focused and social attention of autistic children in interactions with familiar and unfamiliar adults: A comparison of autistic, mentally retarded, and normal children. *Development and Psychopathology, 5,* 403–414.

Kasari, C., Sigman, M. D., Baumgartner, P., & Stipek, D. J. (1993). Pride and mastery in children with autism. *Journal of Child Psychology and Psychiatry and Allied Disciplines, 34,* 353–362.

Kasari, C., Sigman, M., Mundy, P., & Yirmiya, N. (1988). Caregiver interactions with autistic children. *Journal of Abnormal Child Psychology, 16,* 45–56.

Kasari, C., Sigman, M., Yirmiya, N., & Mundy, P. (1992). Affective development and communication in children with autism. In A. P. Kaiser & D. B. Gray (Eds.), *The social use of language: Research foundations for early language interventions.* New York: Brookes.

Kaufman, B. N. (1976). *Son-rise.* New York: Harper and Row.

Keating, D. (1990). *Adolescent thinking.* Cambridge: Harvard University Press.

Keeney, T. J., Cannizzo, S. D., & Flavell, J. H. (1967). Spontaneous and induced verbal rehearsal in a recall task. *Child Development, 38,* 935–966.

Kleitman, N. (1963). *Sleep and wakefulness.* Chicago: University of Chicago Press.

Klin, A., & Volkmar, F. R. (1995). *Guidelines for parents: Assessment, diagnosis and intervention of Asperger's syndrome.* New Haven, CT: Learning Disabilites Association of America.

Klinnert, M., Campos, J. J., Sorce, J., Emde, R. N., & Svejda, M. (1983). Social referencing: Emotional expressions as behavior regulators. In R. Plutchik and H. Kellerman (Eds.) *Emotion: Theory, research and experience.* (Vol. 2, pp. 57–86). New York: Academic Press.

Koegel, R., Koegel, L., & Schreibman, L. (1991). Assessing and training parents in teaching pivotal behaviors. In R. Prinz (Ed.), *Advance in behavioral assessment of families* (pp. 65–82). London: Jessica Kingsley.

Koegel, L. K., Koegel, R. L., Hurley, D., & Frea, W. D. (1992). Improving social skills and disruptive behavior in children with autism through self-management. *Journal of Applied Behavior Analysis, 25,* 341–353.

Koegel, L., & Koegel, R. (1995). Motivating communication in children with autism. In E. Schopler & G. Mesibov (Eds.), *Learning and cognition in autism* (pp. 73–87). New York: Plenum Press.

Koegel, R., & Frea, W. (1993). Treatment of social behavior in autism through the modification of pivotal social skills. *Journal of Applied Behavior Analysis, 26,* 369–377.

Kootz, J. P., & Cohen, D. J. (1981). Modulation of sensory intake in autistic children: Cardiovascular and behavioral indices. *Journal of the American Academy of Child Psychiatry, 20,* 692–701.

Kopp, C. (1982). Antecedents of self-regulation: A developmental perspective. *Developmental Psychology, 18,* 199–214.

Kuhl, P. K., Williams, K. A., Lacerda, F., Stevens, K. N., & Lindblom, B. (1992). Linguistic experiences alter phonetic perception in infants by 6 months of age. *Science, 255,* 606–608.

Labov, W., & Waletzky, J. (1968). Narrative analysis. In W. Labov et al. (Eds.), *A study of the non-standard English of Negro and Puerto Rican speakers in New York City* (pp. 286–338). New York: Columbia University Press.

Lainhart, J. E., & Folstein, S. E. (1994). Affective disorders in people with autism: A review of published cases. *Journal of Autism and Developmental Disorders, 24,* 587–601.

Landry, S. H., & Loveland, K. A. (1989). The effect of social context on the functional communication skills of autistic children. *Journal of Autism and Developmental Disorders, 19,* 283–299.

Langlois, J. (1986). From the eye of the beholder to behavioral reality: Development of social behaviors and social relations as a function of physical attractiveness. In C. P. Herman, M. P. Zanna, & E. T. Higgins (Eds.), *Physical appearance, stigma, and special behavior: The Ontario Symposium.* Hillsdale, NJ: Erlbaum.

Laski, K., Charlop, M., & Schreibman, L. (1988). Training parents to use the natural language paradigm to increase their autistic children's speech. *Journal of Applied Behavior Analysis, 21,* 391–400.

Lave, J., & Wenger, E. (1991). *Situated learning: Legitimate peripheral practice.* New York: Cambridge University Press.

Layton, T. L., & Stutts, N. (1985). Pragmatic usage by autistic children under different treatment modes. *Australian Journal of Human Communication Disorders, 13,* 127–142.

Leekam, S., & Perner, J. (1991). Does the autistic child have a metarepresentational deficit? *Cognition, 40,* 203–218.

Lelord, G., Callaway, E., Muh, J. P., Arlot, J. C., Sauvage, D., Garreau, B., & Domenech, J. (1978). Modifications in urinary homovanillic acid after ingestion of vitamin B6: Functional study in autistic children. *Revue Neurologique, 134,* 797–801.

Leont'ev, A. N. (1981). *The problem of activity in psychology.* Armonk, N.Y.: M. E. Sharpe.

Lerner, R. M. (1991). Changing organism-context relations as the basic process of development: A developmental contextual perspective. *Developmental Psychology, 27,* 27–32.

Leslie, A. M. (1987). Pretense and representation: The origins of "theory of mind." *Psychological Review, 94,* 412–426.

Leslie, A. M. (1994). Pretending and believing: Issues in the theory of theory of mind. *Cognition, 50,* 211–238.

Leslie, A. M., & Frith, U. (1988). Autistic children's understanding of seeing, knowing and believing. *British Journal of Developmental Psychology, 6,* 315–324.

Leslie, A. M., & Frith, U. (1990). Prospects for a cognitive neuropsychology of autism: Hobson's choice. *Psychological Review, 97,* 122–131.

Leslie, A. M., & Happé, F. (1989). Autism and ostensive communication: The relevance of metarepresentation. *Development and Psychopathology, 1,* 205–212.

Leslie, A. M., & Roth, D. (1993). What autism teaches us about metarepresentation. In S. Baron-Cohen, H. Tager-Flusberg, & D. J. Cohen (Eds.), *Understanding other minds: Perspectives from autism* (pp. 83–111). Oxford: Oxford University Press.

Leslie, A. M., & Thaiss, L. (1992). Domain specificity in conceptual development: Evidence from autism. *Cognition, 43,* 225–251.

Lewin, D. I. (1995). From mind to molecule: Researchers try to unravel the complexity of autism. *Journal of the National Institute of Health Research,* 44–48.

Lewis, M., & Brooks-Gunn, J. (1979). *Social cognition and the acquisition of self.* New York: Plenum Press.

Lewis, M., & Freedle, R. (1973). Mother-infant dyad: The cradle of meaning. In P. Pliner, L. Krames, & T. Alloway (Eds.), *Communication and affect: Language and thought.* New York: Academic Press.

Lewis, V., & Boucher, J. (1988). Spontaneous, instructed and elicited play in relatively able autistic children. *British Journal of Developmental Psychology, 6,* 325–339.

Lewy, A., & Dawson, G. (1992). Social stimulation and joint attention in young autistic children. *Journal of Abnormal Child Psychology, 20,* 555–566.

Lipsitt, L. P. (1977). Taste in human neonates: Its effects on sucking and heart rate. In J. M. Weiffenbach (Ed.), *Taste and development: The genesis of sweet preference.* Washington, DC: U.S. Government Printing Office.

Lockyer, L., & Rutter, M. (1970). A five to fifteen year follow-up study of infantile psychosis: IV. Patterns of cognitive ability. *British Journal of Social and Clinical Psychology, 9,* 152–163.

Lord, C. (1984). Development of peer relations in children with autism. In F. Morrison, C. Lord, & D. Keating (Eds.), *Applied developmental psychology* (Vol. 1, pp. 166–230). New York: Academic Press.

Lord, C. (1985). Autism and the comprehension of language. In E. Schopler & G. Mesibov (Eds.), *Communication problems in autism* (pp. 257–281). New York: Plenum Press.

Lord, C., & Schopler, E. (1987). Neurobiological implications of sex differences in autism. In E. Schopler & G. B. Mesibov (Eds.), *Neurobiological issues in autism. Current issues in autism* (pp. 191–211). New York: Plenum Press.

Lord, C., & Schopler, E. (1989). Stability of assessment results of autistic and non-autistic language-impaired children from preschool years to early school age. *Journal of Child Psychology and Psychiatry and Allied Disciplines, 30,* 575–590.

Lord, C., Schopler, E., & Revicki, D. (1982). Sex differences in autism. *Journal of Autism and Developmental Disorders, 12,* 317–330.

Lord, C., & Venter, A. (1992). Outcome and follow-up studies of high-functioning autistic individuals. In E. Schopler & G. B. Mesibov (Eds.), *High-functioning individuals with autism. Current issues in autism* (pp. 187–199). New York: Plenum Press.

Lotter, V. (1966). Epidemiology of autistic conditions in young children: I. Prevalence. *Social Psychiatry, 1,* 124–137.

Lotter, V. (1967). Epidemiology of autistic conditions in young children: II. Some characteristics of the parents and children. *Social Psychiatry, 1,* 163–173.

Lotter, V. (1974). Factors related to outcome in autistic children. *Journal of Autism and Childhood Schizophrenia, 4,* 263–277.

Lotter, V. (1978). Follow-up studies. In M. Rutter & E. Schopler (Eds.), *Autism: A reappraisal of concepts and treatment* (pp. 475–495). New York: Plenum Press.

Lotter, V. (1980). Methodological problems in cross-cultural epidemiologic research: Illustrations from a survey of childhood autism in Africa. In F. Earls (Ed.), *Studies of children* (pp. 126–144). New York: Prodist.

Lovaas, I. (1987). Behavioral treatment and normal educational and intellectual functioning in young autistic children. *Journal of Abnormal Child Psychology, 20,* 555–566.

Lovaas, O. I., Berberich, J. P., Perloff, B. F., & Schaeffer, B. (1991). Acquisition of imitative speech by schizophrenic children. *Focus on Autistic Behavior, 6,* 1–5.

Lovaas, O. I., Koegel, R., Simmons, J. Q., & Long, J. S. (1973). Some generalization and follow-up measures on autistic children in behavior therapy. *Journal of Applied Behavior Analysis, 6,* 131–166.

Lovaas, O. I., Schaefer, B., & Simmons, J. O. (1965). Experimental studies in childhood schizophrenia. *Journal of Experimental Research and Personality, 1,* 99–109.

Loveland, K. (1991). Social affordances and interaction II: Autism and the affordances of the human environment. *Ecological Psychology, 3,* 99–120.

Loveland, K., & Landry, S. (1986). Joint attention and language in autism and developmental language delay. *Journal of Autism and Developmental Disorders, 16,* 335–349.

Loveland, K. A., Landry, S. H., Hughes, S. O., Hall, S. K., & McEvoy, R. E. (1988). Speech acts and the pragmatic deficits of autism. *Journal of Speech and Hearing Research, 31,* 593–604.

Loveland, K., McEvoy, R., Tunali, B., & Kelley, M. (1990). Narrative story telling in autism and Down syndrome. *British Journal of Developmental Psychology, 8,* 9–23.

Loveland, K., & Tunali, B. (1991). Social scripts for conversational interactions in autism and Down Syndrome. *Journal of Autism and Developmental Disorders, 21,* 177–186.

Loveland, K., & Tunali, B. (1993). Narrative language in autism and the theory of mind hypothesis: A wider perspective. In S. Baron-Cohen, H. Tager-Flusberg, & D. Cohen (Eds.), *Understanding other minds: Perspectives from autism* (pp. 247–266). Oxford: Oxford University Press.

Loveland, K. A., Tunali, B., McEvoy, R. E., & Kelley, M. L.

(1989). Referential communication and response adequacy in autism and Down's syndrome. *Applied Psycholinguistics, 10*, 301–313.

Loveland, K., Tunali-Kotoski, B., Pearson, D. A., Brelsford, K. A., Ortegon, J., & Chen, R. (1994). Imitation and expression of facial affect in autism. *Development and Psychopathology, 6*, 433–443.

Luria, A. R. (1961). *The role of speech in the regulation of normal and abnormal behavior.* New York: Pergamon Press.

Luria, A. R. (1976). *Cognitive development.* Cambridge: Harvard University Press.

MacDonald, H., Rutter, M., Howlin, P., Rios, P., LeConteur, A., Evered, C., & Folstein, S. (1989). Recognition and expression of emotional cues by autistic and normal adults. *Journal of Child Psychology and Psychiatry and Allied Disciplines, 30*, 865–877.

MacFarlane, A. (1975). Olfaction in the development of social preferences in the human neonate. Paper presented at the Parent-Infant Interaction (CIBA Foundation symposium 33), New York.

Mahler, M. S. (1968). *On human symbiosis and the vicissitudes of individuation: I. Infant psychosis.* New York: International Universities Press.

Main, M., & Solomon, J. (1986). Discovery of an insecure-disorganized/disoriented attachment pattern. In T. B. Brazelton & M. W. Yogman (Eds.), *Affective development in infancy* (pp. 95–124). Norwood, NJ: Ablex Publishing Corp.

Main, M. (1991). Metacognitive knowledge, metacognitive monitoring, and singular (coherent) vs. multiple (incoherent) model of attachment: Findings and directions for future research. In C. M. Parkes, J. Stevenson-Hinde, & P. Marris (Eds.), *Attachment across the life cycle* (pp. 127–159). London: Tavistock-Routledge.

Main, M., & Solomon, J. (1990). Procedures for identifying infants as disorganized/disoriented during the Ainsworth Strange Situation. In M. T. Greenberg, D. Cicchetti, & E. M. Cummings (Eds.), *Attachment in the preschool years: Theory, research, and intervention* (pp. 121–160). Chicago: University of Chicago Press.

Mandler, J. (1984). *Stories, scripts, and scenes: Aspects of schema theory.* Hillsdale, NJ: Erlbaum.

Martineau, J., Garreau, B., Barthelemy, C., Callaway, E., & Lelord, G. (1981). Effects of vitamin B6 on averaged evoked potentials in infantile autism. *Biological Psychiatry, 16,* 627–641.

Maurice, C. (1993). *Let me hear your voice: A family's triumph over autism.* New York: Fawcett Columbine.

McCabe, A., & Peterson, C. (1991). *Developing narrative structure.* Hillsdale, NJ: Erlbaum.

McCarthy, J. D., & Hodge, D. R. (1982). Analysis of age effects in longitudinal studies of adolescent self-esteem. *Developmental Psychology, 18,* 372–379.

McEachen, J., Smith, T., & Lovaas, O. (1993). Long term outcome for children with autism who received early intensive behavioral treatment. *American Journal on Mental Retardation, 97,* 359–372.

McEvoy, R. E., Rogers, S. J., & Pennington, B. F. (1993). Executive function and social communication deficits in young autistic children. *Journal of Child Psychology and Psychiatry and Allied Disciplines, 34,* 563–578.

McHale, S. (1983). Social interactions of autistic and non-handicapped children during free play. *American Journal of Orthopsychiatry, 53,* 81–91.

McNeill, D. (1970). *The acquisition of language: The study of developmental psycholinguistics.* New York: Harper and Row.

Mead, G. H. (1934). *Mind, self, and society.* Chicago: University of Chicago Press.

Meltzoff, A. N. (1988). Infant imitation and memory: Nine-month-olds in immediate and deferred tests. *Child Development, 59,* 217–225.

Meltzoff, A. N., & Gopnik, A. (1993). *The role of imitation in understanding persons and developing a theory of mind.* Oxford: Oxford University Press.

Meltzoff, A. N., & Moore, M. K. (1977). Imitation of facial and manual gestures by human neonates. *Science, 198,* 75–78.

Meltzoff, A. N., & Moore, M. K. (1992). Early imitation within a functional framework: The importance of person identity, movement, and development. *Infant Behavior and Development, 15,* 479–505.

Menyuk, P. (1978). Language: What's wrong and why. In M. Rutter & E. Schopler (Eds.), *Autism: A reappraisal of concepts and treatment* (pp. 105–116). New York: Plenum Press.

Mesibov, G. B. (1995). Facilitated communication: A warning for pediatric psychologists. *Journal of Pediatric Psychology, 20,* 127–130.

Miedzianik, D. C. (1986). *My autobiography.* (Intro. by E. Newson). Nottingham, Eng.: Child Development Research Unit, University of Nottingham.

Mikkelsen, E. (1982). Efficacy of neuroleptic medication in pervasive developmental disorders of childhood. *Schizophrenia Bulletin, 8,* 320–328.

Miller, S. A., Shelton, J., & Flavell, J. H. (1970). A test of Luria's hypothesis concerning the development of verbal self-regulations. *Child Development, 41,* 651–665.

Miller, P., & Garvey, C. (1984). Mother-baby role play: Its origins in social support. In I. Bretherton (Ed.), *Symbolic play: The development of social understanding.* New York: Academic Press.

Miller, P., & Sperry, L. L. (1987). The socialization of anger and aggression. *Merrill-Palmer Quarterly, 33,* 1–31.

Miller, P. J., & Sperry, L. (1988). Early talk about the past: The origins of conversational stories of personal experience. *Journal of Child Language, 15,* 293–315.

Minderaa, R. B., Anderson, G. M., Volkmar, F. R., Harcherik, D., Akkerhuis, G. W., & Cohen, D. J. (1987). Urine 5-hydroxy-indoleacetic acid, whole blood serotonin and tryptophan in autistic and normal subjects. *Biological Psychiatry, 22,* 933–940.

Minshew, N. J., Goldstein, G., Muenz, L. R., & Payton, J. B. (1992). Neuropsychological functioning of nonmentally retarded autistic individuals. *Journal of Clinical and Experimental Neuropsychology, 14,* 749–761.

Mittler, P., Gillies, S., & Jukes, E. (1966). Prognosis in psychotic children: report of a follow-up study. *Journal of Mental Deficiency Research, 10,* 73–83.

Moore, C., & Dunham, P. J. (1995). *Joint attention: Its origins and role in development*. Hillsdale, NJ: Erlbaum.

Morrison, T. (1994). *The Nobel lecture in literature*. New York: Alfred A. Knopf.

Morse, P. A. (1972). The discrimination of speech and non-speech stimuli in early infancy. *Journal of Experimental Child Psychology, 14*, 477–492.

Mundy, P. (1995). Joint attention, social-emotional approach in children with autism. *Development and Psychopathology, 7*, 63–82.

Mundy, P., & Drowson, M. (in press). Intervention and autism: Implications of research on early social-communication skills. *Journal of Autism and Development Disorders*.

Mundy, P. & Sigman, M. (1989). The theoretical implications of joint attention deficits in autism. *Development and Psychopathology, 1*, 173–183.

Mundy, P. & Sigman, M. (1989). Specifying the nature of social impairment in autism. In G. Dawson (Ed.), *Autism: New perspectives on diagnosis, natures, and treatment*. New York: Guilford Press.

Mundy, P., Sigman, M., & Kasari, C. (1990). A longitudinal study of joint attention and language development in autistic children. *Journal of Autism and Developmental Disorders, 20*, 115–128.

Mundy, P., Sigman, M., & Kasari, C. (1993). Theory of mind and joint attention deficits in autism. In S. Baron-Cohen, H. Tayer-Flusberg, & D. Cohen (Eds.), *Understanding other minds: Perspectives from autism*. Oxford: Oxford University Press.

Mundy, P., Sigman, M., & Kasari, C. (1994). Joint attention, developmental level and symptom presentation in autism. *Development and Psychopathology, 6*, 389–401.

Mundy, P., Sigman, M., Ungerer, J., & Sherman, T. (1986). Defining the social deficits of autism: The contribution of nonverbal communication measures. *Journal of Child Psychology and Psychiatry and Allied Disciplines, 27*, 657–669.

Mundy, P., Sigman, M., Ungerer, J. A., & Sherman, T. (1987). Nonverbal communication and play correlates of language development in autistic children. *Journal of Autism and Developmental Disorders, 17,* 349–364.

Nelson, K. (1979). Exploration in the development of a functional system. In W. Collins (Ed.), *Children's language and communication.* The Minnesota Symposia on Child Psychology, 12. Hillsdale, NJ: Erlbaum.

Nelson, K. (1981). *Social cognition in a script framework.* Cambridge, Eng.: Cambridge University Press.

Nelson, K. (1986). *Event knowledge: Structure and function in development.* Hillsdale, NJ: Erlbaum.

Nelson, K. (Ed.). (1989). *Narratives from the crib.* Cambridge: Harvard University Press.

Neuman, C., & Hill, S. (1978). Self-recognition and stimulus preference in autistic children. *Developmental Psychobiology, 11,* 571–578.

Newport, E. H., Gleitman, H., & Gleitman, L. R. (1977). Mother, I'd rather do it myself: Some effects and noneffects of maternal speech style. In C. E. Snow & C. A. Furguson (Eds.), *Talking to children: Language input and acquisition.* Cambridge, Eng.: Cambridge University Press.

Novick, B., Kurtzberg, D., & Vaughn, H. G. (1979). An electrophysiologic indication of defective information storage in childhood autism. *Psychiatry Research, 1,* 101–108.

Ochs, E. (1982). Talking to children in Western Samoa. *Language in Society, 11,* 77–104.

Ochs, E. (1993). Constructing social identity: A language socialization perspective. *Research on Language and Social Interaction, 26,* 287–306.

Ochs, E. (1993). *Stories that step into the future.* Oxford: Oxford University Press.

Ochs, E., & Schieffelin, B. (1984). *Language acquisition and socialization. Three developmental stories and their implications.* Cambridge, Eng.: Cambridge University Press.

Ochs, E., & Schieffelin, B. (1989). Language has a heart. *Text, 9,* 7–25.

Ochs, E., Taylor, C., Rudolph, D., & Smith, R. (1992). Story-telling as a theory-building activity. *Discourse Processes, 15,* 37–72.

Offer, D., Ostrov, E., Howard, K. I., & Atkinson, R. (1988). *The teenage world: Adolescents' self-image in ten countries.* New York: Plenum Press.

Ogawa, T., Sugiyama, A., Ishiwa, S., Suzuki, M., Ishihara, T., & Sato, K. (1982). Ontogenic developmemt of EEG-asymmetry in early infantile autism. *Brain and Development, 4,* 439–449.

Oller, D. K. (1978). *The emergence of the sounds of speech in infancy.* New York: Academic Press.

Olsson, I., Gillberg, C., & Steffenburg, S. (1988). Epilepsy in autism and autistic-like conditions: A population-based study. *Archives of Neurology, 45,* 666–668.

Ornitz, E. M. (1985). Neurophysiology of infantile autism. *Journal of the American Academy of Child Psychiatry, 24,* 251–262.

Ornitz, E. M., Ritvo, E. R., Tanguay, P. E., & Walter, R. D. (1969). EEG spikes and the averaged evoked response to clicks and flashes. *Electroencephalography and Clinical Neurophysiology, 27,* 387–391.

Osherson, D. N., & Markman, E. M. (1975). Language and the ability to evaluate contradictions and tautologies. *Cognition, 2,* 213–226.

Osterling, J. & Dawson, G. (1994). Early recognition of children with autism: A study of first birthday home videotapes. *Journal of Autism and Developmental Disorders, 24,* 247–257.

Ozonoff, S., & McEvoy, R. E. (1994). A longitudinal study of executive function and theory of mind development in autism. *Development and Psychopathology, 6,* 415–431.

Ozonoff, S., Pennington, B. F., & Rogers, S. J. (1990). Are there emotion perception deficits in young autistic children? *Journal of Child Psychology and Psychiatry and Allied Disciplines, 31,* 343–361.

Ozonoff, S., Pennington, B. F., & Rogers, S. J. (1991). Executive function deficits in high-functioning autistic children: Relationship to theory of mind. *Journal of Child Psychology and Psychiatry and Allied Disciplines, 32,* 1081–1106.

Ozonoff, S., Strayer, D. L., McMahon, W. M., & Filloux, F. (1994). Executive function abilities in autism and Tourette syndrome: An information processing approach. *Journal of*

Child Psychology and Psychiatry and Allied Disciplines, 35, 1015–1032.

Palkowitz, R. W., & Wiesenfeld, A. R. (1980). Differential autonomic responses of autistic and normal children. *Journal of Autism and Developmental Disorders, 10,* 347–360.

Panskepp, J. (1979). A neurochemical theory of autism. *Trends in Neuroscience, 2,* 174–177.

Papousek, M., & Papousek, H. (1981). Musical elements in the infant's vocalization: Their significance for communication, cognition, and creativity. *Advances in Infancy Research, 1,* 163–224.

Pascual-Leone, J. (1988). Organismic processes for neo-Piagetian theories: A dialetical causal account of cognitive development. In A. Demetriou (Ed.), *The neo-Piagetian theories of cognitive development: Toward an integration.* Amsterdam: Elsevier.

Paul, R. (1987). Communication. In D. J. Cohen, A. M. Donnellan, & R. Paul (Eds.), *Handbook of autism and pervasive developmental disorders* (pp. 61–84). New York: Wiley.

Perner, J., Frith, U., Leslie, A. M., & Leekam, S. R. (1989). Exploration of the autistic child's theory of mind: Knowledge, belief, and communication. *Child Development, 60,* 689–700.

Piaget, J. (1932). *The moral judgment of the child.* New York: Harcourt Brace.

Piaget, J. (1952). *The origins of intelligence in children.* New York: International Universities Press.

Piaget, J. (1954). *The construction of reality in the child.* New York: Basic Books.

Piaget, J. (1962). *Play, dreams and imitation.* New York: W. W. Norton.

Piaget, J. (1972). Intellectual evolution from adolescence to adulthood. *Human Development, 15,* 1–12.

Piaget, J., & Inhelder, B. (1969). *The psychology of the child.* New York: Basic Books.

Pierce, S., & Bartolucci, G. (1977). A syntactic investigation of verbal autistic, mentally retarded, and normal children. *Journal of Autism and Developmental Disorders, 7,* 121–134.

Piven, J., Berthier, M. L., Startkstein, S. E., Nehme, E., Pearlson,

& Folstein. (1990). Magnetic resonance imaging evidence for a defect of cerebral cortical development in autism. *American Journal of Psychiatry, 147,* 734–739.

Premack, D. (1988). "Does the chimpanzee have a theory of mind" revisited. In R. W. Byrne & A. Whiten (Eds.), *Machiavellian intelligence: Social expertise and the evolution of intellect in monkeys, apes, and humans* (pp. 160–179). Oxford: Clarendon Press.

Premack, D. (1990). The infant's theory of self-propelled objects. *Cognition, 36,* 1–16.

Prior, M. R., & Bradshaw, J. L. (1979). Hemisphere functions in autistic children. *Cortex, 15,* 73–81.

Prior, M. R., & Hall, L. C. (1979). Comprehension of transitive and intransitive phrases by autistic, mentally retarded and normal children. *Journal of Communication Disorders, 12,* 103–111.

Prizant, B. M. (1983). Language acquisition and communicative behavior in autism: Toward an understanding of the "whole" of it. *Journal of Speech and Hearing Disorders, 48,* 296–307.

Propp, V. (1968). *The morphology of the folktale* (T. Scott, Trans.). (2nd ed.). Austin, TX: University of Texas Press.

Ricks, D. M. (1979). Making sense out of sensible sounds. In M. Bullowa (Ed.), *Before speech: The beginning of interpersonal communication* (pp. 245–268). Cambridge, Eng.: Cambridge University Press.

Ricks, D. M., & Wing, L. (1975). Language, communication, and the use of symbols in normal and autistic children. *Journal of Autism and Childhood Schizophrenia, 5,* 191–221.

Ricoeur, P. (1988). *Time and narrative.* Chicago: University of Chicago Press.

Rimland, B. (1988). Controversies in the treatment of autistic children: Vitamin and drug therapy. *Journal of Child Neurology, 3,* 68–72.

Rimland, B. (1994). The modern history of autism: A personal perspective. In J. L. Matson (Ed.), *Autism in children and adults: Etiology, assessment, and intervention.* Pacific Grove, CA: Brooks-Cole.

Ritvo, E. R., Ritvo, E. C., & Mason-Brothers, M. A. (1982).

Genetic and immunohematologic factors in autism. *Journal of Autism and Developmental Disorders, 12,* 109–114.

Rogers, S. J., Ozonoff, S., & Maslin-Cole, C. (1991). A comparative study of attachment behavior in young children with autism or other psychiatric disorders. *Journal of the American Academy of Child and Adolescent Psychiatry, 30,* 483–488.

Rogers, S. J., & Pennington, B. F. (1991). A theoretical approach to the deficits in infantile autism. *Development and Psychopathology, 3,* 137–162.

Rogoff, B. (1990). *Apprenticeship in thinking: Cognitive development in social context.* Oxford: Oxford University Press.

Rubin, Z. (1980). *Children's friendships.* Cambridge: Harvard University Press.

Rumsey, J. M., & Hamburger, A. D. (1988). Neuropsychological findings in high-functioning men with infantile autism, residual state. *Journal of Clinical and Experimental Neuropsychology, 10,* 201–221.

Rumsey, J. M., & Hamburger, S. D. (1990). Neuropsychological divergence of high-level autism and severe dyslexia. *Journal of Autism and Developmental Disorders, 20,* 155–168.

Rumsey, J. M., Rapoport, M. D., & Sceery, W. R. (1985). Autistic children as adults: Psychiatric, social, and behavioral outcomes. *Journal of the American Academy of Child Psychiatry, 24,* 465–473.

Rutter, M. (1970). Autistic children: Infancy to adulthood. *Seminars in Psychiatry, 2,* 435–450.

Rutter, M. (1978). Diagnosis and definition. In M. Rutter & E. Schopler (Eds.), *Autism: A reappraisal of concepts and treatment* (pp. 1–25). New York: Plenum Press.

Rutter, M. (1983). Cognitive deficits in the pathogenesis of autism. *Journal of Child Psychology and Psychiatry and Allied Disciplines, 24,* 513–531.

Rutter, M. (1985). Infantile autism and other pervasive developmental disorders. In M. Rutter & L. Hersov (Eds.), *Child and adolescent psychiatry* (pp. 545–566). Oxford: Blackwell.

Rutter, M., & Lockyer, L. (1967). A five to fifteen year follow-up study of infantile psychosis. I. Description of sample. *British Journal of Psychiatry, 113,* 1169–1182.

Saarni, C. (1979). Children's understanding of display rules for expressive behavior. *Developmental Psychology, 15,* 424–429.

Sachs, J., & Devin, J. (1973). Young children's knowledge of age-appropriate speech styles. Paper presented at the Linguistic Society of America.

Sacks, H. (1987). *On the preferences for agreement and contiguity in sequences in conversation.* Clevedon, Eng.: Multilingual Matters.

Sacks, H., Schegloff, E. A., & Jefferson, G. (1974). A simplest systematics for the organization of turn-taking for conversation. *Language, 50,* 696–735.

Sacks, O. (1995). *An anthropologist on Mars.* New York: Knopf.

Sagi, A., & Hoffman, M. L. (1976). Empathic distress in the newborn. *Developmental Psychology, 12,* 175–176.

Sandman, C. A., Patta, P. C., Banon, J., Hoehler, F. K., Williams, C., Williams, C., & Swanson, J. M. (1983). Naloxone attenuates self-abusive behavior in developmentally disabled clients. *Applied Research in Mental Retardation, 4,* 5–11.

Sapir, E. (1924). Culture, genuine and spurious. *Journal of Sociology, 29,* 401–29.

Saxe, G. B. (1991). *Culture and cognitive development: Studies in mathematical understanding.* Hillsdale, NJ: Erlbaum.

Scaife, M., & Bruner, J. S. (1975). The capacity for joint visual attention in the infant. *Nature, 253*(5489), 265–266.

Scanlon-Jones, S., Collins, K., & Hong, H. W. (1991). An audience effect on smile production in 10-month-old infants. *Psychological Science, 2,* 45–49.

Schieffelin, B. B. (1990). *The give and take of everyday life: Language socialization of Kaluli children.* Cambridge, Eng.: Cambridge University Press.

Schopler, E., Mesibov, G. B., & Hearsey, K. (1995). Structured teaching in the TEACCH system. In E. Schopler & G. B. Mesibov (Eds.), *Learning and cognition in autism. Current issues in autism* (pp. 243–268). New York: Plenum Press.

Schuler, A., & Prizant, B. M. (1985). *Echolalia.* New York: Plenum Press.

Seidner, L. B., Stipek, D. J., & Feshbach, N. D. (1988). A developmental analysis of elementary school-aged children's concepts of pride and embarrassment. *Child Development, 59,* 367–377.

Shapiro, T., Sherman, M., Calamari, G., & Koch, D. (1987). Attachment in autism and other developmental disorders. *Journal of the American Academy of Child and Adolescent Psychiatry, 26,* 480–484.

Shatz, M., & Gelman, R. (1973). The development of communication skills: Modification in the speech of young children as a function of listener. *Monographs of the Society for Research in Child Development, 38*(5, Serial No. 152).

Shatz, M., Wellman, H. M., & Silber, S. (1983). The acquisition of mental verbs: A systematic investigation of the first reference to mental state. *Cognition, 14,* 301–321.

Shell, J., Campion, J. F., Minton, J., Caplan, R., & Campbell, M. (1984). A study of three brothers with infantile autism: A case report with follow-up. *Journal of the American Academy of Child Psychiatry, 23,* 498–502.

Sigman, M. (1989). The application of developmental knowledge to a clinical problem: The study of childhood autism. In D. Cicchetti (Ed.), *The emergence of a discipline: Rochester symposium on developmental psychopathology,* Vol. I. Hillsdale, NJ: Erlbaum.

Sigman, M. (1995, March). Early social understanding and later development of autistic children. Paper presented at the Society for Research in Child Development, Indianapolis, IN.

Sigman, M. (1996). Behavioral resarch in childhood autism. In M. Lenzenweger & J. Haugaard (Eds.), *Frontiers of developmental psychopathology.* Oxford University Press.

Sigman, M., & Kasari, C. (1995). Joint attention across contexts in normal and atypical children. In C. Moore & P. Dunham, (Eds.), *Joint attention: Its origin and role in development.* Hillsdale, NJ: Erlbaum.

Sigman, M., & Mundy, P. (1987). Symbolic processes in atypical children. In D. Cicchetti & M. Beeghly (Eds.), *Symbolic development in atypical children.* San Francisco, CA: Jossey-Bass.

Sigman, M., & Mundy, P. (1989). Social attachments in autistic children. *Journal of the American Academy of Child and Adolescent Psychiatry, 28*, 74–81.

Sigman, M., Mundy, P., Sherman, T., & Ungerer, J. (1986). Social interactions of autistic, mentally retarded and normal children and their caregivers. *Journal of Child Psychology and Psychiatry and Allied Disciplines, 27*, 647–656.

Sigman, M., & Ungerer, J. (1981). Sensorimotor skills and language comprehension in autistic children. *Journal of Abnormal Child Psychology, 9*, 149–165.

Sigman, M. & Ungerer, J.A. (1984a). Cognitive and language skills in autistic, mentally retarded, and normal children. *Developmental Psychology, 20*, 293–302.

Sigman, M., & Ungerer, J. A. (1984b). Attachment behaviors in autistic children. *Journal of Autism and Developmental Disorders, 14*, 231–244.

Sigman, M., Ungerer, J., Mundy, P., & Sherman, T. (1986). Cognition in autistic children. In D. J. Cohen, A. M. Donnellan & R. Paul (Eds.), *Handbook of autism and pervasive developmental disorders.* New York: Wiley.

Sigman, M. D., Kasari, C., Kwon, J., & Yirmiya, N. (1992). Responses to the negative emotions of others by autistic, mentally retarded, and normal children. *Child Development, 63*, 796–807.

Sigman, M. D., Yirmiya, N., & Capps, L. (1995). Social and cognitive understanding in high-functioning children with autism. In E. Schoper & G. B. Mesibov (Eds.), *Learning and cognition in autism.* New York: Plenum Press.

Silliman, E. R., Campbell, M., & Mitchell, R. S. (1989). Genetic influences in autism and assessment of metalinguistic performance in siblings of autistic children. In G. Dawson (Ed.), *Autism: Nature, Diagnosis and Treatment* (pp. 225–259). New York: Guilford Press.

Simmons, R. G., & Blythe, D. A. (1987). *Moving into adolescence: The impact of pubertal change in school context.* New York: A. de Gruyter.

Smalley, S. L. (1991). Genetic influences in autism. *Psychiatric Clinics of North America, 14*, 125–139.

Snow, C. (1977). The development of conversation between mothers and babies. *Journal of Child Language, 4,* 1–22.

Snow, M. E., Hertzig, M. E., & Shapiro, T. (1987). Expression of emotion in young autistic children. *Journal of the American Academy of Child and Adolescent Psychiatry, 26,* 836–838.

Sodian, B., & Frith, U. (1992). Deception and sabotage in autistic, retarded and normal children. *Journal of Child Psychology and Psychiatry and Allied Disciplines, 33,* 591–605.

Sparrow, S. S., Balla, D. A., & Cicchetti, D. V. (1984). *Vineland Adaptive Behavior Scales.* Circle Pines, MN: American Guidance Service.

Spiker, D., & Ricks, M. (1984). Visual self-recognition in autistic children: Developmental relationships. *Child Development, 55,* 214–225.

Spring, D. R., & Dale, P. S. (1977). Discrimination of linguistic stress in early infancy. *Journal of Speech and Hearing Research, 20,* 224–232.

Steffenburg, S., & Gillberg, C. (1986). Autism and autistic-like conditions in Swedish rural and urban areas: A population study. *British Journal of Psychiatry, 149,* 81–87.

Steiner, J. E. (1977). *Facial expressions of the neonate infant indicating the hedonics of food related chemical stimuli.* Washington, DC: U.S. Government Printing Office.

Steinhausen, H.-C., Gobel, D., Breinlinger, M., & Wohleben, B. (1983). A community survey of infantile autism. Paper presented at the 30th annual meeting of the American Academy of Child Psychiatry, San Francisco.

Stern, D. (1985). *The interpersonal world of the infant: A view from psychoanalysis and developmental psychology.* New York: Basic Books.

Stern, D. N., Spieker, S., Barnett, R. K., & MacKain, K. (1983). The prosody of maternal speech: Infant age and context related changes. *Journal of Child Language, 10,* 1–15.

Stone, W. L., & Caro-Martinez, L. M. (1990). Naturalistic observations of spontaneous communication in autistic children. *Journal of Autism and Developmental Disorders, 20,* 437–453.

Strain, P., Kerr, M., & Ragland, E. (1979). Effects of peer-mediated social initiations and prompting/reinforcement procedures on the social behavior of autistic children. *Journal of Autism and Developmental Disorders, 9*, 41–54.

Sugarman, S. (1983). *Children's early thought.* Cambridge, Eng.: Cambridge University Press.

Super, C. M., & Harkness, S. (1972). *The infant's niche in rural Kenya and metropolitan America.* New York: Academic Press.

Swisher, L., & Demetras, M. J. (1985). The expressive language characteristics of autistic children compared with mentally retarded or specific language-impaired children. In E. Schopler & G. Mesibov (Eds.), *Communication problems in autism* (pp. 147–162). New York: Plenum Press.

Szatmari, P., Bartolucci, G., Bremner, R. S., Bond, S., & Rich, S. (1989). A follow-up study of high functioning autistic children. *Journal of Autism and Developmental Disorders, 19*, 213–226.

Szatmari, P., & Jones, M. B. (1991). IQ and the genetics of autism. *Journal of Child Psychology and Psychiatry and Allied Disciplines, 32*, 897–908.

Tager-Flusberg, H. (1981a). On the nature of linguistic functioning in early infantile autism. *Journal of Autism and Developmental Disorders, 11*, 45–54.

Tager-Flusberg, H. (1981b). Sentence comprehension in autistic children. *Applied Psycholinguistics, 2*, 5–24.

Tager-Flusberg, H. (1982). Pragmatic development and its implications for social interaction in autistic children. In D. Park (Ed.), *Proceedings of the International Symposium for Research in Autism* (pp. 103–108). Washington, DC: National Society for Autistic Children.

Tager-Flusberg, H. (1985a). Basic level and superordinate level categorization in autistic, mentally retarded and normal children. *Journal of Experimental Child Psychology, 40*, 450–469.

Tager-Flusberg, H. (1985b). The conceptual basis for referential word meaning in children with autism. *Child Development, 56*, 1167–1178.

Tager-Flusberg, H. (1986). Constraints on the representation of word meaning: Evidence from autistic and mentally retarded children. In S. Kuczaj & M. Barrett (Eds.), *The development of word meaning* (pp. 139–166). New York: Springer-Verlag.

Tager-Flusberg, H. (1989). A psycholinguistic perspective on language development in the autistic child. In G. Dawson (Ed.), *Autism: Nature, diagnosis and treatment* (pp. 92–115). New York: Guilford Press.

Tager-Flusberg, H. (1993). What language reveals about the understanding of minds in children with autism. In S. Baron-Cohen, H. Tager-Flusberg, & D. Cohen (Eds.), *Understanding other minds: Perspectives from autism* (pp. 138–157). Oxford: Oxford University Press.

Tager-Flusberg, H., Calkins, S., Nolin, T. L., Anderson, M. J., & Chadwick-Dias, A. M. (1990). A longitudinal study of language acquisition in autistic and Down Syndrome children. *Journal of Autism and Developmental Disorders, 20,* 1–20.

Tanguay, P. E. (1976). *Clinical and electrophysiological research.* New York: Spectrum.

Taylor, C. (1989). *Sources of the self.* Cambridge: Harvard University Press.

Thoman, E. B., & Whitney, M. P. (1989). Sleep states of infants monitored in the home: Individual differences, developmental trends, and origins of cyclicity. *Infant Behavior and Development, 12,* 59–75.

Tietjen, A. M. (1989). *The ecology of children's social support networks.* New York: Wiley.

Tomasello, M. (1992). The social bases of language acquisition. *Social Development, 1,* 67–87.

Tomasello, M. (1995). Joint attention as social cognition. In C. Moore & P. Dunham (Eds.), *Joint attention: Its origins and role in development* (pp. 103–130). Hillsdale, NJ: Erlbaum.

Tomasello, M., & Farrar, J. (1986). Joint attention and early language. *Child Development, 57,* 1454–1463.

Tomasello, M., Kruger, A. C., & Ratner, H. H. (1993). Cultural learning. *Behavioral and Brain Sciences, 16,* 495–552.

Tomasello, M., & Mannle, S. (1985). Pragmatics of sibling speech to one-year-olds. *Child Development, 56,* 911–917.

Tomasello, M., Mannle, S., & Kruger, A. C. (1986). Linguistic environment of 1- to 2-year-old twins. *Developmental Psychology, 22,* 169–176.

Tranel, D., & Hyman, B. (1990). Neuropsychological correlates of bilateral amygdala damage. *Archives of Neurology, 47,* 349–355.

Treffert, D. A. (1970). Epidemiology of infantile autism. *Archives of General Psychiatry, 22,* 431–138.

Trevarthen, C. (1977). *Descriptive analyses of infant communicative behavior.* New York: Academic Press.

Trevarthen, C. (1979). *Communication and cooperation in early infancy: A description of primary subjectivity.* Cambridge, Eng.: Cambridge University Press.

Tronick, E., Als, H., Adamsen, L., Wise, S., & Brazelton, T. (1978). The infant's response to entrapment between contradictory messages in face to face interaction. *Journal of the American Academy of Child Psychiatry, 17,* 1–11.

Ungerer, J. A., & Sigman, M. (1981). Symbolic play and language comprehension in autistic children. *Journal of the American Academy of Child Psychiatry, 20,* 318–338.

Ungerer, J. A., & Sigman, M. (1987). Categorization skills and receptive language development in autistic children. *Journal of Autism and Developmental Disorders, 17,* 3–16.

Valsiner, J. (1988). *Child development within culturally structured environments: Social co-construction and environmental guidance in development.* (Vol. 2). Norwood, NJ: Ablex.

Van Engeland, H., Bodnar, F. A., & Bolhuis, G. (1985). Some qualitative aspects of the social behaviour of autistic children: An ethological approach. *Journal of Child Psychology and Psychiatry and Allied Disciplines, 26,* 879–893.

Van Lancker, D. R., Cornelius, C., & Kreiman, J. (1989). Recognition of emotional-prosodic meanings in speech by autistic, schizophrenic, and normal children. *Developmental Neuropsychology, 5,* 207–226.

Venter, A., Lord, C., & Schopler, E. (1992). A follow-up study of high-functioning autistic children. *Journal of Child Psychology and Psychiatry and Allied Disciplines, 33,* 489–507.

Volkmar, F. R., & Anderson, G. M. (1989). Neurochemical perspectives on infantile autism. In G. Dawson (Ed.), *Autism:*

Nature, diagnosis and treatment (pp. 208–224). New York: Guilford Press.

Volkmar, F. R., & Cohen, D. J. (1985). The experience of infantile autism: A first-hand account by Tony W. *Journal of Autism and Developmental Disorders, 15,* 47–54.

Volkmar, F. R., & Cohen, D. J. (1989). Disintegrative disorder or "late onset" autism. *Journal of Child Psychology and Psychiatry and Allied Disciplines, 30,* 717–724.

Volkmar, F. R., Hoder, E. L., & Cohen, D. J. (1985). Compliance, "negativism," and the effects of treatment structure in autism: A naturalistic, behavioral study. *Journal of Child Psychology and Psychiatry and Allied Disciplines, 26,* 865–877.

Vygotsky, L. S. (1978). *Mind in society.* Cambridge: Harvard University Press.

Walden, T. A., & Baxter, A. (1989). The effect of context and age on social referencing. *Child Development, 60,* 1511–1518.

Walker-Andrews, A. S. (1986). Intermodal perception of expressive behaviors: Relation of eye and voice? *Developmental Psychology, 22,* 373–377.

Waterhouse, L., & Fein, D. (1982). Language skills in developmentally disabled children. *Brain and Language, 15,* 307–333.

Waterhouse, L. (1994). Severity of impairment in autism. In S. H. Broman & J. Grafman (Eds.), *Atypical cognitive deficits in developmental disorders: Implications for brain function* (pp. 159–180). Hillsdale, NJ: Erlbaum.

Watson, M. W., & Fischer, K. W. (1977). A developmental sequence of agent use in late infancy. *Child Development, 48,* 828–835.

Weeks, S. J., & Hobson, R. P. (1987). The salience of facial expression for autistic children. *Journal of Child Psychology and Psychiatry and Allied Disciplines, 28,* 137–151.

Weiss, B., & Weisz, J. R. (1995). Effectiveness of psychotherapy. *Journal of the American Academy of Child and Adolescent Psychiatry, 34,* 971–972.

Weissberg, J. A., & Paris, S. G. (1986). Young children's remem-

bering in different contexts: A reinterpretation of Is-
tomina's study. *Child Development, 57,* 1123–1129.

Weisz, J. R., Weiss, B., Han, S. S., Granger, D. A., et al. (1995).
Effects of psychotherapy with children and adolescents
revisited: A meta-analysis of treatment outcome studies.
Psychological Bulletin, 117, 450–468.

Wellman, H., & Lempers, J. D. (1977). The naturalistic communication abilities of two-year-olds. *Child Development, 48,*
1052–1057.

Wellman, H. M. (1990). *The child's theory of mind.* Cambridge:
MIT Press.

Wetherby, A. M. (1986). Ontogeny of communication functions
in autism. *Journal of Autism and Developmental Disorders,
16,* 295–316.

Wetherby, A. M., Koegel, R. L., & Mendel, M. (1981). Central
auditory nervous system dysfunction in echolalic autistic
individuals. *Journal of Speech and Hearing Research, 24,* 420–
429.

White, H. (1980). *The value of narrativity in the representation of
reality.* Chicago: University of Chicago Press.

Whiten, A. (Ed.). (1991). *Natural theories of mind: Evolution,
development and simulation of everyday mindreading.* Oxford:
Blackwell.

Williams, D. (1992). *Nobody nowhere: The remarkable autobiography of an autistic girl.* London: Doubleday.

Williams, R. S., Hauser, S. L., Purpura, D. P., DeLong, G. R., &
Swisher, C. N. (1980). Autism and mental retardation:
Neuropathologic studies performed in four retarded persons with autistic behavior. *Archives of Neurology, 37,* 749–
753.

Wimmer, H., & Perner, J. (1983). Beliefs about beliefs: Representation and constraining function of wrong beliefs in
young children's understanding of deception. *Cognition,
13,* 103–128.

Wing, L. (1976). Kanner's syndrome: A historical perspective.
In L. Wing (Ed.), *Early childhood autism* (pp. 3–14). Oxford:
Pergamon Press.

Wing, L. (1981). Language, social, and cognitive impairments in autism and severe mental retardation. *Journal of Autism and Developmental Disorders, 11,* 31–44.

Wing, L., & Gould, J. (1979). Severe impairments of social interaction and associated abnormalities in children: Epidemiology and classification. *Journal of Autism and Developmental Disorders, 9,* 11–29.

Wing, L., Yeates, S. R., Brierly, L. M., & Gould, J. (1976). The prevalence of early childhood autism: Comparison of administrative and epidemiological studies. *Psychological Medicine, 6,* 89–100.

Winner, E. (1988). *The point of words.* Cambridge: Harvard University Press.

Wittgenstein, L. (1918/1966). *Tractatus logico philosophicus* (D. F. Pears and B. F. McGuinness, Trans.). New York: Humanities Press.

Wolf, D. P., Rygh, J., & Altshuler, J. (1984). *Agency and experience: Actions and states in play narratives.* Orlando, FL: Academic Press.

Wulff, S. B. (1985). The symbolic and object play of children with autism: A review. *Journal of Autism and Developmental Disabilities, 15,* 139–148.

Yarczower, M., & Daruns, L. (1982). Social inhibition of spontaneous facial expressions in children. *Journal of Personality and Social Psychology, 43,* 831–837.

Yirmiya, N., Kasari, C., Sigman, M., & Mundy, P. (1989). Facial expressions of affect in autistic, mentally retarded and normal children. *Journal of Child Psychology and Psychiatry and Allied Disciplines, 30,* 725–735.

Yirmiya, N., & Sigman, M. (1991). High functioning individuals with autism: Diagnosis, empirical findings and theoretical issues. *Clinical Psychology Review, 11,* 668–683.

Yirmiya, N., Sigman, M., Kasari, C., & Mundy, P. (1992). Empathy and cognition in high-functioning children with autism. *Child Development, 63,* 150–160.

Yirmiya, N., Sigman, M., & Zacks, D. (1994). Perceptual perspective-taking and seriation abilities in high-functioning children with autism. *Development and Psychopathology, 6,* 263–272.

Young, J. G., Kavanagh, M. E., Anderson, G. M., Shaywitz, B. A., & Cohen, D. J. (1982). Clinical neurochemistry of autism and associated disorders. *Journal of Autism and Developmental Disorders, 12,* 147–165.

Yuwiler, A., Geller, E., & Ritvo, E. (1985). Biochemical studies of autism. In E. Lejtha (Ed.), *Handbook of neurochemistry* (Vol. 10, pp. 671–691). New York: Plenum Press.

Zahn-Waxler, C., & Radke-Yarrow, M. (1982). *The development of altruism: Alternative research strategies.* New York: Academic Press.

Index

Abilities, variation in, 2, 4
Abstract reasoning, 111–112, 117–118
Academic skills, 88–90, 96–97, 119
Adolescence, 110–130, 134–137
Adulthood, 137–140
Ainsworth, Mary, 42, 56
Alpha-blocking methods, 165
American Psychiatric Association, 6
Amphetamines, 171
Amygdala, 168–169
Arousal, regulation of, 18–19, 24–25, 158–159
Asperger, Hans, 3–5, 7
Asperger Syndrome, 3–6, 25, 97, 106, 193n4
Attachment security, 9, 42–43, 54–58, 150
Attention, problems of, 158–159
Attention Deficit Disorder, 100, 157
Auditory Integration Training, 187
Autism: defined, 2, 7–8; early observers of, 3–5; infantile, 3; and schizophrenia, 4–5; variations in, 5–7; high-functioning, 5–6; developmental perspective, 8–16; not diagnosed in infants, 12–14; and mental retardation, 14–16, 94–96, 115–116; development of physiological regulation, 24–33; development of perception, 24–33; development of cognition, 24–33; social development, 44–60; emotional development, 44–60; language acquisition/use, 72–85; in middle childhood, 94–109; in adolescence, 115–130; longitudinal research on, 131–146; development from childhood to adolescence, 134–137; development from childhood to adulthood, 137–140; core psychological deficits in, 152–163; theories about, 159–163; core biological deficits in, 163–171; causes of, 171–174; interventions, 175–190
Autonomic responses, 166–167

Baker, L., 140
Baltaxe, C. A. M., 78, 81
Baron-Cohen, Simon, 30, 154–155
Bartolucci, G., 73
Bayley Scales of Infant Development, 194n3
Behavior therapy, 179–183
Bettelheim, Bruno, 49, 172
Biological deficits, core, 163–171
Bosch, G., 82
Boucher, Jill, 31
Bowlby, John, 42
Brain abnormalities, 136
Brain functioning in autism, 164–167